MICROCOMPUTER
ESSENTIALS

MICROCOMPUTER ESSENTIALS

SARAH E. HUTCHINSON

STACEY C. SAWYER

IRWIN
Advantage
Series for
Computer
Education

Homewood, IL 60430
Boston, MA 02116

We recognize that certain terms in this book are trademarks, and we have made every effort to print these throughout the text with the capitalization and punctuation used by the holder of the trademark.

WordPerfect® is a registered trademark of WordPerfect Corporation.
dBASE IV® is a registered trademark of Ashton-Tate.
Lotus® and Lotus 1-2-3® are registered trademarks of Lotus Development Corporation.
Microsoft Windows® and Microsoft Word for Windows® are registered trademarks of Microsoft Corporation.

Sponsoring editors:	Rick Williamson
Developmental editor:	Rebecca Johnson
Project editor:	Stacey C. Sawyer
Production:	Stacey C. Sawyer, Sawyer & Williams
Designer:	Maureen McCutcheon
Cover designer:	Michael Rogondino
Cover art:	Pat Rogondino
Artists:	Rolin Graphics and GTS Graphics
Compositor:	GTS Graphics
Typeface:	$10\frac{1}{2}$/12 Electra
Printer:	Webcrafters, Inc.

Library of Congress Cataloging-in-Publication Data

Hutchinson, Sarah E.
    Microcomputer essentials / Sarah E. Hutchinson, Stacey C. Sawyer
        p.   cm.
    Includes index.
    ISBN 0-256-14294-7
    1. Microcomputers.   2. Computer software   I. Sawyer, Stacey C.
II. Title.
QA76.758.H88   1993
004.16—dc20   92–46873

Printed in the United States of America
1 2 3 4 5 6 7 8 9 0 WC 9 8 7 6 5 4 3

SUPPLEMENTS

FOR THE INSTRUCTOR

Instructor's Manual with Transparency Masters

Color Transparencies

Test Bank

Irwin's Computerized Testing Software

PREFACE

WHY WE WROTE THIS BOOK: MEETING THE NEEDS OF USERS

Microcomputer Essentials is written for future microcomputer *users*, also called *end-users*—people for whom the computer will be an everyday tool for working with reports, spreadsheets, databases, and the like. It is not intended for specialists who will write programs or design computer systems.

We wrote this book in order to provide instructors and students with the most useful information possible in a microcomputer course. Specifically, we offer the following five important features.

PRACTICALITY AND COMPLETENESS

A textbook, we feel, should above all be *practical and complete*. It should give users all the information they need to effectively use a microcomputer at work or at home. Thus, for example, we try to avoid the weaknesses we've seen elsewhere of stressing software to the detriment of hardware coverage, or of being too brief or too encyclopedic. We try to give users just what they need to know to use a microcomputer competently for business or personal purposes. Some examples:

- We present up-to-date PC and Macintosh hardware information and compatibility issues so users can understand the capabilities of the computer systems they are using.
- We offer "bonus" information users may find useful on the job, such as the different RAM requirements of different color monitors

FLEXIBLE, REASONABLY PRICED SOFTWARE LABS

We realize that students (and instructors) have a great deal of concern about the cost of textbooks. Accordingly, we offer many *reasonably priced*, separately bound software tutorials. These hands-on tutorials, now available or shortly to be available from *Irwin's Advantage Series for Computer Education*, include the following:

dBASE III Plus	Lotus 1-2-3 release 2.4
dBASE IV	Lotus 1-2-3 release 3.1
DOS 3.3	Microsoft Works
DOS 5.0	Microsoft Works for Windows
Excel for the Macintosh	Paradox 3.5
Excel 3.0 for Windows	Quattro 1.01
Filemaker Pro for the Macintosh	Quattro Pro 3.0
Lotus 1-2-3 release 2.01 and 2.2	QuickBASIC/QBASIC
Lotus 1-2-3 release 2.3	System 7.0 for the Macintosh

VisualBASIC   Word 2.0 for Windows
Windows 3.1   WordPerfect 5.1
Word for the Macintosh

Additional tutorials will be added to the series as the need arises.

Instructors adopting any of these tutorials are entitled to receive a free copy of Irwin's class-organizing software, written by Glen Coulthard.

AVOIDANCE OF CLUTTER

Our market research finds that many instructors have become tired of the cluttered, over-illustrated look and style of many introductory texts. Thus, you will not find margin notes, cartoons, wild colors, and other such distractions here.

Also, we have attempted to use color to enhance content, not overpower it. For example, as Figure 1.2 on page 4 shows, we use four specific colors to indicate input (red), storage (blue/green), processing (brown), and output (gold).

INTERESTING, READABLE STYLE

We are gratified that reviewers have consistently found our writing style praiseworthy. Our primary goal is to reach students by making our explanations as clear, relevant, and interesting as possible.

EFFECTIVE PEDAGOGY

We have carefully developed our learning aids to maximize students' comprehension and learning:

- *Chapter outlines and previews*: Each chapter opens with an outline of the chapter's content and a section called "Why Is This Chapter Important?" which explains why the material in the chapter is important to the user.
- *Chapter summaries*: Each chapter concludes with a useful summary section to help students review.
- *Key terms*: All the important terms covered—and the numbers of the pages on which they are defined—appear in a section called Key Terms at the end of each chapter. All key terms are also listed and defined in the glossary in the back of the book.
- *Self-tests and exercises*: Fill-in-the-blank tests, short-answer exercises, and projects test students' comprehension and encourage them to learn more about microcomputers on their own.
- *Career boxes*: One-page boxes in Chapters 2 through 12 show students how computers are used in some common and uncommon ways in business and other professions.

SUPPLEMENTS THAT WORK

It's not important how many supplements a book has but whether they're truly useful, accurate, and of high quality. We offer a number of supplements that you will find useful. These supplements, prepared for the parent text *Microcomputer Fundamentals*, can also be used for *Microcomputer Essentials*.

INSTRUCTOR'S MANUAL WITH TRANSPARENCY MASTERS

This supplement contains:

- Student profile sheet
- Course planning guidelines
- Chapter outlines
- Teaching tips
- 29 transparency masters
- Suggestions for using transparency masters and full-color overhead transparencies

COLOR TRANSPARENCIES

77 full-color overhead transparencies of key illustrations and tables are available to qualified adopters.

TEST BANK

For each lesson, this supplement, prepared by L. Anne Breene, contains:

- True/false, multiple-choice, and fill-in-the-blank questions, graded in difficulty
- Sample midterm exam
- Sample final exam of the entire text
- All answers to the test-bank questions

IRWIN'S COMPUTERIZED TESTING SOFTWARE

This computer-based test bank is available to qualified adopters.

THE DEVELOPMENTAL MODEL FOR THIS BOOK

ACQUISITION AND DEVELOPMENTAL EDITORS

Microcomputer Essentials is published as a companion to our *Computers: The User Perspective* and follows the excellent developmental model our publisher has devised for that book. We're grateful for the assistance of our acquisition and developmental editors, who served in an invaluable capacity to guarantee the quality control of this book. Few, if any, publishers offer this high degree of editorial assistance and attention to detail. Special appreciation goes to Larry Alexander, Rick Williamson, Tom Casson, Bill Setten, and Rebecca Johnson for assistance beyond the call of duty. In addition, we thank Micky Lawler for her careful line-by-line analysis of all our books.

We are also grateful to our many reviewers, who provided helpful comments over the course of several drafts. In addition, we are appreciative of the efforts of the photo researcher, Judy Mason, and the proofreader/copyeditors, Linda McPhee and Toni Murray, whose work significantly improved the quality of this book. The staff at GTS Graphics, typesetter and producer of the new illustrations—especially

Elliott Derman, Sherrie Beyen, Daniel Casquilho, and Christina Rogers—are at the top of their field in providing electronic typesetting and graphics services in record time.

WRITE TO US

Finally, we need to know: Was this book truly useful to students? We'd like to hear from you about any improvements we might make. Write to us in care of our publisher, Richard D. Irwin.

SARAH E. HUTCHINSON
STACEY C. SAWYER

CONTENTS

CHAPTER 1

MICROCOMPUTERS: POWER TOOLS FOR AN INFORMATION AGE

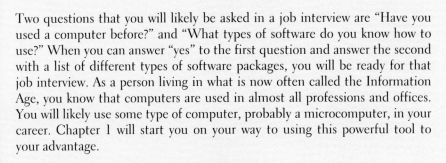

Two questions that you will likely be asked in a job interview are "Have you used a computer before?" and "What types of software do you know how to use?" When you can answer "yes" to the first question and answer the second with a list of different types of software packages, you will be ready for that job interview. As a person living in what is now often called the Information Age, you know that computers are used in almost all professions and offices. You will likely use some type of computer, probably a microcomputer, in your career. Chapter 1 will start you on your way to using this powerful tool to your advantage.

PREVIEW

When you have completed this chapter, you will be able to:

Explain what a computer system is by focusing on hardware, software, data/information, procedures, and people

Distinguish the four main types of computer systems

Describe the basic components of a microcomputer

Describe the types of tasks microcomputers are used for in business today

CHAPTER OUTLINE

This text focuses on microcomputers. By 1995, more than 185 million microcomputers will be in use in companies worldwide. But what is a microcomputer? How does this computer compare to other types of computers? Why do you need to know more about microcomputers than about other types of computers?

Chapter 1 defines terms, answers some questions, and puts the microcomputer into perspective by providing an overview of all types of computers. It also prepares you to learn about computer hardware and software as you progress through the text.

This chapter may mark your first step toward becoming computer literate. The meaning of **computer literacy**—also called **computer competency**—has rapidly changed. In the early 1980s, most **computer professionals** (those people who have had formal education in the technical aspects of computers) thought of it simply as *technical knowledge*; to **users** (those people without much technical knowledge of computers but who make decisions based on reports and other results produced by computers), it usually meant only *computer awareness*. Today, however, to be considered computer literate you must have a solid understanding of what a computer is and how it can be used as a resource. In addition, to be computer literate you must know how to use a microcomputer as a business or professional tool to assist in producing the information necessary to make intelligent and timely decisions.

The change in the definition of computer literacy during the 1980s is a direct result of the greatly increased use of microcomputers in business. Because many management professionals already know how to use microcomputers, your success in the business or professional world may mean that you also must master this skill.

WHAT IS A COMPUTER SYSTEM?

The term **computer** is used to describe a device made up of a combination of electronic and electromechanical (part electronic and part mechanical) components. By itself, a computer has no intelligence and is referred to as **hardware**. A computer doesn't come to life until it is connected to other parts of a computer system. A **computer system** (Figure 1.1) is a combination of five elements:

- Hardware
- Software
- Data/information
- Procedures
- People

When one computer system is set up to communicate with another computer system, **connectivity** becomes a sixth system element. In other words, the manner in which the various individual systems are connected—for example, by phone lines, microwave transmission, or satellite—is an element of the total computer system. In the 1990s, business professionals will direct a tremendous amount of attention and financial resources toward enabling different computer systems to communicate. We talk about connectivity in more detail in Chapter 8.

Software is the term used to describe the instructions that tell the hardware how to perform a task. Without software instructions, the hardware doesn't know what to do.

The purpose of a computer system is to convert data into information. **Data** is raw, *unevaluated* facts and figures, concepts, or instructions. This raw material is processed into useful **information**. In other words, information is the product of **data processing**. This **processing** includes refining, summarizing, categorizing, and otherwise manipulating data into a useful form for decision making.

People (you), however, constitute the most important component of the computer system. People operate the computer hardware; they create the computer software instructions and respond to the **procedures** that those instructions present. People "capture" data in a variety of ways—for example, by reading, listening, or seeing. Then they may record the data on a document. For instance, Roger Shu records his name on an employee timecard by first entering the letter R. This letter, and each of the remaining letters in his name, is an element of data, as are the numbers 12/22 and 5, used to indicate the date and the number of overtime hours worked. By themselves, these data elements are useless; we must process them to make them mean something. The report produced when Roger's data is run through a computer-based employee records system gives us information— for example, the amount of money due Roger for his overtime work.

Now we'll discuss the basics about the hardware devices that convert data into information in a typical computer-based system.

COMPUTER HARDWARE

If, at a job interview, you are asked about what kind of computer equipment you've used before or what you know about hardware and you don't have an answer, your interviewer will probably perceive you as a person who doesn't take an active role in what's going on around you—a perception that could dramatically hurt your chances of getting the job you want. In today's business world, not

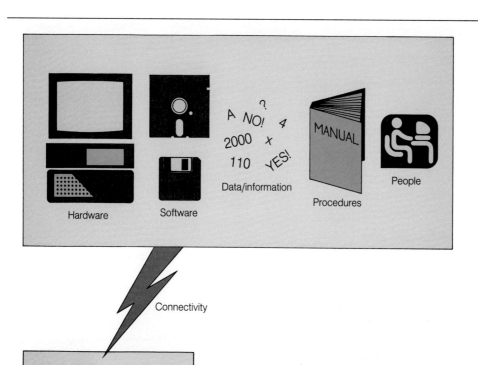

FIGURE 1.1

A computer system combines five elements: hardware, software, data/information, procedures, and people. Connectivity is a sixth element when two or more separate computer systems are set up to communicate.

knowing what computer hardware is and what typical hardware components do is similar to being a taxi driver and not knowing what a car is and that it has components such as an engine, doors, windows, and so on.

Computer hardware can be divided into four categories:

1. Input hardware
2. Processing hardware
3. Storage hardware
4. Output hardware

Figure 1.2 shows the typical configuration of computer hardware.

In this section, we provide a brief description of the components found in each of these categories so you can see how each component relates to others. In Chapters 2 through 5 we talk about input, processing, storage, and output hardware in more detail.

INPUT HARDWARE

The purpose of **input hardware** is to collect data and convert it into a form suitable for computer processing. The most common input device is a **keyboard**. It looks very much like a typewriter keyboard with rows of keys arranged in the typical typewriter layout, as well as a number of additional keys used to enter special computer-related codes. Although it isn't the only type of input device available, the computer keyboard is the one most generally used by the business community. In Chapter 2, we describe the microcomputer keyboard in detail, along with other types of popular input devices.

FIGURE 1.2

The four categories of computer hardware are input, processing, storage, and output.

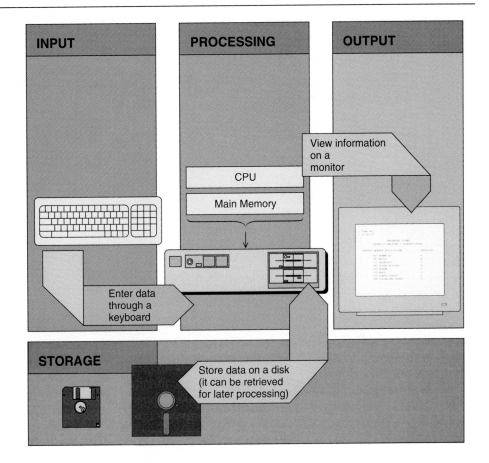

PROCESSING HARDWARE

The purpose of **processing hardware** is to retrieve, interpret, and direct the execution of software instructions provided to the computer. The most common components of processing hardware are the central processing unit and main memory.

The **central processing unit (CPU)** is the brain of the computer. It reads and interprets software instructions and coordinates the processing activities that must take place. The design of the CPU affects the processing power and the speed of the computer, as well as the amount of main memory it can use effectively. With a well-designed CPU in your computer, you can perform highly sophisticated tasks in a very short time.

Main memory (also called *random access memory* [RAM], *internal memory*, *primary storage*, or just *memory*) can be thought of as an electronic desktop. The more desk surface you have in front of you, the more you can place on it. Similarly, if your computer has a lot of memory, you can place more software instructions in it. (Some of these instructions and data are retrieved by the computer from storage on disk or tape; others are input directly by the user—for example, through the keyboard.) The amount of memory available determines whether you can run simple or sophisticated software; a computer with a large memory is more capable of holding the thousands of instructions that are contained in the more sophisticated software programs. In addition, it also allows you to work with and manipulate great amounts of data and information at one time. Quite simply, the more main memory you have in your computer, the more you can accomplish. However, the data and instructions in main memory are **volatile**—that is, they are lost when the computer's power is turned off, unless the user had saved them to a storage device. In Chapter 3, we describe processing hardware in more detail.

STORAGE HARDWARE

The purpose of **storage hardware** is to provide a means of storing computer instructions and data in a form that is relatively permanent, or **nonvolatile**—that is, the data is not lost when the power is turned off—and easy to retrieve when needed for processing. Storage hardware serves the same basic functions as do office filing systems except that it stores data as electromagnetic signals or laser-etched spots, commonly on disk or tape, rather than on paper. Storage devices are discussed in Chapter 4.

OUTPUT HARDWARE

The purpose of **output hardware** is to provide the user with the means to view information produced by the computer system. Information is output in either **hardcopy** or **softcopy** form. Hardcopy output can be held in your hand—an example is paper with text (words or numbers) or graphics printed on it. Softcopy output is displayed on a **monitor,** a television-like screen on which you can read text and graphics. We describe output devices in Chapter 5.

Communications hardware, which is used to transmit output among and receive input from different computer systems, is discussed in Chapter 8.

COMPUTER SOFTWARE

A computer is an inanimate device that has no intelligence of its own and must be supplied with instructions so that it knows what to do and how and when to do it. These instructions are called *software*. The importance of software can't be overestimated. You might have what most people consider the best computer sitting on your desk; however, without software to "feed" it, the computer will do nothing more than take up space.

Software is made up of a group of related **programs,** each of which is a group of related instructions that perform very specific processing tasks. These instructions are represented on disk or tape using a binary coding scheme. In Chapter 4, we describe in detail how instructions and data are represented on storage devices.

Software acquired to perform a general business function is often referred to as a **software package**. Software packages, which are usually created by professional software writers, are accompanied by **documentation**—users' manuals—that explains how to use the software.

Software can generally be divided into two categories:

1. Systems software
2. Applications software

SYSTEMS SOFTWARE

Programs designed to allow the computer to manage its own resources are called **systems software**. This software runs the basic operations; it tells the hardware what to do and how and when to do it. However, it does not solve specific problems relating to a business or a profession. For example, systems software will not process a prediction of what your company's tax bill will be next year, but it will tell the computer where to store the data used during processing; systems software will not process the creation of the animation strip for your next film, but it will manage how it is output.

APPLICATIONS SOFTWARE

Any instructions or collection of related programs designed to be carried out by a computer to satisfy a user's *specific* needs are **applications software**. A group of programs written to perform payroll processing is one type of applications software, as are programs written to maintain personnel records, update an inventory system, help you calculate a budget, or monitor the incubation temperatures at your poultry farm.

Applications software can be purchased off the shelf—that is, already programmed, or written—or it can be written to order by qualified programmers. If, for example, a company's payroll processing requirements are fairly routine, it can probably purchase one or more payroll applications software programs off the shelf to handle the job. However, if a company has unique payroll requirements, such as a need to handle the records of hourly employees, salaried employees, and commissioned employees, then off-the-shelf software may not be satisfactory. It may be more cost-effective to have the payroll programs written to exact specifications by a computer programmer.

Figure 1.3 shows a variety of packaged applications software available at computer stores. Many of these products are also available through vendors and mail-order sources.

Chapters 6 and 7 explore the categories of applications software and systems software.

TYPES OF COMPUTER SYSTEMS: WHAT'S THE DIFFERENCE?

Microcomputer users often come into contact with other types of computer systems. To provide a basis for comparing their capabilities, computers are generally grouped into four basic categories:

1. Supercomputers, which are the powerful giants of the computer world;
2. Mainframe computers, which are large, extremely powerful computers used by many large companies;

3. Minicomputers, which are the next most powerful;

4. Microcomputers, which are the least powerful—but which you most likely will be required to use in business.

It's hard to assign a worthwhile definition to each type of computer because definitions can get bogged down in potentially confusing technical jargon. Nevertheless, the following definitions can suffice:

- A **supercomputer** (Figure 1.4) can handle gigantic amounts of scientific computation. It's maintained in a special room or environment, may be about 50,000 times faster than a microcomputer, and may cost as much as $20 million. As a user in business, you probably would not have contact with a supercomputer. However, you might if you worked in the areas of defense and weaponry, weather forecasting, or scientific research; at one of several large universities; or for the National Aeronautics and Space Administration.

FIGURE 1.3

Need help with your budget? Want to design and print some greeting cards or your own newsletter? Want to set up a large bank of cross-referenced, business-related data? Buying software is almost like buying records, tapes, and CDs. Most computer stores offer a wide variety of applications software packages. But be sure you know what you want to accomplish before you make your selection.

■ A **mainframe computer** (Figure 1.5) is a large computer, usually housed in a controlled environment, that can support the processing requirements of hundreds and often thousands of users and computer professionals. It may cost from several hundred thousand dollars up to $10 million. If you go to work for an airline, a bank, a large insurance company, a large accounting company, a large university, or the Social Security Administration, you will likely have contact—through your individual workstation—with a mainframe computer.

■ A **minicomputer,** also known as a *midsized* or *low-end mainframe computer* (Figure 1.6), is similar to but less powerful than a mainframe computer. It

FIGURE 1.4

Supercomputer. This supercomputer (center), capable of performing 1.8 billion calculations a second, is the centerpiece of the National Test Bed. It was installed in mid-1988 at Colorado Springs for the U.S. Strategic Defense Initiative.

FIGURE 1.5

Mainframe. The mainframe computer is front left, between two printers. At the back left are disk-drive storage units; tape storage units are at the back and back right. These units, or peripherals, are connected to the mainframe by under-floor cables.

can support 2 to about 50 users and computer professionals. Minicomputers and mainframe computers can work much faster than microcomputers and have many more storage locations in main memory. Minicomputers cost from about $10,000 to several hundred thousand dollars. Many small and medium-sized companies today use minicomputers.

- The **microcomputer** (Figure 1.7) is the type of computer that you undoubtedly will be dealing with as a user. You may already be familiar with the microcomputer, also known as a *personal computer* (*PC*). Microcomputers cost between $500 and about $20,000. They vary in size from small portables, such as *notebook computers* and *laptop computers* that you can carry around like a briefcase, to powerful desktop *workstations*, such as those used by engineers and scientists. A microcomputer, which is generally used by only one person at a time but which can often support more—uses a **chip** as its CPU. This chip is referred to as the **microprocessor**. As small as one quarter of an inch square (Figure 1.8), a chip is made of silicon, a material made from sand. Silicon is referred to as a **semiconductor** because it sometimes conducts electricity and sometimes does not (*semi* means "partly"). (Silicon by itself conducts electricity poorly, but when impurities such as arsenic and indium are added, it can be used to form electrical circuits.)

Table 1.1 compares the four basic types of computers. In general, a computer's type is determined by the following seven factors:

1. *The type of CPU.* As noted, microcomputers use microprocessors. The larger computers tend to use CPUs made up of separate, high-speed, sophisticated components.

2. *The amount of main memory the CPU can use.* A computer equipped with a large amount of main memory can support more sophisticated programs and can even hold several different programs in memory at the same time.

FIGURE 1.6

Minicomputer. Four to more than 100 personal computers (workstations) can be linked to a minicomputer. (The minicomputer in this photo is on the floor to the left of the desk. The computers on the desks are linked to it.)

3. *The capacity of the storage devices.* The larger computer systems tend to be equipped with higher-capacity storage devices (covered in Chapter 4).

4. *The speed of the output devices.* The speed of microcomputer output devices tends to be rated in terms of the number of **characters per second (cps)** that can be printed—usually in tens and hundreds of cps. Larger computers' output devices are faster and are usually rated at speeds of hundreds or thousands of lines that can be printed per minute.

FIGURE 1.7

Microcomputer. This photo shows an IBM PS/2 Model 90 XP486 microcomputer; the three main components are the monitor, the system unit, and the keyboard. This unit also has a mouse.

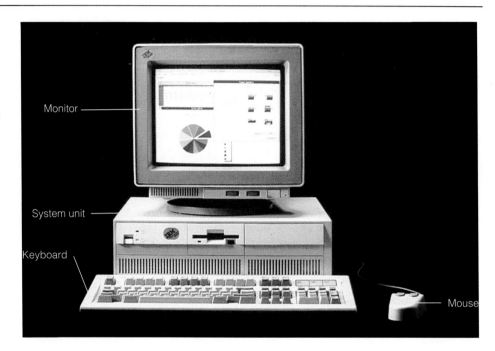

FIGURE 1.8

This photo of a microprocessor gives you an idea of how small a chip is.

5. *The processing speed in* **millions of instructions per second (mips).** The term *instruction* is used here to describe a basic task that the software asks the computer to perform while also identifying the data to be affected. The processing speed of the smaller computers ranges from 3 to 5 mips. The speed of large computers can be 70 to 100 mips or more, and supercomputers can process from 200 million up to billions of instructions per second. In other words, a mainframe computer can process your data a great deal faster than a microcomputer can.

6. *The number of users that can access the computer at one time.* Most small computers can support only a single user; some can support as many as two or three at a time. Large computers can support hundreds of users simultaneously.

7. *The cost of the computer system.* Business systems can cost as little as $1,500 (for a microcomputer) or as much as $10 million (for a mainframe)—and much more for a supercomputer.

It's difficult to say exactly what kind of computer you'll be using in the business environment. Some companies use a combination of computers. For instance, a company with branch offices around the country might use a mainframe computer to manage companywide customer data. To access information from the mainframe, the user might use a microcomputer that sits on his or her desktop. In addition to accessing information from the mainframe computer, the microcomputer can be used to perform specialized tasks such as generating invoices or drafting letters to customers. Although it is still relatively easy to find a company that doesn't use a supercomputer, a mainframe, or a minicomputer to process data, it is difficult to locate a company that doesn't use a microcomputer for some of its processing. Because microcomputers are generally versatile, increasingly powerful, and more affordable than the other types of computers, they provide a practical tool for the business that wants to computerize.

Chances are that, when you enter the business environment, you will be required to know how to use a microcomputer to perform many of your job-related functions. To use a microcomputer effectively and talk about it intelligently, you

---

TABLE 1.1 The Four Kinds of Computers*

	Microcomputer	Minicomputer	Mainframe	Supercomputer
Main memory	512,000– 32,000,000 characters	8,000,000– 50,000,000 characters	32,000,000– 200,000,000 characters	100,000,000– 2,000,000,000 characters
Storage	360,000– 300,000,000 characters	120,000,000– 1,000,000,000+ characters	500,000,000–? characters	No limitation
Processing speed	700,000– 10,000,000 instructions per second	8–40 mips	30 mips and up	200 mips and up
Cost	$500–20,000	$10,000– $475,000	$250,000 and up	$10,000,000 and up

*The figures in this table represent average approximations. These numbers change rapidly as changing technology blurs the distinctions between categories.

must understand the typical components of a microcomputer system. The more you know about them, the more valuable you will be to an employer. In the following section, we concentrate a bit more on microcomputer components.

THE ANATOMY OF A MICROCOMPUTER

To understand the tremendous role microcomputers now play in business, it's helpful to look at how that role has developed. With the introduction of the Apple II and the Radio Shack Model I and II systems in the late 1970s, the business community began to adopt microcomputers. Then a number of additional vendors, including Atari, Commodore, Osborne, and Kaypro, entered the marketplace with computers designed to be used in the office or in the home. The interest in microcomputers grew rather slowly at first for several reasons: (1) The initial cost for some microcomputer systems was quite high, ranging up to $6,000; (2) only a limited amount of software was commercially available, and the average person was not able to write his or her own software; (3) the average person did not have sufficient background in computer-related subjects to use the computer without difficulty; and (4) there were no industrywide standards to ensure the **compatibility**—that is, the usability—of data and software on different types of microcomputer systems.

However, when IBM introduced the IBM PC in 1981, so many businesses adopted the product that an industry standard was set. Most vendors now design their products to be compatible with this standard—these products are referred to as IBM **clones**. The only other relatively successful microcomputer product lines today that have maintained their own unique standards are the Apple II and the Macintosh. The Apple II retains a loyal group of users who have supported it since its introduction in the late 1970s. Although the Apple II has been overshadowed in the business world by IBM-compatible products, the powerful and versatile Apple Macintosh line of microcomputers is now commonly used in desktop publishing operations. (We'll discuss desktop publishing in more detail in Chapter 6.)

The large number of different types of microcomputer systems in the marketplace makes it difficult to select one best system. As a result, our discussion of the microcomputer will center on the three basic hardware devices found in most desktop microcomputer systems used in business today: the keyboard, the monitor, and the system unit (Figure 1.9).

KEYBOARD

The microcomputer input device that you will use the most—the keyboard—is made up of a circuit board and related electronic components that generate a unique electronic code when each key is pressed. The code is passed along the keyboard cord to the computer system unit, where it is translated into a usable form for processing. The number of keys and their positions on the keyboard vary among machines. You should select a keyboard that is comfortable for you to use. (A mouse is also frequently used to input data, but we will describe the mouse in Chapter 2.)

MONITOR

The term *monitor* is used interchangeably with *screen, video display screen,* and *cathode-ray tube* (CRT). This output device provides your principal visual contact with the microcomputer system. When you enter commands or data from the keyboard, you see the results on the monitor. A **monochrome monitor** displays text and, in some cases, graphics in a single color—commonly green or amber— usually on a dark background. A **color monitor,** often referred to as an **RGB monitor** (for red, green, blue), can display text and graphics in various colors. Most of the capabilities of the monitor, including image clarity and the ability to do graphics, are determined by the sophistication of the video display circuit board, if any, contained within the system unit.

System Unit

The main computer system cabinet, called the **system unit** (Figure 1.10), usually houses the power supply, the system board, and the storage devices (although

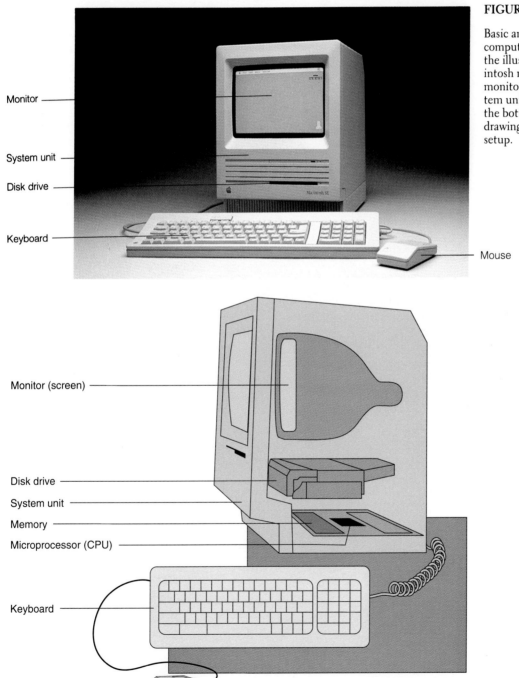

Monitor

System unit

Disk drive

Keyboard

Mouse

Monitor (screen)

Disk drive

System unit

Memory

Microprocessor (CPU)

Keyboard

Mouse

FIGURE 1.9

Basic anatomy of a microcomputer. The top part of the illustration shows a Macintosh microcomputer with monitor, keyboard, and system unit with disk drive; on the bottom is a cutaway drawing of the same basic setup.

some storage devices—disk drives, for example—are often housed in cabinets outside the system unit). These elements can be defined as follows:

1. The **power supply** provides electrical power to all components housed in the system unit. In some microcomputers—such as the Macintosh—it also provides power to the monitor.

2. The **system board,** also known as the **motherboard,** is the main circuit board of the microcomputer system. It normally includes (1) the microprocessor chip (or CPU), (2) main memory chips, (3) all related support circuitry, and (4) the expansion slots where additional components can be plugged in.

3. The **storage devices** are usually one or more floppy disk drives and usually a high-capacity hard disk drive. A **floppy disk,** or **diskette,** is a thin plastic disk enclosed in a paper or plastic covering that can be magnetically encoded with data. **Hard disks** are rigid disks capable of storing much more

---

FIGURE 1.10

This illustration shows the basic parts of the microcomputer's system unit. (The system board continues under the diskette drive.)

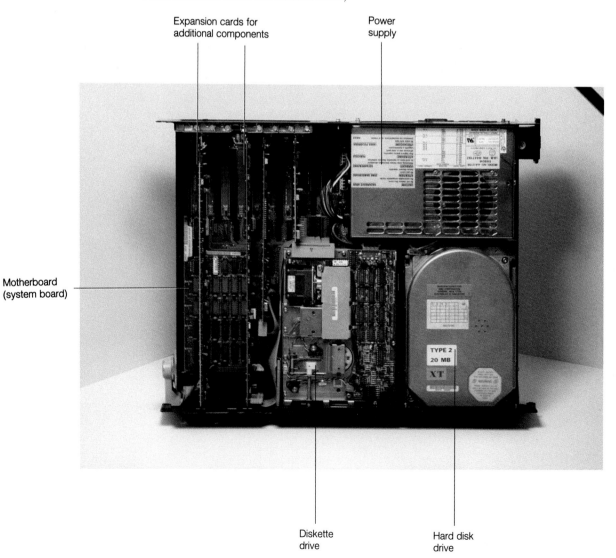

Expansion cards for additional components

Power supply

Motherboard (system board)

Diskette drive

Hard disk drive

data than a floppy disk. (And hard disk drives access data faster than do floppy disk drives.) Hard disks are more expensive than floppy disks. Since most hard disks are permanently installed in the system unit, floppy disks, which can be carried around, are often used to move data from one computer to another.

4. *Additional components:* The expansion slots on the system board allow users to add new components to their computer systems. The most popular add-on components include:
   - A memory card containing main memory chips that give you additional main memory
   - An internal modem to facilitate data communications between computers over phone lines and similar cables
   - A battery-powered clock and calendar mechanism
   - Additional printer ports (hook-ups) that allow you to communicate with several types of output devices
   - Video display boards

Don't worry about remembering what all these components are right now. They will be explained in detail later in the book. Just remember that microcomputers are likely to become an important part of your career. Pay attention to them and focus on what they can do for you.

MICROCOMPUTERS AT WORK

No longer are jobs that require computing experience the sole domain of the computer professional. Today, job applicants on any level may need personal computer experience. In most businesses, microcomputers are viewed as standard business tools for all employees, from the president of the company to the clerks in the typing pool. As the following excerpts from ads in a newspaper's Job Opportunities section demonstrate, many jobs require personal computing experience.

- Accounting—A/R (Accounts Receivable) Supervisor. "Knowledge of PC-based accounting system is a must."
- Consulting. "Prioritize work loads and manage office. Experience with word processing software required."
- Administrative Assistant. "Must have strong background in WordPerfect and Lotus."
- Banking—Loan Service Manager. "Personal computers and basic accounting skills required."
- Contracts Administrator. "Experience required in all aspects of contract administration, including contract and proposal preparation, scheduling, expediting, tracking, and closing. PC experience required."
- Data Entry Operator. "Prior experience on personal computer required."
- Copywriter. "Knowledge of word processing a must."
- Financial Operations. "Computer skills required."
- Loan Processor Trainee. "High-volume mortgage company is looking for qualified individual to train. Must have prior PC experience."
- Sales. "Growth-oriented new software engineering company seeks a results-oriented individual. PC experience preferred."
- Telemarketer. "Professional high-spirited team seeks telemarketer with microcomputer background."

- Production Editor. "Should be knowledgeable about latest desktop publishing techniques, preferably Ventura. Multimate and Lotus a plus."

For each of these jobs—and for many others—unless you have experience using a microcomputer, you probably won't even be considered (Figure 1.11)!

Microcomputing technology is being used across many nations in many different environments. Medical, education, and government sites account for approximately 42% of all installed personal computers in the United States. Other types of businesses—in the areas of banking, savings and loan, transportation, utilities, finance, insurance, process manufacturing, agriculture, data processing, publishing, wholesale and retail businesses—use microcomputers the most. As stated, no matter where you work, you will most likely use a microcomputer to perform some of your job-related tasks. Because of this likelihood, you should be asking yourself the following kinds of questions: What types of tasks are microcomputers being used for? Why are they so popular? How can a business justify the costs of hardware, software, and training? To answer these questions, the following sections

FIGURE 1.11

These job ads from real newspapers and magazines represent only a few ways computers are used in business and the professions.

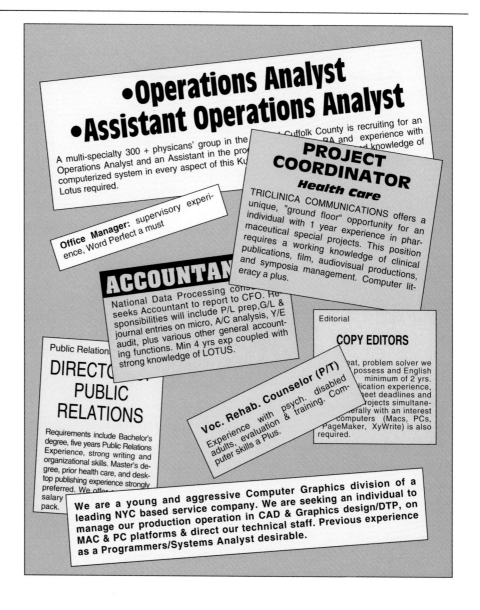

describe the types of tasks that microcomputers are typically used for in business. Most businesses perform one or more of these tasks.

MANAGING DOCUMENTS

Word processing software—software that enables the user to electronically create, edit, store, and print documents—is one of the most popular types of microcomputer applications in business. In fact, many microcomputers are used *only* for word processing. Because word processing software makes creating, changing, "dressing up," duplicating, and printing documents much quicker and easier than it used to be, it saves the business professional a lot of time and money. Thus when a business purchases a microcomputer, it typically purchases word processing software. As a result, word processing software sales have climbed steadily over the last five years—and they continue to do so.

MANAGING DATABASES

Another major reason businesses bring microcomputers in-house is to help them manage, and draw conclusions about, huge amounts of data—their company **database**. Before dBASE II was introduced in 1982, computer-based database management activities were performed principally by mainframes and minicomputers. Because of the huge expenses associated with purchasing and operating these large systems, most businesses couldn't afford to computerize the management of company data. In addition, the computer systems weren't easy to use, and they required that experienced programmers be hired to first write the software for the system and then run the system. For most businesses, using microcomputers and dBASE II represented an astonishing alternative to managing the company database by hand. Data could now be kept up to date easily, and reports were more comprehensive and more readily available than they previously were. And the system didn't have to be run by trained programmers. Because of this new and valuable software tool, sales of microcomputers skyrocketed.

Today, database management is a common application for microcomputers in business. Sales of **database management software** continue to rise at the same rate as sales of word processing software.

COMMUNICATIONS

One of the major reasons microcomputers are so popular in business is that they facilitate efficient communication. In more and more companies and professions, microcomputers are being "tied" together so they can share data and information. In such environments, microcomputers are used to enable people in offices around the country and around the world to communicate without playing "telephone tag." In addition, when microcomputer systems are connected, it's easy to distribute announcements and reports, thereby reducing the amount of paper shuffling that goes on. Some experts predict that soon 90% of all microcomputers in business will be part of a **network,** or connected to one or more other computers.

Microcomputers with **facsimile (fax)** capabilities—the ability to "read" text and graphics and transmit them over telephone lines to other microcomputers with fax capabilities—are being used by more and more businesses every day. Faxing documents instead of sending them via a messenger service or an overnight shipping service saves some companies thousands of dollars monthly. And, instead of having to wait one or two days to receive important documents, fax users have to wait only a few minutes.

ACCOUNTING AND FINANCE

Recently the personal computer has had a highly visible influence on how finances are managed in businesses. According to a study conducted by the National Association of Accountants, Arthur Young & Co., and Digital Equipment Corporation, most financial functions in business—including planning, forecasting, budgeting, and management reporting—are performed by microcomputers. Of 510 senior executives surveyed (from companies of more than $50 million in revenues), 83% used microcomputers routinely to receive up-to-date financial information.

From major stock exchanges around the world to individual businesses and households, computers are affecting the way huge amounts of money are being handled each day. In investment brokerage houses across the United States, microcomputers are being used to make brokers more efficient. For example, in 1987, Merrill Lynch & Co. replaced its mainframe computer with 20,000 IBM PS/2 microcomputers. The move was designed to provide brokers at the 500 offices around the world with more useful information. In 1991, Shearson Lehman had nearly 70 Sun 360 and Compaq 386 microcomputers working together on the floor of the New York Stock Exchange. Also, it is estimated that 8 out of 10 accountants use microcomputers to do their jobs. **Electronic spreadsheet software**—software that allows users to easily perform complicated calculations on large amounts of data—is used extensively to perform accounting and finance-related tasks.

MICROCOMPUTERS IN THE FUTURE

In retrospect, the development of the microcomputer into an integral part of business and North American culture seems to have progressed predictably over the past decade or so. But this is not really true. No one in the early 1980s could have foreseen what the microcomputer would look like and be able to do today. The collective effort of thousands of innovators and investors has helped to define the modern microcomputer, and it has ultimately been business that has determined what technologies stay and go and what technologies are needed.

What is the point? It is hard to foresee exactly what the microcomputer will evolve into during the next decade. However, it certainly will play an important role in your career. With each passing year, the technologies that allow all types of computers to communicate are improving so that the issue of compatibility will no longer be an issue. It won't matter whether you are using an IBM PS/2, a Macintosh, a mainframe, or some other type of computer—each one will be able to process data from the others.

You can also be sure that the microcomputers of tomorrow will be able to process data faster. It seems that, with each day, some technological advance is made that increases the speed with which microcomputers can process data into information. The faster a computer can process data, the greater the amount of work that can be done in the same amount of time—that is, if the work is being done in an appropriate manner. Even though microcomputers are becoming more and more powerful, their cost has been going down. Indeed, the microcomputer industry is one of the few industries in which the product's price goes down as the product becomes more powerful and more useful. It is predicted that by 1994, microcomputers will be as powerful as the mainframes of 10 years ago, and the cost of processing on microcomputers will be 80 times less than it was in 1984.

In short, microcomputers will continue to get better and better. When referring to the microcomputers of the 1990s, Edward M. Esber, the chairman and CEO of a prominent software company, said: "It goes without saying that the dinosaurs won't survive. It's going to be an exciting new world."

SUMMARY

- Being *computer literate*—that is, being familiar with computers and their uses—is necessary today because it is virtually inevitable that you will be using a computer in your career. As the uses of computers in business and the professions increase, graduating students will be required to have more advanced computer training.

- A computer is a device made up of electronic and electromechanical parts; by itself it has no intelligence and is referred to as *hardware*.

- A computer must be part of a system to be useful. A *computer system* has five parts:
  1. *Hardware*
  2. *Software*
  3. *Data/information*
  4. *Procedures*
  5. *People*

- *Hardware* comprises the electronic and the electromechanical parts of the computer system.

- *Software* is the instructions—electronically encoded on disk or tape—that tell the hardware what to do.

- *Data* is raw, unevaluated facts, concepts, or instructions. Through *data processing* data becomes *information*, which is data transformed into a form useful for decision making. Processing can include refining, summarizing, categorizing, and listing, as well as other forms of data manipulation.

- *Procedures* are specific sequences of steps, usually documented, that users follow to complete one or more information processing activities.

- *People*—the most important part of the computer system—operate the computer hardware, create the software instructions, and establish *procedures* for carrying out tasks.

- Computer hardware is categorized as:
  1. *Input hardware*—used to collect data and input it into the computer system in computer-usable form. The *keyboard* is the most common input device.
  2. *Processing hardware*—retrieves, interprets, and directs the execution of software instructions. The main components of processing hardware are the *central processing unit* (CPU), which is the "brain" of the computer, and *main memory*, the computer's primary storage area, where data and instructions currently being used are stored. These data and instructions are *volatile*—that is, they will be lost when the computer's power is turned off, unless they are saved to a storage device.
  3. *Storage hardware*—usually disk or tape devices for relatively permanent (*nonvolatile*) storage of data and instructions for later retrieval and processing.
  4. *Output hardware*—provides a means for the user to view information produced by the computer system—either in *hardcopy* form, such as printouts from a printer, or *softcopy* form, such as a display on a monitor, a TV-like screen that can be color (*RGB*) or *monochrome*, usually amber, green, or black and white.

- *Software*, which is usually written by professional programmers, is made up of a group of related *programs*, each of which is a group of related instructions that perform specific processing tasks. Software that runs the hardware and allows the computer to manage its resources is *systems software*; software that is written to perform a specific function for the user—such as preparing payroll or doing page-makeup for a magazine—is *applications software*. Applications software can be purchased *off the shelf* as a *software package*, or it can be *custom written* to solve the unique needs of one company or business. Software is accompanied by *documentation*, or users' manuals.

- Computers are categorized from the largest and most powerful to the smallest and least powerful:
  1. *Supercomputer*
  2. *Mainframe computer*
  3. *Minicomputer*
  4. *Microcomputer*

- A computer's type is determined by seven factors:
  1. Type of CPU
  2. Amount of main memory the CPU can use
  3. Storage capacity
  4. Speed of output devices
  5. Processing speed
  6. Number of users that can access the computer at one time
  7. Cost

- The microcomputer (*personal computer*, or *PC*) is the computer used most by business professionals. Microcomputers range in size from small *notebooks* and *laptops* to powerful desktop *workstations*, which are hooked up to a larger computer. The microcomputer has a small *semiconductor* (*silicon*) *chip*, or *microprocessor*, as its CPU.

- A microcomputer main system cabinet—the *system unit*—usually houses the *power supply*, the *system board* (*motherboard*), and some storage devices, such as one or more floppy disk drives and a high-capacity hard disk drive. The system board includes the *microprocessor chip*, *main memory chips*, *related support circuitry*, and *expansion slots*.

- Microcomputers are used for, among other things, *word processing*—creating, editing, storing, and printing documents; *database management*—creating and managing huge "banks" of data; *communications*—facilitating immediate communication and document transmission capabilities through the use of *networks*, *fax*, and *modems*; and *financial management* through the use of electronic *spreadsheets*.

KEY TERMS

applications software, p. 6
central processing unit (CPU), p. 5
characters per second (cps), p. 10
chip, p. 9
clone, p. 12
color monitor, p. 12
compatibility, p. 12
computer, p. 2
computer literacy, p. 2
computer professional, p. 2
computer system, p. 2
connectivity, p. 2

data, p. 2
data processing, p. 3
database, p. 17
database management software, p. 17
diskette, p. 14
documentation, p. 6
electronic spreadsheet software, p. 18
facsimile (fax), p. 17
floppy disk, p. 14
hardcopy, p. 5
hard disk, p. 14
hardware, p. 2
information, p. 3
input hardware, p. 4

keyboard, p. 4
mainframe computer, p. 8
main memory, p. 5
microcomputer, p. 9
microprocessor, p. 9
millions of instructions per second (mips), p. 11
minicomputer, p. 8
monitor, p. 5
monochrome monitor, p. 12
motherboard, p. 14
network, p. 17
nonvolatile, p. 5

EXERCISES

SELF-TEST

1. (Figure 1.12) Label the components of the microcomputer.
2. The term _____ is used to describe a device made up of electronic and electromechanical parts.
3. List four categories of hardware:
   a. _____   b. _____   c. _____   d. _____
4. Main memory is a software component. (true/false)
5. _____ _____ includes programs designed to enable the computer to manage its own resources.
6. Softcopy output can be displayed on a _____, or TV-like screen.
7. Related programs designed to be carried out by a computer to satisfy a user's *specific* needs are called _____ _____.
8. Computers are generally grouped into one of the following four basic categories:
   a. _____   b. _____   c. _____   d. _____

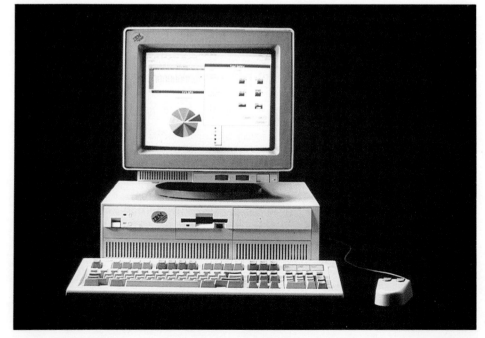

FIGURE 1.12

9. You are more likely to use a microcomputer in business than a supercomputer. (true/false)
10. The _____ _____ of a microcomputer usually houses the power supply, the system board, and the storage devices.
11. _____ monitors display images in a single color or black and white.
12. Hard disks have greater storage capacities than diskettes. (true/false)
13. _____ _____ software offers capabilities for creating, editing, storing, and printing documents.
14. Users' manuals that accompany computer hardware and software are referred to as _____.
15. Mainframe computers process faster than microcomputers. (true/false)
16. The CPU of a microcomputer is referred to as the _____.
17. Chips are made of silicon, which is referred to as a semiconductor because it sometimes conducts electricity and sometimes does not. (true/false)
18. As a result of data processing, _____ (what you put into the computer) is often processed into useful _____ (what is output by the computer).
19. List the five parts of a computer system:
    a. _____ b. _____ c. _____ d. _____ e. _____
20. To be _____ _____ you must have a solid understanding of what a computer is and how it can be used as a resource.

SOLUTIONS (1) see Figure 1.7; (2) computer; (3) input, processing, storage, output; (4) false; (5) systems software; (6) monitor; (7) applications software; (8) supercomputer, mainframe, minicomputer, microcomputer; (9) true; (10) system unit; (11) monochrome; (12) true; (13) word processing; (14) documentation; (15) true; (16) microprocessor; (17) true; (18) data, information; (19) hardware, software, data/information, procedures, people; (20) computer literate

SHORT ANSWER

1. What is a microcomputer?
2. Describe the function of each of the five main components of a computer system.
3. What does it mean to be computer literate? Why is computer literacy, or competency, important?
4. Why do you think many companies spend a lot of money training their employees how to use computers?
5. What is the difference between systems software and applications software?
6. What is the meaning of the term *connectivity*?
7. What is a microprocessor?
8. What factors determine a computer's type (supercomputer, mainframe, minicomputer, microcomputer)?
9. What is the function of storage hardware in a computer system?
10. What is the purpose of main memory?
11. What types of tasks are microcomputers used for?
12. What is the purpose of the system unit in a microcomputer system?
13. How is a computer *user* different from a *computer specialist*?

14. What are two main differences between floppy disks and hard disks?

15. Is main memory volatile or nonvolatile? What does that mean?

16. What is word processing software? Spreadsheet software? Database management software?

PROJECTS

1. Determine what types of computers are being used where you work or go to school. Are microcomputers being used? Minicomputers? Mainframes? All types? What are they being used for? How are they connected, if at all?

2. Look in the job opportunities section of several newspapers to see if many jobs require applicants to be familiar with using microcomputers. What types of experience are required? What kinds of computer skills do you think you'll need in your chosen job or career? (Note: A school advisor in your major or field may be able to help you answer the last question.)

3. Many people are afraid of or resistant to learning about computers. Are you one of them? If so, make a list of all the factors that you think are affecting your attitude, then list reasons to refute each point. Keep your list and review it again after you have finished the course. What do you still agree with? Have you changed your mind about computers?

4. Although more new information has been produced in the last 30 years than in the previous 5,000, information isn't knowledge. In our quest for knowledge in the Information Age, we are often overloaded with information that doesn't tell us what we want to know. Richard Wurman identified this problem in his book *Information Anxiety*; Naisbitt, in his books *Megatrends* and *Megatrends 2000*, said that "uncontrolled and unorganized information is no longer a resource in an information society. Instead, it becomes the enemy of the information worker."

   Identify some of the problems of information overload in one or two departments in your school or place of employment—or in a local business, such as a real estate firm, health clinic, pharmacy, or accounting firm. What types of problems are people having? How are they trying to solve them? Are they rethinking their use of computer-related technologies?

CHAPTER 2

INPUT HARDWARE

Do you know how to type?

Perhaps it may not be necessary to learn. Methods exist for inputting data and software instructions to a microcomputer system that do not require a keyboard. We believe, however, that if you do know how to type, you are much better off. No matter what company or organization you join, it will most likely want to hire people who can handle a microcomputer keyboard—not just clerks and typists, but managers and executives as well.

PREVIEW

When you have completed this chapter, you will be able to:

Describe the different keys on the microcomputer keyboard

Name the main direct-entry (nonkeyboard) input devices used with a microcomputer and describe how they are used

CHAPTER OUTLINE

WHY IS THIS CHAPTER IMPORTANT?

In most jobs, you will not be able to avoid entering data of some sort into a computer system. Thus, the more you understand about input hardware, the better you will be able to do your job. If you find keyboards somewhat cumbersome, be glad you are entering the job market now rather than back in the 60s. Then, the principal means of inputting data to a computer system was on punched cards—the so-called IBM cards that a generation of college students were admonished never to "fold, spindle, or mutilate." Although these cards are still in use in some quarters, their numbers are very few compared to the 150,000 tons of them that were used every year in the 1960s—enough, put end to end, to stretch 8 million miles.

In this chapter, we describe the input hardware components you will probably encounter in your career. One of the easiest ways to categorize input hardware is according to whether or not it uses a keyboard. We have focused special attention on the keyboard, because it will probably be your principal input device. In addition, we describe the following nonkeyboard input devices, called *direct-entry devices:* scanners, fax, mice, trackballs, light pens, touch screens, and voice recognition equipment.

FIGURE 2.1

This figure shows two common kinds of computer keyboards—(a) an IBM PC keyboard and (b) an enhanced keyboard (which has a numeric keypad separate from the cursor-movement keys).

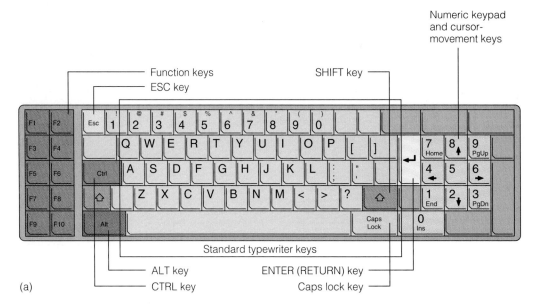

1. Esc   ESC key: This key can be thought of as the "undo" key. Pressing it when using many of the applications software packages in use today will move you out of a command that you didn't want to be in.

2. Ctrl   CTRL key: This key, pressed along with another key, is often used to issue commands from within applications software packages (key combinations differ according to package).

3. Alt   ALT key: This key, pressed along with another key, is often used to issue commands from within applications software packages.

4. F1 F2   Function keys: Software packages use these keys to perform certain commands. What each key does is determined by the software package you use.
    etc.

THE KEYBOARD

A computer **keyboard** (Figure 2.1) is a sophisticated electromechanical component designed to create special standardized electronic codes when a key is pressed. The codes are transmitted along the cable that connects the keyboard to the computer system unit or the terminal (a monitor connected to a system unit in another location), where the incoming code is analyzed and converted into the appropriate computer-usable code. If you can use a typewriter keyboard, you should find it easy to work with a computer keyboard. Except for a few differences, the layout of the keys is similar.

Because a code is sent to the computer every time a key is pressed, in most cases you should only *tap* the keys on the keyboard instead of holding them down. For example, if you press the letter "A" and keep your finger pressed down on the key, you will see something like "AAAAAAAAAAAAAAAAAAAA" on the screen. The same is true of issuing commands. For example, if you are trying to print a document and keep the keys pressed down that initiate the PRINT command, you may be sending multiple print instructions to the printer. As a result, with some computers, multiple copies of your document will print out on the printer.

(continued)   **FIGURE 2.1**

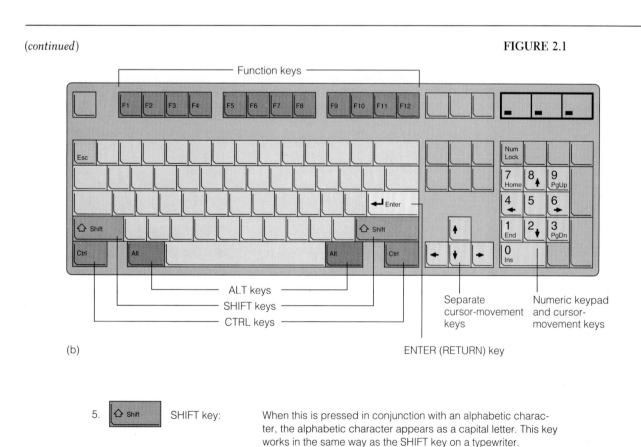

(b)

5. ⇧ Shift   SHIFT key: When this is pressed in conjunction with an alphabetic character, the alphabetic character appears as a capital letter. This key works in the same way as the SHIFT key on a typewriter.

6. ↵ Enter   ENTER key: This key is usually pressed to tell the computer to execute a command.

7. 4   Numeric keypad and cursor-movement keys: These keys are used to either enter numbers or to move the cursor around the screen. If the NUM LOCK key has been depressed, when you press these keys, numbers will appear on the screen. Otherwise, pressing these keys will cause your cursor to move around the screen in the direction of the arrows.

THE KEYS

Keyboards come in a variety of sizes and shapes, but most keyboards used with microcomputer systems have a certain number of features in common.

1. Standard typewriter keys
2. Function keys
3. Special-purpose keys
4. Cursor-movement keys
5. Numeric keys

You need to understand the purpose of these keys so that you can use the keyboard effectively.

The typewriter-like keys are used to type in text and special characters such as $, *, and #. In general, these keys are positioned in much the same location as the keys on a typewriter. People often refer to this layout as the **QWERTY** layout, because the first six characters on the top row of alphabetic keys spell "QWERTY."

The **function keys,** labeled F1, F2, F3, and so on, are used to issue commands (Figure 2.1). (Function keys are also called *programmable keys.*) Most keyboards are configured with from 10 to 12 function keys. The software program you are using determines how the function keys are used. For example, using one software program, you would press the F2 key to print your document. However, in a different software program, you would use the F2 key to save your work to disk. The user's manual (documentation) that comes with the software tells you how to use the function keys.

Computer keyboards also have some special-purpose keys such as Ctrl (Control), Alt (Alternate), Shift, Del (Delete), Ins (Insert), Caps Lock, and Enter. The **Ctrl key,** the **Alt key,** and the **Shift key** are modifier keys. By themselves they do nothing. But when pressed along with another key, they modify the function of the other key.

The **Ins key** and the **Del key** are used for editing what you type. Word processing software uses them frequently to insert and delete text.

The **Caps Lock key** is used to place all the alphabetic keys into an uppercase position (that is, capital letters only). This key is similar to the shift lock key on a typewriter, with one difference. The shift lock key allows you to type the upper character on any typewriter key, whereas the Caps Lock key affects *only* the alphabetic keys on the computer keyboard.

The **Enter key** is usually pressed to tell the computer to execute a command entered by first pressing other keys.

Cursor-movement keys (arrow keys) are used to move the **cursor** around the screen. (The cursor is the symbol on the video screen that shows where data will be input next; see Figure 2.2.) On the keyboards used with the early IBM PC-compatible microcomputers (which are still used in many businesses today), the keys for cursor movement were combined with the **numeric keypad**—the keys used to enter numbers (Figure 2.1a). When you turn it on, your microcomputer system "assumes" that the numeric keypad keys will be used for cursor movement. Therefore, you have to remember to press the **Num Lock key** or a Shift key before using these keys to enter numbers. On these older keyboards, it's easier to enter numerals by using the numbers across the top of the keyboard.

Most of today's keyboards have cursor-movement keys that are separate from the numeric keypad keys (Figure 2.1b). These keyboards are often referred to as *101-key enhanced keyboards.* When a microcomputer system that uses an enhanced keyboard is turned on, the assumption made by your computer system is that the Num Lock key is active—that is, the numeric keypad will be used for entering numbers.

FIGURE 2.2

The cursor shows the position on the screen where the next character, space, or command instruction will be entered. The cursor-movement (arrow) keys are used to move the cursor up, down, right, and left. The cursor can also be moved with a mouse.

The Macintosh extended keyboard   **FIGURE 2.3**

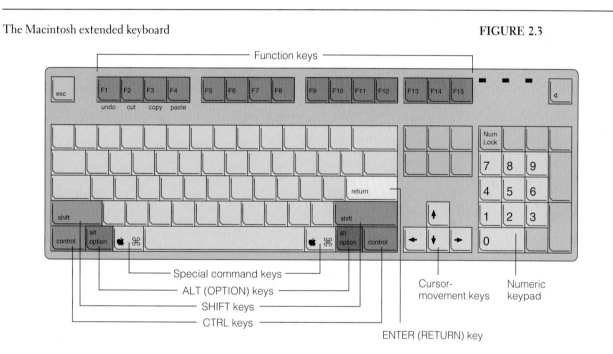

Figure 2.3 identifies the common types of keys on the Apple Macintosh keyboard.

NONKEYBOARD INPUT DEVICES

Some of the most exciting kinds of input systems don't use a keyboard. For example, did you know that you can touch a video display screen or use a "magic" wand to input data? Talk to a computer? Even use the movement of your eyes to tell the computer what to do? Nonkeyboard, or **direct entry,** data entry systems minimize the amount of human activity required to get data into a computer-usable form. The ones receiving the most attention today are

1. Scanning devices that "read" data
2. Voice input devices
3. So-called "pointing" devices

Most direct-entry input devices are used in conjunction with a keyboard because these specialized devices can't be used to input all types of data and instructions. An exception may be the Eyescan Communicator, which translates eye movements into signals for a computer. This innovation—still being refined—allows people who cannot speak or use keyboards to communicate using a computer.

SCANNING SYSTEMS

A **scanning system** consists of a microcomputer (PC), a scanner, and scanning software (Figure 2.4). These systems enable users to convert (digitize) a hardcopy picture or a photograph into a computer-usable graphics file that can be understood by a desktop publishing or graphics package (such as Aldus PageMaker or Adobe Illustrator). In addition, they enable users to convert hardcopy (printed) text into a text file that can be used by a word processing package (such as WordPerfect or Microsoft Word). Scanned images can be stored in a computer system, manipulated (changed), and/or output in a different form.

The software required to scan graphics is usually packaged with the scanner when you purchase it. The software required to scan characters, or text, called **optical character recognition (OCR) software,** isn't normally packaged with the scanner.

One factor to consider when choosing a scanner is whether you plan to scan graphics and/or text. If you typically scan graphics to be used by a desktop publishing or graphics package, you want your scanner to scan images at a high resolution—**resolution** refers to the clarity of an image. In addition, you want your scanner to support scanning as many shades of gray as possible; this is called *grayscale scanning.* The more shades of gray that a scanner is capable of scanning, the more natural the scanned image is, which is important if you're working with pho-

FIGURE 2.4

Scanning system. The scanner (left) converts the hardcopy photo into computer-usable form so it can be manipulated by desktop publishing or graphics software.

tographs. Color scanners and slide scanners are available for users who are using desktop publishing to produce sophisticated magazines and books.

Another factor to consider when purchasing a scanner is the physical format of the material you plan to scan. If you will often scan text or graphics from a bound volume, you should consider a **flatbed scanner** (Figure 2.5a). To use a flatbed scanner, the user must hold the material to be scanned in place on a piece of glass while the scanning mechanism, referred to as the **scanhead,** passes over it in a fashion similar to that of a copy machine. If you are working with loose sheets, consider a **sheet-fed scanner** (Figure 2.5b), which uses mechanical rollers to move the paper past the scanhead. Another type of scanner is the **hand-held scanner** (Figure 2.5c), which relies on the human hand to move the scanhead over the material to be scanned.

Scanners are also used for specialized purposes, such as identifying an individual by his or her fingerprints (Figure 2.6).

FAX

A **fax (facsimile) machine** uses a built-in scanner to read text and graphics and transmit them over phone lines to another fax machine or a computer with a fax board in its system unit. One factor to consider before purchasing a fax capability is your need to fax graphics, such as photos. If you do need to fax graphics, make sure the fax scanner can support displaying halftones, or shades of gray. If you are only faxing text, it doesn't matter if your computer can support shades of gray. Fax machines are described in greater detail in Chapter 8.

VOICE INPUT DEVICES

In an effort to increase worker productivity, a substantial amount of research is being done in voice recognition—programming the computer to recognize spoken commands. **Voice input devices** (Figure 2.7), or **voice recognition systems,** convert spoken words into computer-usable code by comparing the electrical patterns produced by the speaker's voice with a set of prerecorded patterns. If a matching pattern is found, the computer accepts this pattern as a part of its standard "vocabulary."

Voice input technology is used today in a number of successful business applications. NASA has developed experimental space suits that use microprocessors and storage devices to allow astronauts to view computerized displays across their helmet visors. These displays are activated and manipulated by spoken commands—convenient when both hands are busy on a repair job in space! The brokerage house of Shearson Lehman uses a voice input technology called the Voice Trader to enable brokers to communicate trades verbally rather than writing them down on scraps of paper that are often illegible or become lost. The medical industry has also been using voice recognition products to help physicians, hospitals, and clinics minimize the huge quantities of paperwork and handwritten notes they would otherwise have to deal with.

Voice technology is also used by people whose jobs do not allow them to keep their hands free and by handicapped people, such as the blind, who may not be able to use traditional input devices. A blind person, for example, can enter commands verbally rather than using the keyboard. In a system with this capability, computer output is typically communicated to the user using text-to-speech capabilities—that is, the computer responds to the user with spoken words. (A blind skipper reportedly used a voice-navigational system to successfully navigate a boat!) For the physically handicapped, the ability to control computers without using a keyboard is crucial. Voice input technology is now used by quadriplegics and people with severe arthritis to control computers, telephones, and other devices.

FIGURE 2.5   (a) Flatbed scanner; (b) sheet-fed scanner; (c) hand-held scanner. Photo (b) also shows the documentation that accompanies the software necessary to use the scanner with a computer and the expansion card that must be put in the computer's expansion slot. The computer needs the software and the circuitry on the expansion card to be able to interact with the scanner; (d) Slide scanner.

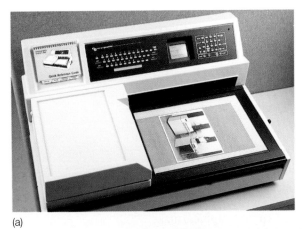

(a)

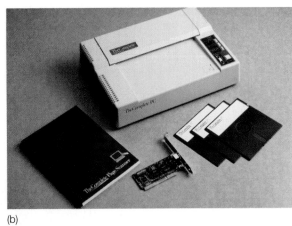

(b)

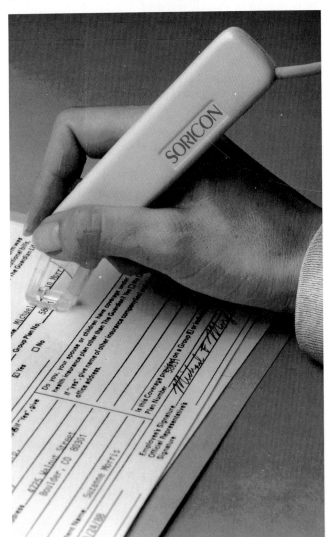

(c)

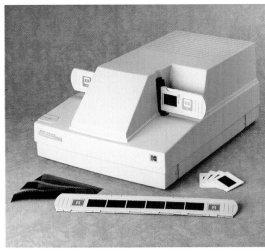

(d)

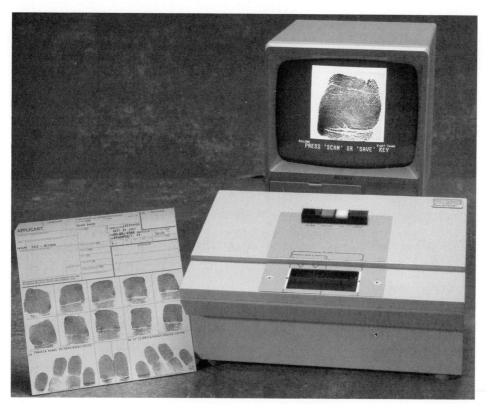

FIGURE 2.6

Fingerprint reader—a type of scanner that is used to identify an individual's fingerprint for security purposes. After a sample is scanned, access to the computer or other restricted system is granted if the user's fingerprint matches the stored sample.

FIGURE 2.7

Voice recognition. (a) This diagram gives you a basic idea of how voice input works (adapted by permission of Wide World Photos); (b) Texas Instruments voice input system.

How does it work?

Speech
A person speaks into a microphone connected to the computer.

Signal Processing
The sound wave is transformed into a sequence of codes that represent speech sounds.

1. Phonetic Models
Describe what codes may occur for a given speech sound.
In the word *how*, what is the probability of the "aw" sound appearing between an H and a D?

2. Dictionary
Defines the phonetic pronunciation (sequence of sounds) of each word
How does it work
haw   daz   it werk

3. Grammar
Defines what words may follow each other, using part of speech
How does <it> [work]
adv   vt   pron   v

Output
Computer recognizes word string and prints it on the screen.

Recognition Search
Using the data from 1, 2, and 3, the computer tries to find the best matching sequence of words as learned from a variety of examples.

(b)

To date, the biggest problems with voice technology involve limitations on the size of the computer's vocabulary, pronunciation differences among individuals, and the computer's inability to accept continuous speech. However, research continues at a fast pace. Several voice input units are currently available for use with microcomputers. For example, Covox, Inc. introduced a voice recognition system that lets IBM PC and IBM PS/2 users replace keystroke entries with spoken commands. This system requires users to use the keyboard to type in a word they want the system to listen for, type in the command keystrokes they want the system to execute when the word is spoken, and to then say the word into a microphone that is built into the Covox system. When the words are spoken at a later time, the appropriate keystrokes will automatically execute.

POINTING DEVICES

Data input also involves not only typing in text but also entering commands and selecting options. The mouse, the trackball, the light pen, the touch screen, and the digitizer tablet were all developed to make these functions easy. Each of these devices allows the user to identify and select the necessary command or option by, in effect, moving the cursor to (pointing at) a certain location on the screen or tablet and sending a signal to the computer. For this reason they are sometimes called *pointing devices*.

Systems that enable users to use their eyes to point at the screen to specify screen coordinates are being used by the handicapped (Figure 2.8). A system that has this capability is typically referred to as a **line-of-sight** system.

FIGURE 2.8

Line of sight. To track the position of the eye's pupil, a video camera is mounted beneath the monitor. These positions are then translated into screen coordinates, thus allowing the eyes to "point." This technology is being used by the handicapped to enable them to direct computer processing.

MOUSE

When using applications software, you can often select menu options by using a mouse to choose a picture, or graphic, (called an *icon*) that represents the processing option you want. The **mouse** (Figure 2.9) is a hand-held device connected to the computer by a small cable. As the mouse is rolled across the desktop, the cursor moves across the screen. When the cursor reaches the desired location, the user usually pushes a button on the mouse once or twice to signal a menu selection or a command to the computer.

Mouse technology is often used with graphics-oriented microcomputers like the Macintosh and the Macintosh portable, as well as with new graphics-oriented programs for the IBM. Indeed, graphical user interfaces such as those used on the Macintosh line of computers are becoming commonplace. As a result, the emphasis will shift from the keyboard as the principal input device to pointing devices such as the mouse to select screen objects and functions. The keyboard, however, will still be used to type in characters and to issue some commands, depending on the software.

When mice were first introduced, they functioned mainly as cursor-movement devices that enabled users to choose menu options. Although they are still used this way today, they are increasingly used to create graphics. The technology has improved so that mice can be used to move tiny *picture elements*—called **pixels**—on the screen one by one. In other words, the mouse can be used like a pen or a paintbrush to draw figures and create patterns directly on the video display screen. Used with a monitor capable of displaying high-quality graphics, a sophisticated mouse enables users to generate very complex and precise images. A sophisticated mouse can manipulate extremely small pixels, influencing the clarity of an image.

(a)

(b)

FIGURE 2.9

Nonkeyboard input control. (a) When the user rolls the mouse around the desktop, the pointer moves correspondingly on the screen. By rolling the mouse to move the pointer to an icon and clicking the mouse button once or twice, the user can select and open the file that the icon represents. By pointing at a particular place on a text line and clicking the mouse button, the user can move the cursor to the desired place. (The use of multiple mouse buttons is determined by the software; the accompanying documentation explains the uses.) (b) Examples of icons.

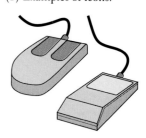

A type of mouse that may soon become popular is built into a pen-like body. It works in the same basic way as does the traditional mouse; however, it is shaped like a pen. It's small enough to fit into a shirt pocket and is capable of working on most surfaces. As a result, this type of mouse is well-suited for use with portable microcomputers.

TRACKBALL

Trackballs have all the functionality of a mouse but don't need to be rolled around on the desktop. The ball is held in a socket on the top of the stationary device (Figures 2.10, 2.11). Instead of moving the ball by rolling the device around on the desktop, you move the ball with your fingers. Trackballs have become especially popular in offices where crowded desktops are the norm and on airplanes, where space is limited.

FIGURE 2.10

MAC Portable with reversible numeric keypad and trackball. The positions of the numeric keypad and the trackball can be swapped to accommodate left-handed trackball users.

FIGURE 2.11

Kensington TurboMouse 4.0 trackball

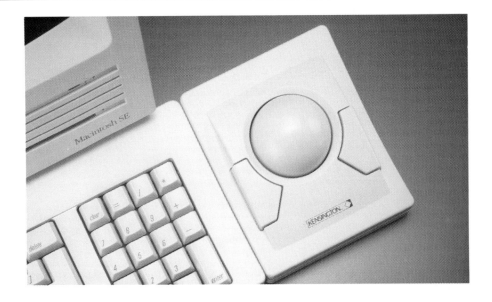

*N*ot *planning to make a career in computers and information processing? Think computers will have only the barest presence in your professional life? We're guessing otherwise. In every line of work, computers have become nearly as commonplace as pencil and paper, even in those fields that seem to be mostly rooted in intuition, emotions, and creativity. In this box, the first of several on computers and different career fields, we show how these instruments of logic are used in the arts, sports, and entertainment.*

The casting agent is looking for an actor who can speak Spanish, owns cowboy gear, and can shoot a rifle while riding a horse. She turns to her computer and feeds her request into RoleCall, a computerized casting service for film, theater, and television. Almost instantly the computer screen produces the names of 40 actors who fit the bill.

In rehearsals, the director uses a Macintosh computer and a program called TheaterGame to go through the process of staging ("blocking") a scene. The program offers a choice of sets, props (such as furniture, trees), and costumed characters that can be moved around on the screen by using a mouse to direct the cursor. If a chair gets in the way of the action, the director can use the mouse to push it aside. Characters can be manipulated so that they turn their heads to talk, sit, fall down, and so on. Afterward, the director can play back the staging to see how it looks.

In the television studio, there are no longer headphone-wearing operators rolling three or four cameras back and forth. Rather, there are now robotic cameras linked to a central computer called the "cue computer," which prompts the cameras. The cue computer is operated by an engineer, who keeps his or her eyes on several wall monitors to keep each camera in focus. Standard shots, such as an overhead view of the set, can be programmed in advance and called up on the computer as needed.

Examples of how computers can be used in nonscientific ways are found in other artistic fields. Dancers may use computers to choreograph their movements. Musicians may use them to write out musical scores while they compose them on a piano keyboard. Computer artists don't use bristles and pigments but rather metal-tipped styluses, with which they "paint" on slate-like digitizing pads, which in turn transmit their movements and colors to a computer screen. Art dealers may use the Omnivex electronic art catalogue, which stores images of artwork on videodisk and allows dealers to view them by calling them up on high-resolution computer screens.

Viewers of televised sports have become accustomed to seeing all kinds of statistics and percentages flashed on the screen. Now, however, coaches and athletes can receive this kind of computerized analysis even for sports such as tennis, using a program called Computennis. And cyclists can use computer-generated three-dimensional maps, called Terragraphics guidebooks, which give the rider a preview of a planned route. Even people who like to fish can improve their odds with the use of a computerized sonar device, called Specie Select, which, using software based on information from over 1,000 professional anglers and guides, can home in on the fish-locating information pertinent to a particular species.

Computers are an important part of all sectors of the entertainment industry. Just one example: Computer-based animation has come of age to produce spectacular new images, from glowing, flying, spinning station call letters to cartoon characters. ■

COMPUTERS AND CAREERS

THE ARTS, SPORTS, AND ENTERTAINMENT

LIGHT PEN

The **light pen** uses a photoelectric (light-sensitive) cell to signal screen position to the computer (Figure 2.12). The pen, which is connected to the computer by a cable, is pressed to the video display screen at the desired location. The switch on the pen is pushed to close the photoelectric circuit, thereby indicating the x-y (horizontal and vertical) screen coordinates to the computer. The computer stores these coordinates in main memory (RAM). Depending on the applications software you are using, you can then edit the data stored in RAM and save it onto a disk. Light pens are frequently used by graphics designers, illustrators, and drafting engineers.

TOUCH SCREEN

Limited amounts of data can be entered into the computer via a **touch screen** (Figure 2.13). The user simply touches the screen at the desired locations, marked by labeled boxes, to "point out" choices to the computer. The software determines the kinds of choices the user has. Of course, not all microcomputers have touch screens. Some touch screens are built into the monitor and others can be snapped on to certain kinds of existing monitors.

FIGURE 2.12

Light pen. This user is employing a light pen to analyze an angiogram of certain blood vessels and arteries.

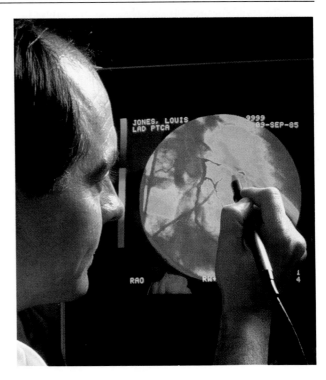

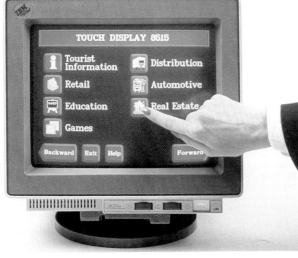

FIGURE 2.13

Touch screen

DIGITIZER

An specialized method of input that is used in drafting and mapmaking is the **digitizer,** or **digitizing tablet** (Figure 2.14). The tablets, which come in different sizes, are the working surface. Each is covered by a grid of many tiny wires that are connected to the computer by a cable. (Wacom, Inc. has produced a digitizer that is cordless.) Drawings placed over this grid can be traced and entered into the computer by the use of a special pen or a mouse-like device with cross hairs that opens and closes electrical circuits in the grid and thus identifies x-y coordinates. Original drawings also can be entered. As it progresses, the drawing is displayed on the screen; it can later be stored or printed out. Digitizers are also used in design and engineering businesses—such as those that develop aircraft or computer chips.

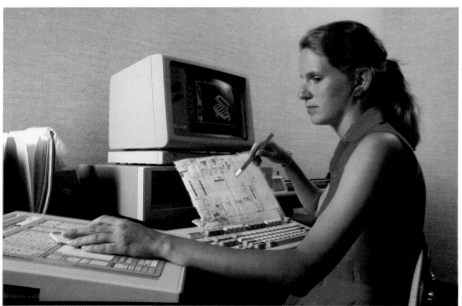

(a)

FIGURE 2.14

Digitizer. (a) This engineer is creating a blueprint using a mouse-like digitizer on a grid with electronic wires that is connected to the computer. (b) A student in the School of Visual Arts in New York City is using a 3-space Isotrack digitizer to draw a freehand 3-D project viewed on the monitor.

(b)

PEN-BASED COMPUTING

Pen-based computing is a recent development by which special software interprets handwriting done directly on a special type of computer screen (Figure 2.15). As the computer—such as Go Corporation's PenPoint and Tandy's Grid System—interprets the handwriting, it displays what was written on the screen in a computer typeface. Users can edit what they have entered and give commands by circling words, checking boxes, and using symbols developed by the manufacturer. This type of small computer is used by police officers to record tickets and by salespeople to record sales.

FIGURE 2.15   Pen-based computing. The chart shows 11 basic handwriting gestures used to issue commands and move around on the screen and within files.

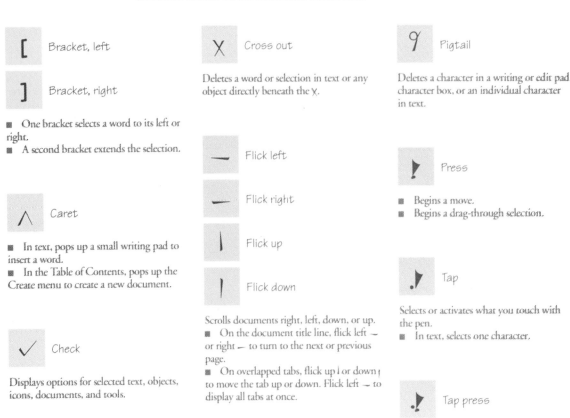

[Bracket, left

] Bracket, right

■ One bracket selects a word to its left or right.
■ A second bracket extends the selection.

∧ Caret

■ In text, pops up a small writing pad to insert a word.
■ In the Table of Contents, pops up the Create menu to create a new document.

✓ Check

Displays options for selected text, objects, icons, documents, and tools.

○ Circle

Opens an edit pad for a word or selection in text, text fields, and labels.

X Cross out

Deletes a word or selection in text or any object directly beneath the X.

— Flick left

— Flick right

| Flick up

| Flick down

Scrolls documents right, left, down, or up.
■ On the document title line, flick left — or right — to turn to the next or previous page.
■ On overlapped tabs, flick up | or down | to move the tab up or down. Flick left — to display all tabs at once.

L Insert space

■ In text, adds a space.
■ In writing and edit pads, adds one or more spaces.

9 Pigtail

Deletes a character in a writing or edit pad character box, or an individual character in text.

▶ Press

■ Begins a move.
■ Begins a drag-through selection.

▶ Tap

Selects or activates what you touch with the pen.
■ In text, selects one character.

▶ Tap press

Begins a copy.

PenPoint has eleven basic gestures for commands and navigation. Most gestures have menu equivalents. See the user manuals for more details.

SUMMARY

- Input hardware is categorized either as *keyboard-based* or *direct-entry* (non-keyboard).
- The keyboard is the most widely used input device. It includes five basic types:
  1. *Standard typewriter keys*—used to type in text and special characters.
  2. *Function keys*—used to issue commands.
  3. *Special-purpose keys*—Ctrl, Alt, Ins, Del, Caps Lock, and Num Lock, used to modify the functions of other keys. The Enter key is usually pressed to tell the computer to execute a command entered by first pressing other keys.
  4. *Cursor-movement keys*—used to move the *cursor*, which marks the position of the next character to be typed, around the screen. The keys for cursor movement are sometimes combined with the *numeric keypad.*
  5. *Numeric keys*—used to enter numbers.

  The software package dictates how the function keys and special-purpose keys are used (check the documentation that comes with the package).
- Direct-entry devices, which are used in conjunction with a keyboard, include:
  1. *Scanning* devices that "read" data
  2. *Voice input* devices
  3. *Pointing* devices
- Scanners convert hardcopy text or graphics into computer-usable code. The text and/or graphics can then be displayed on the monitor and edited, modified, printed, communicated, and stored for later retrieval.
- A *fax (facsimile) machine* is a type of scanner that "reads" text and graphics and then transmits them over telephone lines to another fax machine or a computer with a fax board in its system unit.
- *Voice input devices*, or *voice recognition systems*, convert spoken words into computer-usable code by comparing the electrical patterns produced by the speaker's voice with a set of prerecorded patterns. After the computer matches the patterns, it executes the appropriate command.
- Pointing devices include:
  1. The *mouse*—a hand-held device connected to the computer by a cable and rolled around the desktop to move the cursor around the screen. When the cursor is placed at the desired location, the user pushes a button on the mouse once or twice to issue a command or select an option. The mouse can be used to move the tiny *pixels*, or *picture elements*, on the screen to create graphics.
  2. The *light pen*—a pen-shaped input device that uses a photoelectric (light-sensitive) cell to signal screen position to the computer. The pen, which is connected to the computer by a cable, is placed on the display screen at the desired location. The switch on the pen is pushed to close the photoelectric circuit, thereby signaling the location to the computer.
  3. The *touch screen*—a special display screen that is sensitive to touch. The user touches the screen at desired locations, marked by labeled boxes, to "point out" choices to the computer.
  4. The *digitizer*—a tablet covered by a grid of tiny wires that are connected to the computer by a cable. Drawings placed on the tablet can be traced with a special pen or mouse-like device to translate the image into computer-usable code. Original drawings also can be entered.
  5. *Pen-based computing* uses special software and hardware to interpret handwriting done directly on the screen.

KEY TERMS

Alt key, p. 28
Caps Lock key, p. 28
Ctrl key, p. 28
cursor, p. 28
cursor-movement keys,
    p. 28
Del key, p. 28
digitizer, p. 39
digitizing tablet, p. 39
direct entry, p. 29
Enter key, p. 28
fax (facsimile) machine,
    p. 31
flatbed scanner, p. 31

function keys, p. 28
hand-held scanner,
    p. 31
Ins key, p. 28
keyboard, p. 27
light pen, p. 38
line-of-sight, p. 34
mouse, p. 35
Num Lock key, p. 28
numeric keypad, p. 28
optical character recog-
    nition (OCR), p. 30
pen-based computing,
    p. 40

pixel, p. 35
QWERTY, p. 28
resolution, p. 30
scanhead, p. 31
scanning system, p. 30
sheet-fed scanner, p. 31
Shift key, p. 28
touch screen, p. 38
trackball, p. 36
voice input device,
    p. 31
voice recognition
    system, p. 31

EXERCISES

SELF-TEST

1. One of the easiest ways to categorize input hardware is whether or not it uses a _____.

2. Most keyboards used with microcomputers include the following types of keys:
   a. _____ b. _____ c. _____ d. _____ e. _____

3. What determines what the function keys on a keyboard do?

4. Cursor-movement keys are used to execute commands. (true/false)

5. The _____ key, the _____ key, and the _____ key are modifier keys.

6. A _____ enables users to convert hardcopy text and graphics into computer-usable code.

7. List three common categories of direct entry (nonkeyboard) input devices.
   a. _____ b. _____ c. _____

8. List four pointing devices commonly used with microcomputer systems.
   a. _____ b. _____ c. _____ d. _____

9. A picture element on the screen is called a *pixel*. (true/false)

10. An input device commonly used in mapmaking is the _____ _____.

11. Light pens enable you to type text faster than do keyboards. (true/false)

12. To date, the biggest problems with voice technology are:
    a. _____ b. _____ c. _____

13. The most popular input hardware component is the _____.

14. QWERTY describes a common keyboard layout. (true/false)

15. Scanners cannot scan color images. (true/false)

16. The most common keyboard layout is called *QWERTY*. (true/false)

17. Function keys are used the same way with every software application. (true/false)

18. Some keyboards have cursor-movement keys that are separate from the numeric keypad. (true/false)

19. A code is sent to the computer *every* time a keyboard key is pressed. (true/false)

20. Pointing devices were developed to make the functions of entering commands and selecting options easy. (true/false)

SOLUTIONS (1) keyboard; (2) standard typewriter keys, function keys, special-purpose keys, cursor-movement keys, numeric keys; (3) software program or applications software; (4) false; (5) Ctrl, Alt, Shift; (6) scanner; (7) scanning devices, voice input devices, pointing devices; (8) mouse, light pen, touch screen, digitizer tablet; (9) true; (10) digitizer tablet; (11) false; (12) size of the computer's vocabulary, pronunciation differences among individuals, computer's inability to accept continuous speech; (13) keyboard; (14) true; (15) false; (16) true; (17) false; (18) true; (19) true; (20) true

SHORT ANSWER

1. What are the two main categories of input hardware?

2. What is a fax machine?

3. What is a mouse and how is it used?

4. What do a mouse, a light pen, and a digitizer have in common?

5. What direct-entry devices are commonly used in conjunction with the microcomputer keyboard?

6. What is an optical character recognition system?

7. What is a digitizer?

8. What are function keys, and what determines what happens when you press one of them?

9. What is a light pen? How does the use of a light pen differ from pen-based computing?

10. What is a voice recognition system?

PROJECTS

1. A new type of keyboard, called the *Mouseboard*, puts the mouse *on* the keyboard, where most keyboards have their cursor-movement (arrow) keys. Do you think this keyboard would be easier to use than the standard keyboard plus mouse or trackball combination? Write or call the manufacturer and ask for brochures and other information about this new development; then describe this new keyboard to the class.
   Cherry Corporation
   Cherry Electrical Products
   3600 Sunset Avenue
   Waukegan, IL 60087
   708/360-3599

2. Research scanning technology. What differentiates one scanner from another? Is it the clarity of the scanned image? Price? Software? If you were going to buy a scanner, which do you think you would buy? Why? What do you need to run a color scanner?

3. Research possible copyright infringement problems arising from first scanning photos and other pictures and then modifying them.

CHAPTER 3

PROCESSING HARDWARE

When you look at a computer, you can see and even touch most of the input, output, and storage equipment—the keyboard and the mouse, the video display screen, the printer and the disk drive doors. But unless you open up the computer, you cannot see the equipment that actually does the processing—the electronic circuitry inside the cabinet of the computer. Although you have no need to puzzle through wiring diagrams and the like, you should have some understanding of the processing hardware, because the type of processing hardware used affects how much the computer can do for you and how quickly it can do it.

PREVIEW

When you have completed this chapter, you will be able to:

Identify the main parts of the microprocessor and describe their functions

Explain the importance of and distinguish between random access memory and the different types of read-only memory

Describe the factors that should be considered when evaluating the processing power of a microcomputer

CHAPTER OUTLINE

As a microcomputer user, you need a basic understanding of the hardware components that enable you to process data into information.

- Just as some people like to work on their own cars, you may decide it's economical for you to do some work on your microcomputer. For instance, you may find that some new software programs are too sophisticated for your computer—that your computer cannot hold enough data or instructions or process them fast enough—and that you need to add some more random access memory. This may well be something you can do yourself.

- More likely, you will some day need to make a buying decision about a microcomputer, either for yourself or for an organization. And, just as when you buy a car, you should learn something about the topic first. It is important to understand processing facts and trends to avoid purchasing a machine that will be obsolete in the near future.

Let's start our discussion of processing with the "brain" of the microcomputer— the microprocessor.

THE MICROPROCESSOR

A central processing unit (CPU) of the 1940s that weighed 5 tons, took up six rooms, processed about 10,000 instructions per second, and cost about $5 million is now 5 millimeters square, about 12 inches thick, can process about 4 million instructions per second, and costs less than $5. This revolution in computer processing was caused by the development of the **microprocessor,** the "brain," or CPU, of the microcomputer system (Figure 3.1). The microprocessor consists of the main processing circuitry on one silicon chip. Today a microcomputer priced at about $5,000 has essentially the same power as an IBM mainframe of more than 10 years ago—but that machine cost $3.4 million at the time. If the automobile industry had advanced this fast since 1982, said Edward Lucente, the head of IBM's Information Systems Group, "Today we'd have cars that go zero to 60 in three seconds, circle the globe on a tank of gas, and cost half as much as they did six years ago. Of course, they would be difficult to get into, because they would be only half the size."

Among other things, a microprocessor's configuration determines whether a microcomputer is fast or slow in relation to other microcomputers. The microprocessor is the most complex computer system component, responsible for directing most of the computer system activities based on the instructions provided. The microprocessor has two main parts: (1) the control unit and (2) the arithmetic/logic unit. The parts of the microprocessor are usually connected by an electronic component referred to as a *bus*, which acts as an electronic path between them (Figure 3.2). To temporarily store data and instructions, the microprocessor has special-purpose storage areas called *registers*.

CONTROL UNIT

The **control unit,** a maze of complex electronic circuitry, is responsible for directing and coordinating all computer system activities. It controls the movement of electronic signals, including the signals between main memory and the input/output devices. Also, it coordinates activities between main memory and the microprocessor.

The control unit (and the entire microprocessor) can deal only with instructions written in **machine language** (Figure 3.3). When programmers write programs, they use high-level (human-language-like) languages. Before the programs can be used, the programmer must convert them into machine language by using a language processor—a type of systems software (language processors are described in more detail in Chapter 7). In machine language, data and instructions are represented in binary form—that is, as 0s and 1s, which stand for the absence or the presence of an electronic pulse. Each type of computer—microcomputer, minicomputer, or mainframe—responds to a unique version of machine language. Once the instructions have been converted into this form, they can be interpreted by the control unit (sometimes referred to as *decoding*). According to each specific instruction, the control unit issues the necessary signals to other computer system components as needed to satisfy the processing requirements. This could involve,

FIGURE 3.1

Intel 80386 microprocessor chip

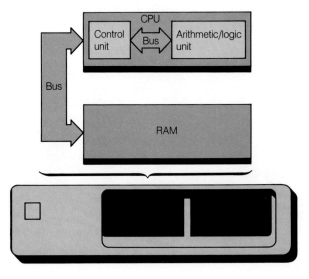

FIGURE 3.2

Buses, a kind of electronic transportation system, connect the main components of the central processing unit and memory.

for example, directing that data be retrieved from a disk storage device, telling the printer to print the letter you just wrote, or simply directing the arithmetic/logic unit to add two numbers.

ARITHMETIC/LOGIC UNIT (ALU)

Without the **arithmetic/logic unit (ALU),** you wouldn't be able to perform any mathematical calculations. In fact, without the ALU, microcomputers would not be able to do most of the tasks that we find useful. The ALU performs all the arithmetic and logical (comparison) functions—that is, it adds, subtracts, multiplies, divides, and does comparisons. These comparisons, which are basically "less than," "greater than," or "equal to," can be combined into several common expressions, such as "greater than or equal to." The objective of most instructions that use comparisons is to determine which instructions should be executed next. The ALU also controls the speed of calculations.

REGISTERS

A **register** is a special temporary storage location within the microprocessor. Registers very quickly accept, store, and transfer data and instructions that are being used *immediately* (random access memory or main memory, to be discussed shortly, holds data that will be used *a little bit later*). To process an instruction, the control unit of the microprocessor retrieves it from main memory and places it into a register. The typical operations that take place in the processing of instructions are part of either the instruction cycle or the execution cycle.

The **instruction cycle,** or I-cycle, refers to the retrieval of an instruction from memory and its subsequent decoding (the process of alerting the circuits in the microprocessor to perform the specified operation). The time it takes to go through the instruction cycle is referred to as *I-time.* The **execution cycle,** or E-cycle, refers to the execution of the instruction and the subsequent storing of the result in a register. The time it takes to go through the execution cycle is referred to as *E-time.* The instruction cycle and the execution cycle together, as they apply to one instruction, are referred to as a **machine cycle** (Figure 3.4). The microprocessor has an internal **clock** that synchronizes all operations in the cycle. The speed is expressed in **megahertz (MHz);** 1 MHz equals 1 million cycles per

FIGURE 3.3

Machine language. This illustration shows the Apple and the IBM instructions for adding two numbers. IBM computers are incompatible with Apple computers because their processors use different versions of machine language instructions. Software written for one machine cannot be used on the other without special conversion software.

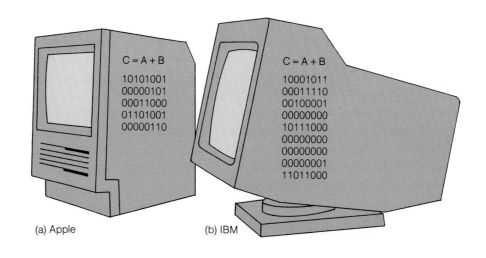

(a) Apple   (b) IBM

second. Generally, the faster the clock speed, the faster the computer can process information. An older IBM PC has a clock speed of 4.77 MHz; an IBM PS/2 Model 50 SX has a clock speed of 16 MHz; the Mac IIci's clock speed is 25 MHz; and the Compaq Deskpro 386/33 has a clock speed of 33 MHz. Some newer microprocessors have a clock speed of 50 MHz.

Typically the faster a microcomputer is (as measured in megahertz), the more expensive it is. Depending on your needs you may (or may not) need a fast computer. Therefore, before purchasing a computer, determine the computer's clock speed by either looking at the documentation that accompanies the computer or asking a salesperson.

Before we continue, we must briefly define a few terms that will help you evaluate the power of processing hardware. Just as inches, feet, and yards are used to measure certain surfaces, bits, bytes, kilobytes, and megabytes are used to measure and compare the processing power and storage capacity of microcomputers. (Each of these terms is described in more detail in Chapter 4.) Data is represented in microcomputers by using a coding scheme that uses groups of **binary digits,** or **bits,** to represent characters. Think of a bit as a light switch. One switch—1 bit—can be either on (1) or off (0)—that is, an electric or light pulse is either present or absent. In microcomputers, it takes 8 bits—known as a **byte**—to form a character. (For example, in some microcomputer coding schemes, A is represented as 01000001.) A **kilobyte (KB, or K)** is equal to 1,024 bytes, and a **megabyte (MB)** is equal to 1,024,000 bytes. A **gigabyte (GB)** is equal to 1,024,000,000 bytes. For simplicity, most users think of a kilobyte as one thousand bytes, a megabyte as one million bytes, and a gigabyte as one billion bytes.

The number and types of registers in a microprocessor vary according to the microprocessor's design. Their size (capacity) and number can dramatically affect the processing power of a computer system. In general, the larger the register (the more bits it can carry at once), the greater the processing power. Some personal computers have general-purpose registers that hold only 8 bits (1 byte) at a time; others hold 16 bits (2 bytes); newer microcomputers have 32-bit registers that hold 4 bytes at once. The difference in processing power due to difference in register

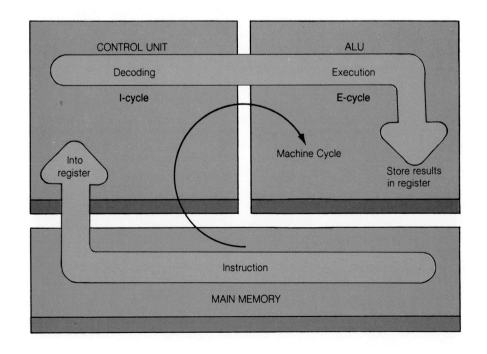

FIGURE 3.4

The machine cycle—the instruction cycle and execution cycle as they apply to the processing of one instruction

size can be illustrated by the difference between trying to put out a fire with a small drinking glass versus a 5-gallon bucket.

BUS

The term **bus** refers to an electrical pathway through which bits are transmitted between the various computer components. Depending on the design of a system, several types of buses may be present. For the user, the most important one is the **data bus,** which carries data throughout the microprocessor. The wider the data bus, the more data it can carry at one time, and thus the greater the processing speed of the computer. The data bus in the Intel 8088 microprocessor is 8 bits wide, meaning that it can carry 8 bits—or one character—at a time. In contrast, the data buses in the Motorola 68030 processor (in the Macintosh IIci microcomputer) and the Intel 80386 processor (in the IBM PS/2 Model 55 SX microcomputer) are 32 bits wide—they can move four times more data through their data buses than the Intel 8088 bus can. An 8-bit computer can do anything a 32-bit computer can, just slower. Table 3.1 shows the data bus capacity and register size of several microprocessor chips.

TABLE 3.1   Comparison of Several Microprocessors

Company	Micro-processor	Data Bus Capacity	Register Size	Clock Speed (MHz)	Microcomputers Using This Chip*
MOS Technology	6502	8	8	4	Apple IIE Atari 800 Commodore 64
Intel	8086	16	16	5–10	Some IBM-compatibles Compaq Deskpro
Intel	8088	8	16	5–8	IBM PC and XT HP 150 touch screen Compaq Portable
Intel	80286	16	32	8–16	IBM AT IBM PS/2 Model 50 Compaq Deskpro 286
Motorola	68000	16	32	8–16	Apple Macintosh SE Commodore Amiga
Motorola	68020	32	32	16–33	Macintosh II
Motorola	68030	32	32	16–50	Macintosh IIex NeXT computer
Motorola	68040	32	32	25–33	Hewlett-Packard workstations
Intel	80386SX	16	32	16–20	NEC PowerMate SC/20 Compaq Deskpro 386s/20
Intel	80386	32	32	16–33	Compaq Deskpro 386 IBM PS/2 Model 80
Intel	80486	32	32	25–50	IBM PS/2 Model 70 Compaq Systempro
Intel	i486 DX2-66	32	32	66	Compaq Deskpro 66i Dell 486P/66

*This table includes a partial list of the microcomputers using each chip.

COPROCESSORS

Additional microprocessors are often used inside a computer to handle some of the CPU's overload. These "pinch hitters," called **coprocessors,** help speed up the operation of your computer. For example, a math coprocessor chip can be installed on the motherboard to perform complex numerical calculations. This kind of a chip can speed up the processing of financial and scientific applications. It can also be used to speed up the calculations a computer uses to display complex graphics on the screen and print them out.

READ-ONLY MEMORY (ROM)

How does your microcomputer know what to do when you turn it on? How does it know to check out your hardware components (such as the keyboard or the monitor) to see that they have been connected correctly? Instructions to perform such operations, which are critical to the operation of a computer, are stored permanently on a **read-only memory (ROM)** chip (Figure 3.5) installed inside the computer by the manufacturer. This ROM chip retains instructions in a permanently accessible, nonvolatile form, which means that when the power in the computer is turned off, the instructions stored in ROM are not lost.

Having basic instructions permanently stored in ROM is both necessary and convenient. For example, if you are using a microcomputer with diskette drives, the more instructions in ROM, the fewer diskettes you may have to handle in order to load instructions into the computer. If you could have *all* the program instructions you'll ever need to use in ROM, you would have everything you need for processing data and information at your fingertips—always. Unfortunately, until recently the process of manufacturing ROM chips and recording data on them was more expensive than the process of producing other types of memory chips. As a result, manufacturers tended to record in ROM only those instructions that were crucial to the operation of the computer. However, in recent years improvements in the manufacturing process of ROM chips have lowered their cost to the point where manufacturers are beginning to include additional software instructions.

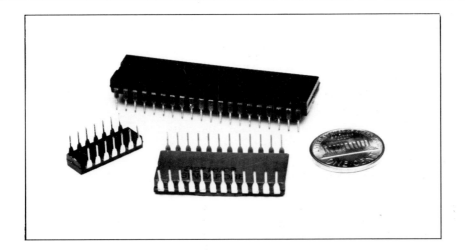

FIGURE 3.5

ROM chips, installed by the manufacturer on the computer's system board, contain instructions that are read by the computer. Since they cannot usually be rewritten, they are called *read-only memory.*

1. All fundamental circuits are designed by people using the rules of Boolean logic. After they have been designed, they reside in disk libraries in the computer system waiting to be selected by the designer.

2. The chip designer selects the appropriate circuits from the library, and the computer generates the physical circuit paths.

3. The circuit paths are refined by a designer. The final results are further inspected to ensure that all the components are aligned properly.

4. The circuitry is turned into several photomasks that will transfer the circuitry design onto chips.

Adapted from *The Computer Glossary*, Alan Freedman, © 1991, Amacom, 135 W. 50th Street, New York, NY 10020.

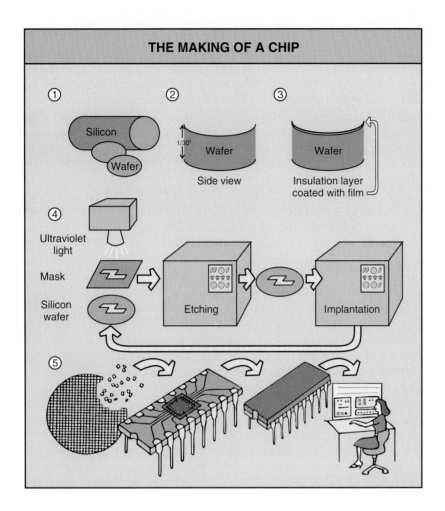

THE MAKING OF A CHIP

①
Silicon
Wafer

②
1/30"
Wafer
Side view

③
Wafer
Insulation layer
coated with film

④
Ultraviolet light
Mask
Silicon wafer
Etching
Implantation

⑤

1./2. Silicon, the raw material of chips, is refined from quartz rocks and purified. It is fabricated into salami-like ingots from 3 to 5 inches in diameter. The ingots are sliced into wafers approximately 1/30th of an inch thick.

3. The wafer is covered with an oxide insulation layer and then coated with film.

4. A design is transferred onto the wafer by exposing it to ultraviolet light through a mask. Wherever light strikes the film, the film is hardened along with the insulation layer beneath it. The wafer is subjected to an acid that etches out the unhardened insulation layer exposing the silicon below. The next step is an implantation process that forces chemicals into the exposed silicon under pressure, creating electrically altered elements below the surface.

Through a series of masking, etching, and implantation steps, the circuitries for many chips are created on the wafer.

5. The finished wafer is tested, and the bad chips are marked for disposal. The wafer is sliced into chips, and the good ones are placed into their final spider-like package. Tiny wires bond the chip to the package's "feet." Each chip is then tested individually. The number of chips that make it through to the very end can be less than the number that don't.

PROM, EPROM, EEPROM

Three additional kinds of nonvolatile memory are used in some microcomputer systems—namely, PROMs, EPROMs, and EEPROMs. **PROM** stands for **programmable read-only memory**. This type of memory functions in the same way a regular ROM component does, with one major exception: PROM chips are custom-made for the user by the manufacturer. In other words, the user determines what data and instructions are recorded on them. The only problem with PROM chips is that, like ROM chips, once data is recorded on them, it can't be changed.

Erasable programmable read-only memory (EPROM) chips were developed as an improvement over PROM chips. EPROM functions exactly the same as PROM; however, with the help of a special device that uses ultraviolet light, in approximately 15 minutes the data or instructions on an EPROM chip can be erased. Once erased, a device generically referred to as a PROM burner is used to reprogram the chip. Unfortunately, to change instructions on an EPROM chip, the chip first must be taken out of the machine and then put back when the changes have been made. This task is one most computer users would prefer to avoid. The alternative to erasing and rerecording an EPROM chip is to replace it with a new EPROM that features the new program code. This is a task best performed by a trained computer professional.

Electrically erasable programmable read-only memory (EEPROM), the latest addition to the ROM family of chips, avoids the inconvenience of having to take chips out of the computer to change data and instructions. Unlike EPROM chips on which changes must be made optically, EEPROM chips allow changes to be made electrically under software control. In other words, they do not need to be taken out of the computer. The only disadvantage of EEPROM chips is they currently cost substantially more than regular ROM chips and disk storage devices. However, Intel and other manufacturers are planning high-volume production, which should push the prices down.

RANDOM ACCESS MEMORY (RAM)

Microprocessors, ALUs, registers, buses, ROM, instructions . . . what good are they if you have no data to work with? You wouldn't have any if it weren't for **random access memory (RAM)** (also called *primary storage, memory,* and *main memory*), the part of the processing hardware that temporarily holds data and instructions needed by the microprocessor.

FUNCTION OF RAM

The principal function of RAM is to act as a buffer between the microprocessor and the rest of the computer system components. It functions as a sort of desktop on which you place the things with which you are about to begin to work. The microprocessor can utilize only those software instructions and data that have been placed in RAM. The name *random access memory* is derived from the fact that data can be stored in and retrieved at random—from anywhere—in the electronic RAM chips in approximately the same amount of time, no matter where the data is.

RAM is an electronic state. When the computer is off, RAM is empty; when it is on, RAM is capable of receiving and holding a copy of the software instructions and data necessary for processing. Because RAM is a volatile form of storage that depends on electric power and because the power can go off during processing, users often save their work frequently onto nonvolatile storage devices such as diskettes or hard disks. In general, RAM is used for the following purposes:

- Storage of a copy of the main systems software program, which controls the general operation of the computer. This copy is loaded into RAM when the computer is turned on (you'll find out how later), and it stays there as long as the computer is on.

- Temporary storage of a copy of applications software instructions (the specific software you are using in your business) to be retrieved by the microprocessor for interpretation and execution.

- Temporary storage of data that has been input from the keyboard or other input device until instructions call for the data to be transferred into the microprocessor for processing.

- Temporary storage of data that has been produced as a result of processing until instructions call for the data to be used again in subsequent processing or to be transferred to an output device such as the screen, a printer, or a disk storage device.

The amount of RAM you have in your microcomputer directly affects the level of sophistication of the software you can use and the amount of data you can process at one time. Sophisticated, or powerful, programs take up a lot of space in RAM. Many of today's software programs require a computer to be configured with 640 K RAM to run. In general, the greater your machine's memory capacity, the better.

RAM Chips

RAM capacity is measured in kilobytes. Early microcomputer systems were not equipped with very much RAM by today's standards. In 1979, they were able to directly access and control only up to 64 K RAM; a microcomputer with 64 K RAM was considered satisfactory. Today a microcomputer system with less than 640 K RAM is considered underpowered. The software available for microcomputers did not require much RAM until certain new products began to appear on the market around 1984. With the introduction of software, called *spreadsheets*, to handle large financial reports, the need for increased RAM grew rapidly (because of the necessity of holding large amounts of numbers and instructions in RAM at one time). Now, for a microcomputer to effectively use many of the newer software products, it should have *at least* 640 K RAM available. In fact, today many microcomputers are configured with 4–8 MB RAM.

Increasing RAM

What if you, like many users, are faced with the need to expand your computer's RAM capacity to be able to use some new software? For instance, what if your microcomputer isn't brand new and has a RAM capacity of only 512 K or 256 K? Unfortunately, you cannot simply pull out two of the 64 K chips and replace them with 256 K chips to increase the amount of RAM available to 640 K. The component that prevents you from doing this is the *dynamic memory access* (DMA) controller. In most older microcomputer systems, the DMA chip was designed to work with only one size of memory chip. However, in newer systems the DMA controller is designed to allow a mix of banks of 64 K, 256 K, 1 MB, 2 MB, and

4 MB memory chips. The DMA chip or module is responsible for managing the use of all RAM. It keeps track of which memory locations are in use (and by what) and which are available for use.

Two basic types of memory are used to increase memory beyond the 640 K limit (Figure 3.6). The type used is influenced by the sophistication of the microprocessor in your machine.

EXPANDED MEMORY

Expanded memory is used in 8088, 8086, 80286, and 80386 computers to increase memory beyond the conventional memory limit of 640 K. Users of early microcomputer systems couldn't increase the amount of RAM directly wired into the motherboard beyond 640 K because of limitations imposed by the systems software (programs designed to allow the computer to manage its own resources— systems software is described in Chapter 7). This situation led to the development of a wide variety of new products allowing the memory to be increased through the use of an **add-on memory board,** or **expansion card** (Figure 3.7). This board is simply pressed into an expansion slot on the motherboard. An **expansion slot** is a plug-in spot specifically meant to support add-on components (Figures 3.8

FIGURE 3.6   Types of RAM: conventional, expanded, extended. Most systems have 384 K of space called *upper memory* above the conventional memory area of 640 K. Upper memory is not considered part of the total memory of your computer because programs cannot use upper memory to store data. This memory is normally reserved for running your system's hardware.

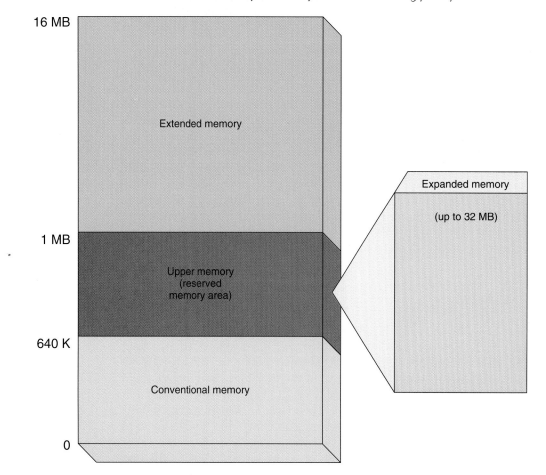

and 3.9). This slot connects the add-on board with the power supply for the computer and links the board with the buses for moving data and instructions.

In order for your computer to know you've added memory, you must also follow special software instructions that come with the board (Figure 3.10). To use expanded memory, you must run applications such as Lotus 1-2-3 (a spreadsheet) that are specifically tailored to address expanded memory.

We do need to mention here that add-on boards or cards can be inserted only in computers with **open architecture**—that is, computers built to allow users to open the system cabinet and make changes. Computers with **closed architecture,** such as the Macintosh SE, do not allow the user to add expansion cards. Thus, you can see that a computer's architecture becomes important to the user if he or she wants to upgrade the system—not only to increase RAM but also to add disk storage, graphics capabilities, some communications capabilities, or to change from a monochrome display screen to a color screen. If you are buying a microcomputer system and think you might want to upgrade it at a later time, make sure you purchase a microcomputer with open architecture.

FIGURE 3.7

This photo shows banks of RAM chips (left) on a memory expansion card that will be plugged into a slot inside the system cabinet.

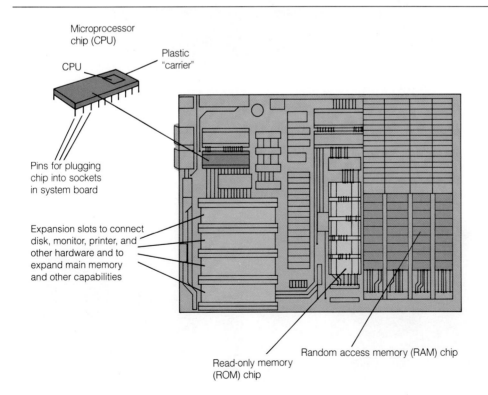

FIGURE 3.8

System board. This illustration shows the usual position of ROM and RAM chips, the CPU, and slots for expansion cards. Expansion cards are often used to increase a computer's RAM capacity.

EXTENDED MEMORY

Extended memory also refers to memory increased above 640 K; however, it can be used only in microcomputers with 80286, 80386, or 80486 microprocessors. Extended memory is also composed of RAM chips that either are plugged directly into the motherboard or are attached to a board that is plugged into an expansion slot. With extended memory, a machine can use up to 16 MB of memory. Like expanded memory, extended memory can be used only by software that recognizes it, such as the extended memory manager in Microsoft Windows. The applications software documentation will specify whether the software is compatible with one or both of these types of memory. Extended memory is accessed under the control of the applications software. For example, software applications that offer limited

FIGURE 3.9

Buy an add-on memory board to plug in an expansion slot and increase your RAM. (The expansion card is at the far left.)

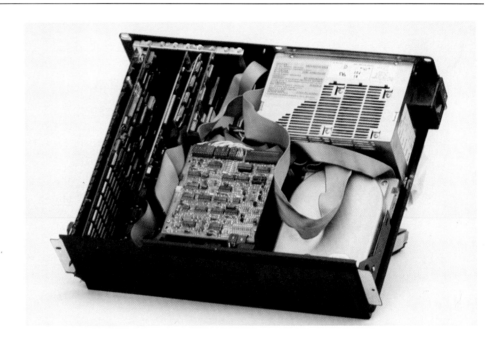

FIGURE 3.10   Expanded memory board and the software required for a computer to use it

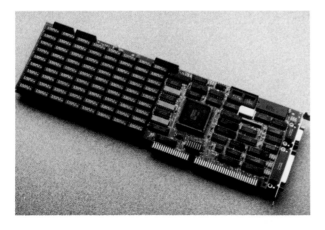

multitasking (the execution of more than one task or program at a time), such as Microsoft Windows and Desqview, can load multiple programs into 640 K (maximum) chunks of extended memory. The more memory, the greater the number of programs that can be run at once.

CACHE MEMORY

Although its definitions differ, basically **cache** (pronounced "cash") **memory** is a special high-speed memory area that the CPU can quickly access. Cache memory is often used with 386 and 486 microprocessors. Cache is a small area of RAM created in addition to the computer's main RAM. A copy of the most frequently used data and instructions is kept in the cache so the CPU can look in the cache first, which makes the computer run faster. Cache memory is usually located right on the microprocessor chip.

VIRTUAL MEMORY

Some microprocessors can also use **virtual memory,** which allows the processor— under control of special software—to use disk storage to simulate a large amount of RAM. For example, virtual memory allows an IBM AT microcomputer to use up to 1 GB (1 billion bytes) of virtual memory. Thus you can run a 4 MB program even if you have only 2 MB of RAM.

MEASURING THE PROCESSING POWER OF A COMPUTER

The proliferation of microcomputers in our society means that more and more people are becoming familiar with the processing power of computers in general. Many individuals are considering the purchase of a microcomputer on their own, with the result that more and more people are asking, "How do you determine how powerful a computer is?"

This question is fairly easy to answer. However, understanding the answer requires knowledge of a few more computer fundamentals.

ADDRESSING SCHEME

The **addressing scheme** is a computer design feature that directly determines the amount of RAM that can be controlled by the microprocessor at any one time. Early microprocessors were limited to 64 K of memory-addressing capability. The popular IBM PC-compatible computers have a memory-addressing capability of 1,024 K. The IBM PS/2 Model P70 uses the 80386 microprocessor, which allows access to approximately 4 GB of RAM—equal to the addressing capability of current minicomputers. (You'll learn in Chapter 7 that systems software prevents users from accessing the full 4 GB.)

REGISTER SIZE

Microcomputers have a number of registers that are used for a variety of purposes, including the temporary storage of results of arithmetic operations. The more of these registers you have and the larger they are, the more processing power you have. The registers in early microcomputers could hold only 8 bits each. Registers in newer computers hold 16 or 32 bits each. Each 32-bit general-purpose register can process twice as much data in each machine cycle per register as a 16-bit register can.

C rime rates have increased, but they might have increased more were it not for the presence of computer technology.

Consider home security. At one time, home-security systems were expensive and notoriously unreliable, with over 90% of alarms triggered being false. Often the alarms were caused by user error, such as a homeowner accidentally tripping a system and forgetting how to deactivate it, but they were also caused by equipment malfunction. Today's computerized home-security systems allow one to turn off some alarms (such as those inside) and turn on others (such as door and window alarms). They can also detect and isolate malfunctioning sensors, eliminating many false alarms.

Police departments, of course, have been using computers for some time, as when an officer in a patrol car calls up on a dashboard-mounted computer the license numbers of suspicious vehicles to check whether they have been stolen. More creative uses of computers have followed. Fingerprint identification, which used to require so many hours of an officer's time that it was virtually not attempted except in the most serious cases, has proved to be extraordinarily successful in those urban police departments that have moved their fingerprint files to a computerized database. The old-fashioned police artist's pad and pencil have been replaced by a software program containing more than 100,000 facial features, allowing officers with no artistic talent to create remarkably professional composite drawings of wanted suspects.

Computers have also helped increase productivity in prosecutors' offices and make the judicial system function better. For instance, a computer system may be used to log all incoming letters and phone calls; the district attorney heading the prosecutor's office can then scan the printouts and find out which callers require return calls and which assistant D.A.s must be reminded to respond to backlogged correspondence. Confidential data can be kept on various cases, and the system can be used to create appropriate legal documents to advance cases through the court system. Weekly calendars of active cases are provided to help prosecutors avoid scheduling conflicts and alert them to necessary actions they must take.

Some prosecutors' offices have a computer system that tracks cases from arrest to disposition. For example, in the Brooklyn, N.Y., district attorney's office, a system called FACTS (Facility for Accurate Case Tracking System) begins to pick up a case when the suspect is first brought to central booking at the police station, where the charges are keyed into a terminal. For misdemeanor cases, a terminal informs the judge about a suspect's prior record, outstanding charges, and the names of prosecuting attorneys. For felonies, the system is used to schedule the first grand jury hearing to determine if the evidence justifies an indictment. Other data includes names of witnesses, bail records, and the like.

Even the U.S. Supreme Court has acquired computer technology. The system is designed to transmit the court's opinion within minutes of its announcement. ■

DATA BUS CAPACITY

As you learned earlier, the data bus is like a pipeline used to move data and instructions among RAM, the microprocessor, and other microcomputer system components. The size of the data bus controls the amount of data that can travel down the pipeline at one time and thus can significantly affect a computer's performance. A data bus is constructed to carry 8, 16, or 32 bits. Hardware and software must be specifically designed for the type of bus used in a microcomputer.

Three basic bus designs, or architectures, are found in IBM and IBM-compatible microcomputer systems today. The Industry Standard Architecture (ISA) bus system is used with the Intel 8088, 80286, and 80386 microprocessors and is capable of passing 8 bits (when using the 8088) or 16 bits (when using the 80286 or 80386) through the data bus. This bus design doesn't fully utilize the 80386 microprocessor—which is capable of supporting 32-bit chunks of data in the data bus. As a result, two bus systems have been developed that enable 80386- and 80486-based machines to pass 32 bits through the data bus: (1) IBM's Micro Channel Architecture (MCA) and (2) Extended Industry Standard Architecture (EISA). There is much debate among industry observers about which of these two bus designs is better. A side-by-side comparison of the two designs reveals more similarities than differences. Unfortunately, users will have to make a choice about which bus system to adopt in their computer because the bus systems aren't compatible—that is, hardware and software must be designed specifically for the bus that will be used.

CLOCK SPEED

The clock, mentioned in the section on the instruction execution cycle, is the part of the microprocessor that synchronizes and sets the speed of all the operations in the machine cycle. The early microcomputers operated at speeds of around 1 MHz. This means that those computers had approximately 1 million processing cycles available per second to perform useful work. Today microcomputers are operating at speeds of 33–66 MHz.

INSTRUCTION SET

The early 8-bit microprocessors were extremely slow when performing mathematical operations. They were designed to handle only addition and subtraction; a more sophisticated operation (such as division or multiplication) had to be performed by a series of special program instructions, often called *subroutines*. For example, to multiply 5 times 3, a subroutine would add the number 3 together 5 times. The more powerful 32-bit microcomputers use additional instructions that handle mathematical operations in a single processing cycle. The 16-bit microprocessors also use single *blocks* of instructions (called *instruction sets*) that can cause whole blocks of data to be moved from one place to another. With the 8-bit microcomputers, this type of operation would also have to be handled by a number of subroutines (lots of "small" individual instructions).

How a microprocessor chip is designed affects how fast it can process. Most microprocessor chips today are designed using the **Complex Instruction Set Computing (CISC)** approach. A multitude of software applications, written for use with this chip design are being used in the business environment today. A new approach to chip design, called **Reduced Instruction Set Computing (RISC)**, allows microcomputers to offer very high speed performance by simplifying the internal design and reducing the number of instruction sets. The RISC design enables a computer to process about twice as fast as one based on the CISC design. The extent to which the RISC design is embraced depends on how the software industry supports it. However, industry observers do agree that the RISC design is definitely in our future.

CHECKLIST

In general, keep these points in mind when trying to determine the processing power of a microcomputer:

- *Addressing scheme:* The larger the addressing capability, the more RAM the computer can control.
- *Register size:* The larger the general-purpose registers, the more data the microprocessor can manipulate in one machine cycle.
- *Data bus:* The larger the data buses, the more efficiently and quickly data and instructions can be moved among the processing components of the computer.
- *Clock speed:* The faster the clock speed, the more machine cycles are completed per second and the faster the computer can perform processing operations.
- *Instruction set:* The more powerful the instruction set, the fewer instructions and processing cycles it takes to perform certain tasks.

SUMMARY

- The *microprocessor* is the "brain"—the CPU—of the microcomputer. It has two main parts:
  1. *Control unit*—directs and coordinates most of the computer system activities.
  2. *Arithmetic logic unit (ALU)*—performs all arithmetic and logical (comparison) functions and controls the speed of the calculations.
- The microprocessor is a ¼-inch to ⅛-inch square *semiconductor chip* that contains complicated circuitry. The power of the microprocessor chip is indicated by its number—generally, the higher the number (for example, 80286, 80386, 80486), the greater the power.
- The parts of the microprocessor and other computer components are connected by *buses*, or electronic pathways. The most important bus is the *data bus*, which carries data throughout the microprocessor.
- *Registers* temporarily store data and instructions for the microprocessor.
- The microprocessor understands only *machine language*, in which data and instructions are represented by 0s and 1s—the off and on states of electrical current or bursts of light. Each 0 or 1 is called a *bit*, short for *binary digit*. Groups of bits represent characters—it takes 8 bits, called a *byte*, to represent 1 character. 1,024 bytes equal a *kilobyte (K)*; 1,024,000 bytes equal a *megabyte (MB)*; and 1,024,000,000 bytes equal a *gigabyte (GB)*.
- The more bits a computer's buses and registers can handle at once (8, 16, or 32), the faster the microcomputer.

- Software instructions are converted into machine language by a *language processor*. Each type of computer uses a unique machine language.

- To process an instruction, the control unit of the microprocessor retrieves it from memory and places it into a register. The *instruction cycle (I-time)* refers to the retrieval of the instruction from memory and its subsequent decoding. The *execution cycle (E-time)* refers to the processing of the instruction and subsequent storing of the result in a register. Together, the instruction cycle and the execution cycle are called the *machine cycle*.

- The microprocessor has an internal *clock* that synchronizes all operations of the machine cycle. Its speed is measured in *megahertz (MHz)*. The faster the clock speed, the faster the computer can process information.

- Many basic computer instructions are stored in *read-only memory (ROM)*, a chip installed by the manufacturer inside the computer. ROM is nonvolatile—the data and instructions are not lost when the power is turned off.

- ROM memory cannot generally be altered. However, special ROM chips exist that allow users to modify ROM.
  1. *Programmable read-only memory (PROM)* allows the user to determine what data and instructions the manufacturer records on the chip—in other words, to customize the chip. However, once the data is recorded, it cannot be changed.
  2. *Erasable programmable read-only memory (EPROM)* not only allows users to determine what data and instructions are recorded on the chip, but it also allows them to erase the data with a special ultraviolet device. Then a trained technician uses a *PROM burner* to reprogram the chip.
  3. *Electrically erasable programmable read-only memory (EEPROM)* allows users to reprogram the chip electrically, under software control.

- *Random access memory (RAM)*, also called *main memory, primary storage*, and just *memory*, refers to the part of the processing hardware that temporarily holds data and instructions needed by the microprocessor. RAM is volatile—unless the data and instructions in RAM have been saved, for example, to disk—they are lost when the power is turned off.

- RAM—sort of a "desktop"—acts as a buffer between the microprocessor and the rest of the computer system components. The microprocessor can utilize only those software instructions and data that have been placed in RAM.

- A copy of the main systems software is stored in RAM when the computer is turned on; it controls the general operation of the computer and stays there as long as the computer is on. A copy of the specific software you are using in your business (applications software) is also temporarily stored in RAM.

- The amount of RAM you have in your computer determines the level of software sophistication your computer can handle because, with more RAM:
  1. It can receive and use larger programs.
  2. It can hold more copies of more than one program in RAM to support sharing of the computer by more than one user.
  3. It can operate faster and more efficiently.
  4. It can hold images for creating graphics and animation.

- Most modern microcomputers need at least 640 K RAM to run today's software. Some software programs require even more RAM—for example, for *multitasking*, the execution of more than one task or program at a time. A user can increase his or her microcomputer's RAM by inserting *add-on memory boards*, also called *expansion cards*, into one of the computer's *expansion slots*.

- Increased memory comes in the form of either *expanded memory* or *extended memory*. The main difference between the two types of memory is the microprocessors each type can be used with. Extended memory can only be used with machines that use at least an 80286 microprocessor.

- Memory expansion cards can be used only by those computers with *open architecture*, which allows users to open the system cabinet and make changes. Computers with *closed architecture* do not allow such changes.
- *Cache memory* is a special high-speed area of RAM created in addition to the computer's main RAM. The CPU looks there first for frequently used data and instructions—thus making the computer run faster.
- *Virtual memory* allows the CPU—under control of special software—to use disk space to simulate a large amount of RAM.
- The processing power of a microcomputer can be measured in terms of:
  1. *Addressing scheme*—determines the amount of RAM that can be controlled by the microprocessor at any one time. The larger the addressing capability, the more RAM the computer can control.
  2. *Register size*—The larger the general-purpose registers, the more data the microprocessor can manipulate in one machine cycle.
  3. *Data bus*—The larger the data buses, the more efficiently and quickly data and instructions can be moved among the processing components of the computer.
  4. *Clock speed*—The faster the clock speed, the more machine cycles are completed per second and the faster the computer can perform processing operations.
  5. *Instruction set*—The more powerful the instruction set, the fewer instructions and processing cycles it takes to perform certain tasks. The design of the chip affects how instruction sets—or blocks of instructions—are processed.

KEY TERMS

add-on memory board, p. 56
addressing scheme, p. 59
arithmetic/logic unit (ALU), p. 48
binary digit, p. 49
bit, p. 49
bus, p. 50
byte, p. 49
cache memory, p. 59
clock, p. 48
closed architecture, p. 57
Complex Instruction Set Computing (CISC), p. 61
control unit, p. 46
coprocessor, p. 51
data bus, p. 50

electrically erasable programmable read-only memory (EEPROM), p. 54
erasable programmable read-only memory (EPROM), p. 54
execution cycle, p. 48
expanded memory, p. 56
expansion card, p. 56
expansion slot, p. 56
extended memory, p. 58
gigabyte (GB), p. 49
instruction cycle, p. 48
kilobyte (KB, or K), p. 49
machine cycle, p. 48

machine language, p. 47
megabyte (MB), p. 49
megahertz (MHz), p. 48
microprocessor, p. 46
multitasking, p. 59
open architecture, p. 57
programmable read-only memory (PROM), p. 54
random access memory (RAM), p. 54
read-only memory (ROM), p. 51
Reduced Instruction Set Computing (RISC), p. 61
register, p. 48
virtual memory, p. 59

EXERCISES

SELF-TEST

1. The _____ _____ performs all the microcomputer's arithmetic and logical functions.
2. In machine language, data and instructions are represented with 0s and 1s. (true/false)
3. The _____ is the CPU of a microcomputer.
4. The _____ _____ directs and coordinates most of the activities in the computer system.
5. The speed of a microprocessor is measured in _____.
6. The more bits a computer's buses and registers can handle at once, the faster the microcomputer. (true/false)
7. Read-only memory is a nonvolatile form of storage. (true/false)
8. A _____ connects the different components in the microprocessor.
9. _____ _____ _____ temporarily holds data and instructions until needed by the microprocessor.
10. Increased memory comes in two forms:
    a. _____   b. _____
11. Expansion cards, or add-on boards, can be used only in computers with _____ architecture.
12. The _____ the data bus, the more efficiently and quickly data can be moved among the processing components of the computer.
13. List three types of ROM chips:
    a. _____   b. _____   c. _____
14. Generally, the more expensive a microprocessor is, the faster it can process data. (true/false)
15. The instruction cycle and the execution cycle together are called the _____ _____.
16. A _____ is composed of 8 _____.
17. The retrieval of an instruction from memory and its subsequent decoding is referred to as the _____ _____.
18. Data and instructions are lost in RAM when the computer is turned off. (true/false)
19. Data and instructions are lost in ROM when the computer is turned off. (true/false)
20. The processing power of a microcomputer can be measured in terms of:
    a. _____   b. _____   c. _____   d. _____   e. _____

SOLUTIONS   (1) arithmetic/logic unit; (2) true; (3) microprocessor; (4) control unit; (5) megahertz; (6) true; (7) true; (8) bus; (9) random access memory; (10) expanded memory, extended memory; (11) open; (12) larger [or wider]; (13) PROM, EPROM, EEPROM; (14) true; (15) machine cycle; (16) byte, bits; (17) instruction cycle; (18) true; (19) false; (20) addressing scheme, register size, data bus, clock speed, instruction set

SHORT ANSWER

1. List and describe the main factors that affect the processing power of a microcomputer.

2. What is the difference between a computer with closed architecture and one with open architecture?

3. What is the function of the ALU in a microcomputer system?

4. What would be a good indication that two computers are incompatible? Why is knowing this important to you?

5. What is the function of a bus in a microcomputer system? How might one bus be better than another?

6. What does the addressing scheme in a microcomputer system affect?

7. Describe why having more RAM in your computer (as opposed to less) is useful.

8. What is a machine cycle and how does it relate to the term *megahertz*? Why would a user be interested in a computer's megahertz rate?

9. What is a coprocessor and what can it be used for?

10. What led to the development of add-on memory boards?

PROJECTS

1. Research the current uses of and the latest advances in ROM technology. How do you think ROM technology will affect the way we currently use microcomputers?

2. Advances are made almost every day in microprocessor chip technology. What are some of the most recent advances? In what computers are these chips being used? How might these advances affect the way we currently use microcomputers? Research the latest advances by reviewing the most current computer magazines and periodicals.

3. Visit a well-equipped computer store and, with the help of a salesperson, decide what microcomputer might be the best one for you to use based on your processing requirements (if necessary, pick a hypothetical job and identify some probable processing requirements). Use the checklist on page 62 to describe the microcomputer you would choose and explain why. Compare this microcomputer to the others you were shown.

4. What does it mean for a microcomputer and related equipment to be "IBM compatible"? Look through some computer magazines and identify advertised microcomputer systems that are IBM compatible. What are their clock speeds? microprocessor model numbers and manufacturers? RAM capacities? register (often called *wordsize*) and data bus capacities? Do you think there are any risks involved in buying an IBM-compatible system instead of an IBM PC?

5. Look through magazines about Apple Macintosh computers and PCs. Compare the Apple Quadra 950 microcomputer and the IBM PS/2 90 microcomputer according to:

        clock speed (MHz): _____

        RAM capacity: _____ (upgradable to: _____)

        data bus capacity: _____

        register (wordsize) capacity: _____

        cost: _____

    Which computer appears to be more powerful? Based on what you know so far, which machine would you prefer?

CHAPTER 4

STORAGE HARDWARE

A great deal of business has to do with keeping score, with record-keeping. Indeed, very few businesses can operate without keeping a running account of daily transactions: who owes what to whom, who collected what, when something is scheduled to happen, and so on. We have already described how data is converted into computer-usable form and processed. Now let us consider how this computerized data is stored and retrieved.

PREVIEW

When you have completed this chapter, you will be able to:

Explain the difference between primary and secondary storage, and how data is represented in each

Describe the secondary storage devices used the most often with microcomputers, including diskettes, hard disks, disk cartridges, and optical storage devices

Explain the importance of backup and the different methods for backing up a microcomputer system

Not understanding the concept of computer storage is like not understanding the concept of a car's gasoline tank. Without using a gasoline tank, you won't be able to get your car to go very far because, of course, without the tank, you can't use gasoline. Similarly, if you don't use a storage device with your computer, you won't have the capability to store the data that will make your computer useful.

As you learned in the previous chapter, the data you are working on—such as a document—is stored in RAM in an electrical state during processing. Because RAM is fueled by electricity, when you turn off the power to your computer, RAM is erased. Therefore, before you turn your microcomputer off, you must save your work onto a permanent storage device that stores data magnetically—such as a diskette or a hard disk—rather than electrically. When stored on a magnetic storage device, your data will remain intact even when the computer is turned off. (Optical storage, which we will cover later, is also an option.)

In general, data is stored in a computer system for three principal reasons.

1. *Current input data needs to be held for processing.* For example, daily sales data might be held in a temporary file until it is processed at the end of the day to produce invoices.

2. *Some types of data are stored on a relatively permanent basis and retrieved as required during processing.* For example, to produce a customer invoice, you need data from the customer file: customer's name, address, billing instructions, and terms.

3. *Data is stored to be periodically updated.* For example, the accounts receivable file (reflecting what customers owe) needs to be updated to reflect the latest purchases.

In addition to all this data, the computer software instructions must be stored in a computer-usable form because a copy of the software must be placed into RAM from a storage device before processing can begin.

In this chapter we describe the different storage devices you should be familiar with to use a microcomputer efficiently. We focus on how they work, as well as their speed, cost, and capacity.

STORAGE FUNDAMENTALS

You know that storage hardware provides the capability to store data and program instructions—either temporarily or permanently—for quick retrieval and use during computer processing. Before we describe the characteristics of the microcomputer storage devices you will likely use in the business environment, you must understand a number of storage fundamentals, including: (1) the difference between primary and secondary storage, (2) how data is represented in a microcomputer system, (3) what a file is, and (4) the general process of storing data on a storage device.

PRIMARY AND SECONDARY STORAGE

The term **primary storage** (main memory) refers to the RAM of a computer, where both data and instructions are temporarily held for immediate access and use by the computer's microprocessor. Although the technology is changing, most primary storage is considered a **volatile** form of storage, meaning that the data and instructions are lost when the computer is turned off. **Secondary storage** (or **aux-**

iliary storage) is any storage device designed to retain data and instructions (programs) in a more permanent form. Secondary storage is **nonvolatile,** meaning that saved data and instructions remain intact when the computer is turned off.

The easiest way to differentiate between primary and secondary storage is to consider the reason data is placed in them. Data is placed in primary storage only when it is needed for processing. Data in secondary storage remains there until overwritten with new data or deleted, and it is accessed when needed. In very general terms, a secondary storage device can be thought of as a file cabinet. We store data there until we need it. Then we open the drawer, take out the appropriate folder (file), and place it on the top of our desk (primary storage, or RAM), where we work on it—perhaps writing a few things in it or throwing away a few papers. When we are finished with the file, we take it off the desktop (out of primary storage) and return it to the cabinet (secondary storage).

DATA REPRESENTATION: BINARY CODE

When you begin to write a report, you have a large collection of symbols to choose from: the letters A–Z, both upper- and lowercase; the numbers 0–9; and numerous punctuation and other special symbols, such as ?, $, and %. People understand what these characters mean; computers cannot.

Computers deal with machine language, data converted into the simplest form that can be processed magnetically or electronically—that is, binary form. The term *binary* is used to refer to two distinct states: on or off, yes or no, present or absent (Figure 4.1). (For example, a light switch can be either on or off, so it can be viewed as a binary device.) A **binary digit (bit)** (Figure 4.2) is either the character 1 (on) or the character 0 (off)—magnetically, electrically, or optically. For example, when data is stored on magnetic tape or disk, it is represented by the presence or absence—"on" or "off"—of magnetic spots.

To store and process data in binary form, a way of representing characters, numbers, and other symbols had to be developed. In other words, *coding schemes*

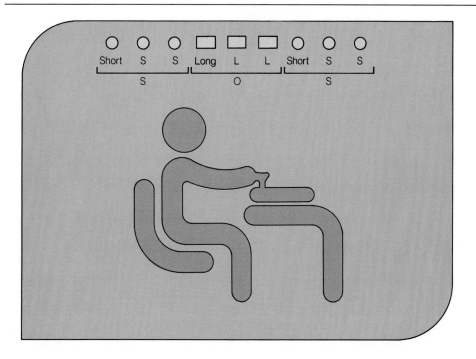

FIGURE 4.1

An early binary code. Samuel F. B. Morse, developer of the Morse code, showed that data elements (characters) could be represented by using two "states"—long and short, otherwise known as dash and dot.

had to be devised as standardized methods of encoding data for use in computer storage and processing. A scheme for encoding data using a series of binary digits is called **binary code**.

Two commonly used binary codes are ASCII (pronounced "as-key") and EBCDIC (pronounced "eb-see-dick") (Figure 4.3). The acronym **ASCII** stands for the **American Standard Code for Information Interchange,** which is widely used to represent characters in microcomputers and many minicomputers. Because microcomputers operate on 8-bit groups, ASCII uses 8 bits to represent a character. For example, the character A in ASCII is 01000001. Eight bits yield 256 possible combinations, enough to represent all the letters of the alphabet, numbers 0–9, and special symbols.

The acronym **EBCDIC** refers to **Extended Binary Coded Decimal Interchange Code,** which is the most popular code used for IBM and IBM-compatible mainframe computers. In EBCDIC, A is 11000001. As you can see in Figure 4.3, characters are coded differently in ASCII and EBCDIC. Because of these differences, transferring data between computers using different coding schemes requires special hardware and software.

PARITY BITS

The term *computer error* is often used when a mistake is caused by a person— inputting data incorrectly, for example. However, errors can be caused by other factors, such as dust, electrical disturbance, weather conditions, and improper handling of equipment. When such an error occurs, the computer may not be able to tell you exactly what and where it is, but it *can* tell you that there is an error.

How does it do this?—by using **parity bits,** or **check bits.** A parity bit is an extra (ninth) bit attached to the end of the byte (Figure 4.4). If you add the number of 1 bits in a byte, you will have either an odd number of 1s or an even

---

FIGURE 4.2

A bit (*binary digit*) is the smallest possible computer signal or impulse; it is used in combination with other signals or impulses to represent data (a character); it is a "1" or a "0"—that is, on or off. Different combinations of 0s and 1s are electronically translated into computerized codes.

A bit is the smallest possible unit of data; it is 1 or 0 — that is, on or off:

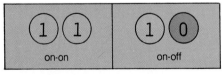

2 bits (2²) can have four possible combinations:

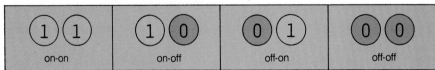

3 bits (2³) can have 8 possible combinations:

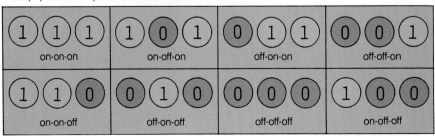

4 bits (2⁴) yield 16 possible combinations. 8 bits (2⁸) yield 256 possible combinations, enough to represent all the letters of the alphabet, numbers 0–9, and special symbols.

number of 1s (for example, ASCII A has two 1s, so it's even). Computers can be designed to use either an *odd-parity scheme* or an *even-parity scheme.* In an odd-parity scheme, a ninth bit, 0 or 1, is added to make the total number of 1s equal an odd number. If any byte turns up with an even number of 1s in an odd-parity scheme, the computer signals an error message on the screen. Similarly, if a byte turns up with an odd number of 1s in an even-parity scheme, an error message appears.

As a user, you won't have to determine whether to use an odd- or an even-parity scheme. The computer manufacturer determines this, and the systems software automatically checks the parity scheme. If your computer signals an error in the parity scheme, a message such as "Parity error" will appear on the screen. At this point, you should have your computer serviced to determine what is causing the problem.

Character	ASCII-8	EBCDIC	Character	ASCII-8	EBCDIC
A	0100 0001	1100 0001	N	0100 1110	1101 0101
B	0100 0010	1100 0010	O	0100 1111	1101 0110
C	0100 0011	1100 0011	P	0101 0000	1101 0111
D	0100 0100	1100 0100	Q	0101 0001	1101 1000
E	0100 0101	1100 0101	R	0101 0010	1101 1001
F	0100 0110	1100 0110	S	0101 0011	1110 0010
G	0100 0111	1100 0111	T	0101 0100	1110 0011
H	0100 1000	1100 1000	U	0101 0101	1110 0100
I	0100 1001	1100 1001	V	0101 0110	1110 0101
J	0100 1010	1101 0001	W	0101 0111	1110 0110
K	0100 1011	1101 0010	X	0101 1000	1110 0111
L	0100 1100	1101 0011	Y	0101 1001	1110 1000
M	0100 1101	1101 0100	Z	0101 1010	1110 1001
0	0011 0000	1111 0000	5	0011 0101	1111 0101
1	0011 0001	1111 0001	6	0011 0110	1111 0110
2	0011 0010	1111 0010	7	0011 0111	1111 0111
3	0011 0011	1111 0011	8	0011 1000	1111 1000
4	0011 0100	1111 0100	9	0011 1001	1111 1001
!	0010 0001	0101 1010	;	0011 1011	0101 1110

FIGURE 4.3

ASCII and EBCDIC. This chart shows some of the printed character codes according to the two most commonly used binary coding schemes for data representation. ASCII originally used 7 bits, but a zero was added in the left position to provide an 8-bit code (more possible combinations to form characters). The ASCII-8 code has enabled the use of many more special characters, such as Greek letters, math symbols, and foreign language symbols.

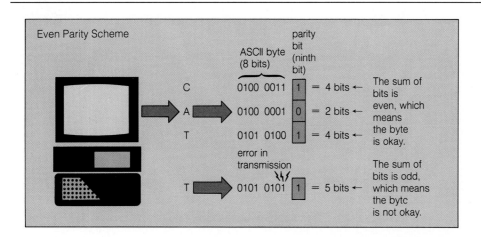

FIGURE 4.4

Parity schemes. This computer was designed to use an even-parity scheme, which means that the computer expects the total number of 1s (in the binary code) to always add up to an even number. In an even-parity scheme, a transmission error is signaled by the computer when the number of 1s adds up to an odd number. (The opposite is true when an odd-parity scheme is used.)

FILES AND DATA HIERARCHY

No matter what size or shape computer you work with, you will be working with files. But before we can put data files in their proper perspective, we need to examine the levels of data, known as the **data storage hierarchy.** If you look at Figure 4.5, at the top of the data hierarchy you'll see the term *file*. A **file** is made up of a group of related records. A **record** is defined as a collection of related fields, and a **field** is defined as a collection of related characters, or bytes, of data. Finally, a byte, or character, of data, as you have learned, is made up of 8 bits.

FIGURE 4.5

Data hierarchy. All data in an information system is stored as bits on a storage device. The data is arranged in hierarchical form: bits, bytes, fields, records, and files.

Examples

A file, made up of records, contains information on a specific topic, or group.

File

Inventory file

A record is made up of related fields.

Records

Snorkels
Boogie boards
Tennis rackets

Fields are items of information about the objects or persons in the file.

Fields

Item or product number
Item or product description
Unit price
Quantity on hand

Each field is composed of a series of bytes.

Bytes

01000001 (Letter A in ASCII)

Each byte is composed of a string of 8 bits.

Bits

1 or 0

FIGURE 4.6

The inventory file contains product records, such as the record for snorkels. Each record contains fields: product number, product description, unit price, and quantity on hand. Each field is made up of characters, or bytes, each of which comprises 8 bits.

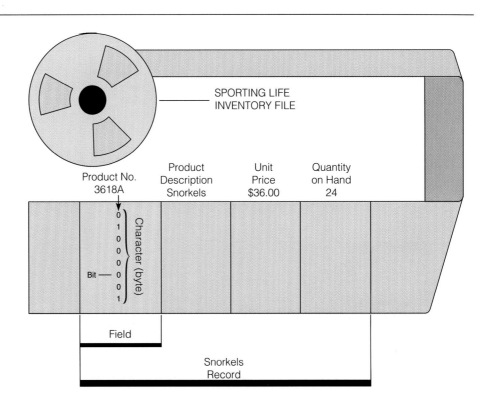

SPORTING LIFE
INVENTORY FILE

Product No.
3618A

Product
Description
Snorkels

Unit
Price
$36.00

Quantity
on Hand
24

Bit

0
1
0
0
0
0
0
1

Character (byte)

Field

Snorkels
Record

To illustrate this concept, let's look at a sample inventory file for a sporting goods store (Figure 4.6). This particular inventory *file* is made up of a group of *records*, one record for each item in inventory, such as snorkels. Each record contains the same number of *fields* such as: (1) product number, (2) product description, (3) unit price, and (4) quantity on hand. Each field contains a number of *characters*, such as the letter A in the product number. In turn, each character is made up of 8 bits, at the low end of the data hierarchy.

Files generally fall into two categories: (1) files containing data (often referred to generically as *data files*) and (2) files containing software instructions (often referred to generically as *program files*).

HOW IS DATA STORED?

To store data for later use you need two things: a storage **medium** (plural = **media**)—the type of material on which data is recorded—and a storage device. The storage device records the data onto the medium, where the data is held until needed. The process of recording data onto media, which is coordinated by software, involves four basic steps (Figure 4.7):

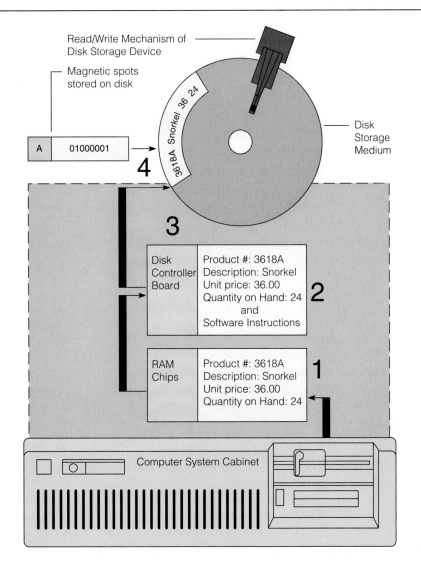

FIGURE 4.7

Data recording process. (1) Data enters RAM from an external device, such as a keyboard. (2) Software instructions determine where the data is to be recorded on the disk. (3) The data goes to the disk controller board. (4) From here it flows to the read/write head in the disk storage device and is recorded on the storage medium.

1. After input, the data to be recorded by a storage device temporarily resides in RAM.

2. Software instructions determine where the data is to be recorded on the storage medium.

3. The controller board for the storage device positions the recording mechanism over the appropriate location on the storage medium. For storage on disk, this mechanism is referred to in most cases as a **read/write head** because it can both "read" (accept) magnetic spots and convert them to electrical impulses and "write" (enter) the spots on the disk; it can also erase the spots.

4. The recording mechanism is activated and converts electrical impulses to magnetic spots placed on the surface of the medium as required to record the data according to the coding scheme being used (ASCII, for example).

DISKETTES

The **diskette, or floppy diskette** is a **direct access storage medium**—meaning that data can be stored and retrieved in no particular sequence. Diskettes are made of a special plastic that can be coated and easily magnetized. Diskettes are often referred to as "floppy" because they are made of flexible material. As Figure 4.8 shows, the disk is enclosed in a protective jacket—either paper or plastic—lined with a soft material specially treated to reduce friction and static. The disk jacket has four openings: (1) hub, (2) data access area, (3) write/protect notch, and (4) index hole. To store and retrieve data from a diskette, you must place it into a **disk drive** (Figure 4.9), which contains special mechanical components for storing and retrieving data.

RETRIEVING AND STORING DATA

The **hub** of the diskette is the round opening in the center. When the diskette is placed into the disk drive, the hub fits over a mount, or spindle, in the drive (Figure 4.9). In some IBM PCs, before you can access any data on the diskette, you must close the **disk drive gate,** or **door,** after you insert the diskette. The act of closing the disk drive gate moves a lever over the drive and clamps the diskette over the spindle of the drive mechanism. Many personal computers today don't have drive doors; the diskette is simply pushed into the drive until it clicks in place. An access light goes on when the disk is in use, and, in many microcomputers, the disk is ejected by pressing the eject button. (In microcomputers without eject buttons, the user simply opens the disk drive door and pulls out the diskette.)

When data is stored and retrieved, the diskette spins inside its jacket, and the read/write head on the actuator arm is clamped on the surface in the **data access area** of the disk (Figure 4.10). Most disk drives are equipped with two read/write heads so that the top and bottom surfaces of the diskette can be accessed simultaneously. The read/write heads are moved back and forth over the data access area in small increments to retrieve or record data as needed.

Just inside the disk drive unit, a small mechanism checks to determine if the user has covered the disk's **write/protect notch**. If the notch is covered, a switch is activated that prevents the read/write head from being able to touch the surface of the diskette, which means no data can be recorded (Figure 4.11). This is a security measure; covering the write/protect notch prevents accidental erasure or overwriting of data.

The **index hole** in the jacket is positioned over a photoelectric sensing mechanism in the disk drive. As the diskette spins in the jacket (when data is being recorded or retrieved), the hole (or holes—some diskettes have more than one) in the diskette repeatedly passes over the hole in the jacket, is sensed, and activates a timing switch. The timing activity is critical because this is how the mechanism determines which portion of the diskette is over or under the read/write heads. The diskette spins at a fixed speed of about 300 revolutions per minute (RPM).

As you'll learn in the next section, diskettes come in a few different sizes and with various storage capacities. The size and capacity of the diskette you use depends on the characteristics of the disk drive in your microcomputer system.

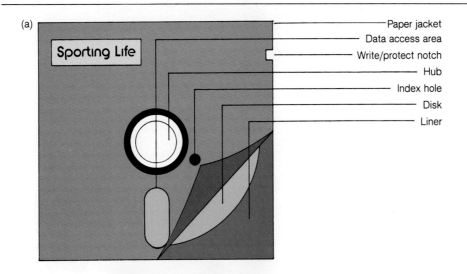

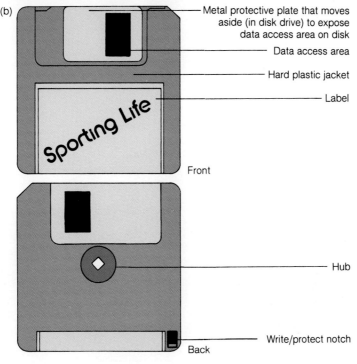

FIGURE 4.8

Diskettes were developed to replace cassette tape as a data storage medium for use with microcomputers. Diskettes provide fast direct access capabilities. IBM PCs and many IBM-compatible microcomputers use (a) the 5¼-inch diskette; the Macintosh line of microcomputers, as well as most portable IBM-compatible computers and IBM PS/2 series microcomputers, use (b) the 3½-inch diskette.

FIGURE 4.9

(a) These cutaway illustrations show the main parts of a 5¼-inch disk drive and a 3½-inch disk drive for diskettes. (b) Inserting a 5¼-inch diskette in a disk drive. (c) Inserting a 3½-inch diskette in a disk drive.

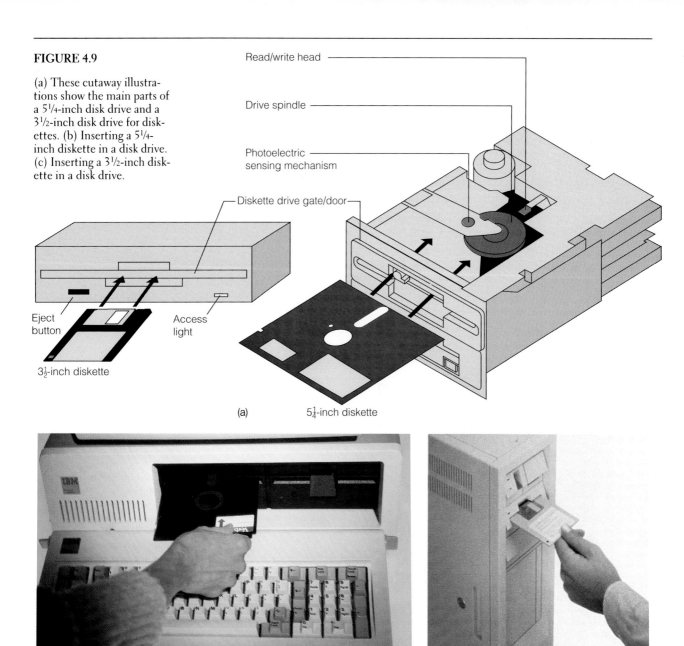

Read/write head

Drive spindle

Photoelectric sensing mechanism

Diskette drive gate/door

Eject button

Access light

3½-inch diskette

(a)

5¼-inch diskette

(b)

(c)

FIGURE 4.10

Inside the drive, the read/write head moves back and forth over the data access area in the protective jacket to read or write data on the disk.

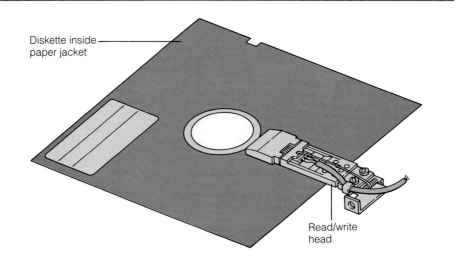

Diskette inside paper jacket

Read/write head

Some disk drives are intended to store and retrieve data from a high-capacity diskette, whereas others have been designed to be used with low-capacity diskettes. Likewise, 3½-inch disk drives are to be used only with 3½-inch diskettes. Don't try putting a 3½-inch diskette in a 5¼-inch disk drive! You could damage the read/write mechanism inside the drive. Later on in the book you will learn how to transfer data between disks of different sizes.

DISKETTE STORAGE CAPACITY

The **byte** is the unit of measure used most often to determine the capacity of a storage device used with any type of computer (Table 4.1). The capacity of a diskette does not necessarily depend on its size. A number of factors affect how much data can be stored on a disk, including:

1. Whether the diskette stores data on only one side (single-sided) or both sides (double-sided)
2. Whether the disk drive is equipped with read/write heads for both the top and the bottom surfaces of the diskette

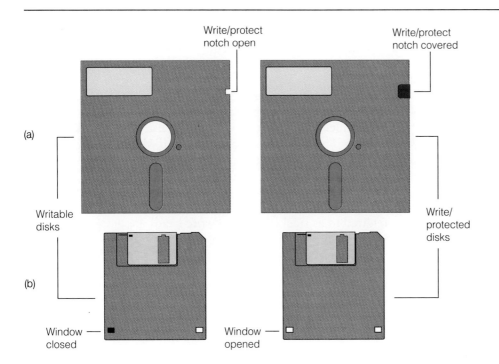

FIGURE 4.11

(a) The write/protect notch of the 5¼-inch disk on the left is open and, therefore, data can be written to the disk. The notch of the 5¼-inch disk on the right, however, is covered (the user has put tape over it). Data cannot be written to this disk. (b) Data cannot be written on the 3½-inch disk on the right because the small black piece of plastic is not covering the window in the lower left corner. Plastic covers the window of the 3½-inch disk on the left, so data can be written on this disk.

Bit	A binary digit; 0 or 1
Byte	8 bits, or 1 character
Kilobyte (K, or KB)	1,024 bytes
Megabyte (MB)	1,024,000 bytes
Gigabyte (GB)	1,024,000,000 bytes
Terabyte (TB)	1,024,000,000,000 bytes

TABLE 4.1

Units of Measurement for Disk Storage

3. What the data-recording density is (the number of bits that can be stored per inch)
4. What the track density is (the number of tracks per inch in which data is recorded)

The first diskettes were **single-sided**. But as the need to store more data became a significant concern in the business community, technology produced the **double-sided** disk, which is capable of storing twice the amount of data as a comparable single-sided disk. To take advantage of a double-sided disk, however, you must have a computer with a double-sided floppy disk drive. Double-sided disk drives are equipped with read/write heads for both the top and the bottom surfaces of a disk. This allows data to be read from or written to both surfaces simultaneously. (The heads move together on the same mechanism so that they are positioned over corresponding locations on the surfaces of the disk.) Disk capacity also depends on the recording density capabilities of the disk drive. **Recording density** refers to the number of bits per inch (bpi) of data that can be written onto the surface of the disk. Disks and drives are typically rated as having one of three recording densities:

1. **Single-density**
2. **Double-density**
3. **Quadruple-density** (often referred to as *quad-density*, or *high-density*)

The specifications for the exact number of bits per inch for each recording density vary from one manufacturer to another. Disk manufacturers use the recording density designation as a measure of the maximum bpi their diskettes can reliably be expected to store.

A double-sided, double-density 5¼-inch diskette (labeled "DS, DD," or "2S/2D") has a storage capacity of 360 K. Using a new technology called *vertical recording*, Toshiba is now producing a 3½-inch extra high-density (ED) diskette that can store 2.88 MB of data. The 3½-inch diskettes for the IBM PS/2 series of microcomputers hold from 720 K (single-density) to 1.44 MB (double-density). Table 4.2 compares the capacities of some popular diskettes.

The final factor affecting disk capacity is the track density. As pictured in Figure 4.12, data is recorded on disks in circular bands—similar to grooves on a phonograph record—referred to as **tracks**. The read/write heads are designed to move in small increments across the data access area of the disk to find the appropriate track. As the precision of positioning the read/write head increases, the widths of the tracks become thinner—that is, less dense. Common **track densities** in use today are 48 tracks per inch (tpi), 96 tpi, and 135 tpi. The recording surface of a 5¼-inch disk is slightly less than 1 inch; therefore, there are 40 or 80 usable tracks per inch in most cases.

TABLE 4.2

Capacities of Widely Used Diskettes

	Bytes	Tracks	Sectors/ Track	Bytes/ Sector
5¼-inch diskettes:				
Double-sided, double-density	360 K	40	9	512
Double-sided, quad-density	1.2 MB	80	15	512
3½-inch diskettes:				
Double-sided, single-density	720 K	80	9	512
Double-sided, double-density	1.44 MB	80	18	512

DISKETTE SIZES AND SHAPES

The use of 5¼-inch diskettes by IBM in their personal computer system in 1981 led to the adoption of this size as the microcomputer industry standard. However, since the Apple Macintosh introduced the 3½-inch diskette and disk drive in 1984 and IBM switched to this size in 1987 in its PS/2 microcomputer systems, the standard has been changing. Although they are smaller in size, the 3½-inch disks are capable of storing more data than 5¼-inch diskettes, and they are also less susceptible to damage because they are covered by a hard plastic jacket rather than a paper jacket. (The care of diskettes is discussed later in this chapter.)

Nearly 80% of all disk drives sold today are used with 3½-inch diskettes. "The 3½-inch is a done deal. The only momentum for 5¼-inch drives comes from clone makers who just copy old products," said James Porter, president of Disk/Trend, Inc. Laptop computers—microcomputers that typically weigh between 5 and 20 pounds and that you can carry around like a briefcase—fueled the ascension of the 3½-inch drive.

SECTORS

Typically a disk is divided into eight or nine **sectors,** or equal, wedge-shaped areas used for storage reference purposes (Figure 4.12). The point at which a sector intersects a track is used by systems software to reference the data location; the track number indicates where to position the read/write head, and the sector number indicates where to activate the read/write head as the disk spins.

Disks and drives are identified as being either hard-sectored or soft-sectored. *Hard-sectored* disks always have the same number and size of sectors, which are fixed by the manufacturer. Today most microcomputer systems use soft-sectored disks. *Soft-sectored* disks are marked magnetically by the user's computer system during a process called **formatting,** or **initializing,** which determines the size and the number of sectors on the disk. Since your diskettes must be adapted to the particular microcomputer and software you are using, you format these diskettes yourself. This is easily done using only a few simple commands on the computer.

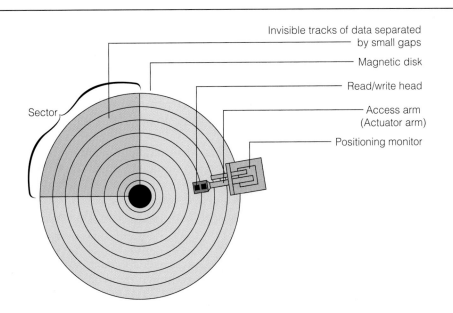

Invisible tracks of data separated by small gaps

Magnetic disk

Read/write head

Access arm (Actuator arm)

Positioning monitor

Sector

FIGURE 4.12

Tracks are circular bands on disks on which data is recorded. The tracks are separated by small gaps and are divided into equal areas called sectors. Tracks and sectors are used to determine addresses of fields of data.

ACCESS TIME

The responsiveness of your computer depends to a great extent on the time it takes to locate the instructions or data being sought and then to load a copy into RAM. The term **access time** refers to the average speed with which this is done. The access time of your computer's disk drive is determined by adding up the time it takes to perform each of the following activities:

1. Positioning the read/write heads over the proper track (the time it takes to do this is called the **seek time**)

2. Waiting for the disk to revolve until the correct sector is under or over the read/write heads (this is called **rotational delay,** or **latency**)

3. Placing the read/write head(s) in contact with the disks

4. Transferring the data from the disk into the computer's RAM (at a speed called the *data transfer rate*)

The average access time for diskettes ranges from 150 milliseconds (150 thousandths of a second) to 300 milliseconds, depending on the operating characteristics of the drive mechanism. This may not seem like very long, but access time can be a major performance factor for the following reasons: (1) Large applications software packages keep only a portion of the instructions in RAM at one time and must retrieve additional instructions from disk periodically to perform specific tasks. (2) The processing of large files is done only a few records at a time, so a substantial amount of time can be spent going back and forth to the disk to retrieve records.

Before you proceed to the next section, you need to know how to care for your diskettes—abuse means lost data. Figure 4.13 shows 5¼-inch diskettes; however, just because the 3½-inch diskettes have hard jackets does not mean that they cannot be damaged, too!

HARD DISKS

The introduction of high-capacity **hard disks**—which can store from 20 MB to more than a gigabyte, or 1,000 MB—solved two serious problems related to the limited storage capacity of diskettes. First, as a business begins to use microcomputers extensively, the amount of software it acquires and data it collects tends to grow substantially. As a result, the number of diskettes it needs to handle increases dramatically. It is not uncommon for one user alone to have a library of 100 or more diskettes. Second, the largest file that can be accessed at one time is limited to the capacity of RAM and the capacity of the storage medium. So, if the capacity of a diskette is 360 K, no file larger than that can be stored on the disk or worked with in RAM.

Hard disks can store much larger files; for example, certain businesses may need to set up an inventory system on a microcomputer that calls for working with a 45,000-item inventory master file. And the 150-page report that didn't fit on one diskette can easily fit on a hard disk. Of course, you could have stored the report in sections in separate files on different diskettes, but that would have been very inconvenient. You would have had to continually swap diskettes, inserting them and ejecting them, to work on your report. The hard disk spares you that trouble.

Just a few years ago, one 20 MB hard disk provided enough storage for most users (Figure 4.14). Today, because of storage-hungry graphical software interfaces, networking software, and more sophisticated software applications and systems software, hard disk storage capacities of 300 MB and larger are becoming increasingly commonplace and necessary. Hard disk drives can store and retrieve data much faster than can diskette drives. Whereas the average access time for diskettes is approximately 300 milliseconds, the average access time for hard disks ranges from 16–70 milliseconds.

Hard disk units have become increasingly smaller while at the same time they have achieved higher storage capacities. The most popular units today use 3½-inch disks; some units still use 5¼-inch disks. The initial 5¼-inch disk drives were approximately 3½-inches high, whereas the new disk drives are just over 1½-inches high; this means that you can put at least twice as much disk capacity in the same

FIGURE 4.13

Handle with care! This illustration shows how to avoid disk damage.

space you used before (Figure 4.15). Two diskette drives can fit where only one used to fit, and two hard disk units can occupy the space that one did. This type of configuration provides a powerful system in a small work space.

FIGURE 4.14

The use of hard disk units on microcomputers has greatly increased their ability to deal with large amounts of data at one time. For example, onc 20 MB hard disk holds the same amount of data as 56 double-sided, double-density diskettes.

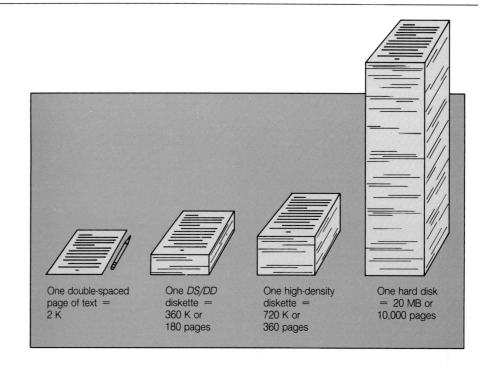

One double-spaced page of text = 2 K

One *DS/DD* diskette = 360 K or 180 pages

One high-density diskette = 720 K or 360 pages

One hard disk = 20 MB or 10,000 pages

FIGURE 4.15

This 1½-inch hard disk drive can be inserted in the computer's system unit to provide the user with high-capacity storage.

The alternative to replacing a diskette drive or taking up desk space with an external hard disk drive is to buy a **hardcard** (Figure 4.16), a circuit board with a disk that plugs into an expansion slot inside the computer. Hardcards store between 40 MB and 105 MB of data and have an average access time of from 9 to 25 milliseconds.

RETRIEVING AND STORING DATA

In hard disk systems, data is stored in the same way as it is on diskettes. A series of tracks are divided into sectors when the disk is formatted. As their name suggests, hard disks are made out of a rigid substance that is capable of storing a greater amount of data than the soft material used for diskettes. Hard disk drives for microcomputers (Figure 4.17) can be *internal* (built into the computer cabinet and nonremovable) or *external* (outside the computer cabinet and connected to it by a short cable) (Figure 4.18).

Hard disks have the following characteristics:

1. They are rigid metal platters connected to a central spindle.
2. The entire disk unit (disks and read/write heads) is placed in a permanently sealed container.
3. Air that flows through the container is filtered to prevent contamination.
4. The disks are rotated at very high speed (usually around 3,600 RPM; floppy disks rotate at about 300 RPM).

These disk drives can have four or more (often eight) disk platters in a sealed unit. In most of these disk units (which are often called *Winchester disk drives*), the read/write heads never touch the surfaces of the disks. Instead, they are designed to float from .5 to 1.25 millionths of an inch from the disk surface; because of this characteristic, the design is often referred to as a *flying head* design. Because the heads float so closely to the sensitive disks, any contamination—such as a dust particle or a hair—can cause a *head crash*, also referred to as a *disk crash*, which destroys some or all of the data on the disk. This sensitivity is the reason why hard disk units are assembled under sterile conditions.

FIGURE 4.16

Hardcard. This hardcard works like a hard disk but plugs into an expansion slot inside the microcomputer cabinet. (The disk is under the cover at the left side of the card.)

FIGURE 4.17

Internal hard disk unit. (a) These illustrations show the main components of a hard disk unit. (b) As you can see from this photo of an IBM PS/2 computer, a hard disk does not have an exterior opening, because the disk(s) is sealed in a unit inside the system cabinet. (The single drive opening you see is for a diskette.)

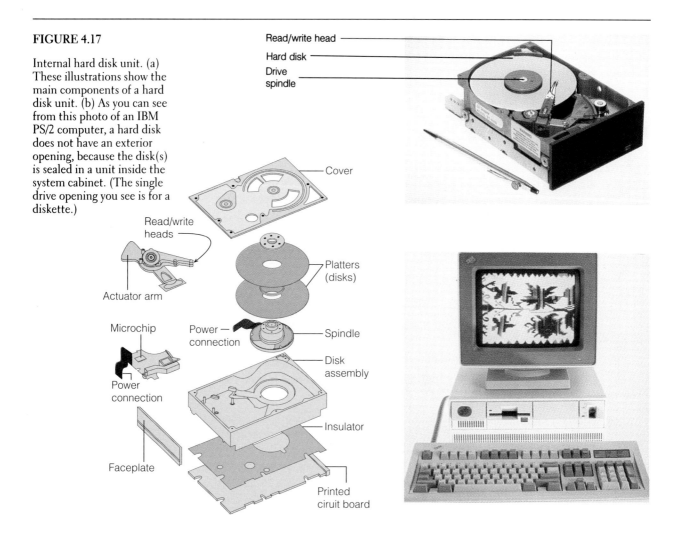

Read/write head
Hard disk
Drive spindle
Cover
Read/write heads
Actuator arm
Microchip
Power connection
Power connection
Faceplate
Platters (disks)
Spindle
Disk assembly
Insulator
Printed ciruit board

FIGURE 4.18

External hard disk drive. This shot of a Mac SE shows it hooked up to an external hard disk drive (the "box" positioned under the computer, directly behind the keyboard). You can also see the diskette drive opening on the front of the system cabinet. Some Mac systems can also include an additional internal hard disk unit and a second floppy disk drive.

All of us know how to eat. Some of us know how to cook. Numerous enterprising people go into the food and beverage business to try cooking for others. And computers have become as essential for restaurant operators as recipes and menus.

Many small eating and drinking establishments get by with just an electronic cash register, a calculator-like machine with a cash drawer that is not much different from the time-honored cash register. Larger food-service operations, however, may go to a point-of-sale (POS) system. A POS system links three areas: the eating and drinking areas, the kitchen or other food-preparation areas, and the back office.

In the eating and drinking areas—what the industry calls the "front of the house"—there may be POS registers with different cash drawers for different waiters, waitresses, and bartenders. Or, if a cash drawer is shared by several servers, separate cash accountability is maintained by the software. Special-purpose software is also available that tells the host or hostess how many customers came in and when, the size of the order, and which server took the order and when. Some software can help servers be more efficient or helpful—for example, by indicating when a particular food or beverage is out of stock or by cueing servers to ask how an order of beef should be cooked.

So-called cash-taking software is important because often the person taking the order is not the cashier. Cash-taking software consolidates bar and food charges, provides information on discounts and senior-citizen specials, and indicates whether payment is by cash or credit card. Different kinds of printers are available for printing out guest checks: dot matrix or impact printers, which are commonplace but noisy; thermal printers, which require special paper; and laser printers, the most recently developed kind, which are quiet and require no special paper.

Servers in the front of the house may use flat-membrane-type keyboards; touch-screen devices; or, sometimes, hand-held terminals. Hardware in the kitchen must be of a hardier sort, capable of working amid heat, water, and grease. If orders are transmitted electronically by servers from terminals in the front of the house via cable to the kitchen, they may appear on a printer or display screen. Software may process the information sent by the server in a way to assist the preparer. For instance, similar food items might be grouped together, cooking instructions might be put in order, special cooking instructions highlighted, and instructions given on when to begin each part of an order. Software can also indicate that a kitchen is properly stocked to meet demand, based on previous experience.

Depending on the kind of eating establishment, a POS system might be hooked up to outside payment processors for credit card charges and check clearing. Or, if the restaurant is in a hotel, it might link front-of-the-house terminals with the front desk, so that food and beverage charges may be posted to a guest's room bill.

Finally, there is the relationship of the POS system to what is called the "back office," the manager's office or the corporate headquarters. A manager may use the back-office terminal to collect information so that the restaurant can regulate the mix of products, adjust prices, and in general run things more efficiently. If the back-office machine is also a microcomputer, it can be used for other tasks, such as doing spreadsheets, word processing, and telecommunications. ∎

DISK CARTRIDGES

Removable hard **disk cartridges** (Figure 4.19) are an alternative to regular hard disks as a form of secondary storage. Whereas hard disks remain inside the computer or the external disk drive, disk cartridges can be removed and replaced easily. The cartridges usually contain one or two platters enclosed in a hard plastic case that is inserted into the disk drive, much like a music cassette tape. The capacity of these cartridges ranges from 5 to 450 MB, somewhat lower than regular hard disk units but still substantially superior to diskettes. They are handy because they give microcomputer users access to amounts of data limited only by the number of cartridges used.

OPTICAL STORAGE

Because they offer practical solutions to large-scale storage requirements, optical storage technologies are increasingly becoming a rival of magnetic storage. **Optical storage technologies** involve the use of a high-power laser beam to pack information densely on a removable disk.

Optical storage technologies offer users a number of advantages. The primary advantage is storage density. You can fit a lot more data on an optical disk than you can on a comparably sized magnetic disk. Because lasers can be focused with such precision, the tracks recorded on an optical disk are much closer together than those recorded on a magnetic disk. Also, the amount of space required to

FIGURE 4.19

Hard disk cartridge. This Tandon hard disk drive has one cartridge in place; another cartridge has been placed on top of the drive.

record an optical bit is much less than that required to record a magnetic bit. As a result, removable optical disk storage capacities range from 600 MB to over 1 GB. Another advantage of optical storage is that the media on which data is stored is much less susceptible to deterioration or contamination than magnetic recording media. The reason for this durability is that nothing touches the optical disk's surface except for a beam of light. Finally, optical disks are also less susceptible to head crashes than are magnetic disks because the optical head is suspended farther from the surface of the disk. Because the heads are so close to the disk's surface in a magnetic hard disk drive, trying to remove the disk would end the life of both the magnetic disk and the drive. Optical disks, however, are easily loaded and removed without risk of damaging either the optical disk or the drive.

Most technologies come with disadvantages; optical storage isn't any different. The primary disadvantage of optical storage is that the time it takes to retrieve data, or the average access time, is much greater than it is with magnetic storage media. In other words, optical disk drives are slow.

Any microcomputer can run an optical disk drive. In the following sections, we describe three types of optical storage disks that are available for use with microcomputers today.

CD-ROM

Compact disk read-only memory (CD-ROM) is the oldest and best-defined optical storage technology. This read-only storage medium is capable of storing 540 to 748 MB of data, images, and sound—the equivalent in storage capacity to about 275,000 pages of text, 1,800 double-density floppy disks, 74 minutes of audio, or thousands of images.

CD-ROMs are imprinted by the disk manufacturer. The user cannot erase or change the data on a CD-ROM or write on the disk—the user can only read the data. The optical disk is used primarily for storing huge amounts of prerecorded information. You will find the following types of information stored on commercial CD-ROMs: (1) encyclopedias, (2) medical reference books, (3) dictionaries, (4) legal libraries, (5) engineering and drafting/design standards, (6) collections of magazine and newspaper articles on specific subjects, and (7) graphic images (called *clip art*, grouped according to subject, that can be copied—"clipped"— and used as illustrations in documents produced by desktop publishing or word processing).

WORM

Write Once, Read Many (WORM) technology goes a step beyond CD-ROM. WORM disks are also imprinted by the manufacturer, but the buyer can determine what is written on them. Once the disks have been written on, however, they can only be read from then on—again, no changes can be made. WORM disks have much greater storage capacities than CD-ROM disks. The storage capacity of a WORM disk ranges from 122 to 6,400 MB. WORM disks are ideal for storing custom data that doesn't need to be updated often.

ERASABLE OPTICAL DISKS

Although ideal for certain situations, CD-ROM and WORM drives aren't general-purpose storage devices, because—once written—the data on them can't be changed. The erasable optical disk is the first optical technology to provide to users the capability of changing data under software control.

Erasable optical disks come housed in removable cartridges (Figure 4.20) and store about 281–3,200 MB each. The data access times are between two and six times slower than those of the high-performance hard disk drives. Erasable optical disks are often used in *magneto-optical* (MO) *disk drives*, which use aspects of both magnetic disk and optical disk technologies. The new MO drives pack up to 122 MB on each removable 3½-inch disk. No matter how much data a hard disk drive can store, its capacity is limited (for example, to 60 MB or 120 MB). However, MO drives have essentially unlimited capacity—that is, limited only by the number of disks the user buys. A 3½-inch MO disk looks like a 3½-inch floppy disk but is twice as thick. MO drives are available as external or internal units.

MO drives are useful to people who need to save successive versions of large documents, handle enormous databases, work in desktop publishing or graphics, or work with sound and/or video.

FIGURE 4.20

(a) Optical disks can store much more data than magnetic diskettes, disks, or tape can. They are also cheaper. Optical storage devices are available for all sizes of computer systems. This photo shows a Maxtor erasable optical disk in a cartridge along with an optical disk drive (which may be internal or external). (b) NEC W-CDR-74 optical disks and disk drive, plus speakers for outputting sound.

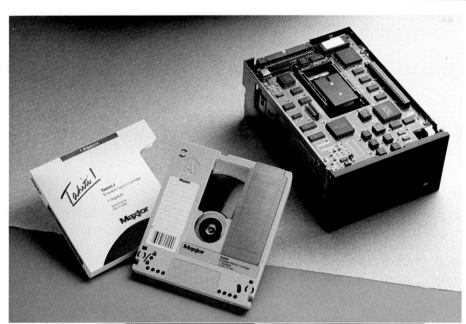

(a)

(b)

BACKING UP A MICROCOMPUTER SYSTEM

As high-capacity hard disk units increased in popularity, the problem of making backup copies of disk contents became a significant concern. *Users should make backup copies of all stored data files to ensure that they don't lose their data if the hard disk is damaged or destroyed.* Many users neglect this step and live to regret it: How would you feel if your 400-page masterpiece novel was lost forever because your hard disk crashed? Or if two weeks' worth of tax computations turned to dust because your disk storage units were electrocuted by a power surge? But it takes about twenty 3½-inch diskettes to back up the contents of one 20 MB hard disk, and 100 diskettes for a 144 MB disk! Something more efficient was needed.

This concern prompted the development and refinement of **cartridge-tape units** (also called *tape streamers* and *streaming tape*) to back up high-capacity hard disks (Figure 4.21). Tape cartridges have a capacity (per cartridge) ranging from 20 MB to 525 MB. The copying speeds of tape backup units vary; it takes approximately 12 minutes to copy the contents of a 60 MB hard disk. (In addition to tape units, hard disk cartridges are also used to back up regular hard disk units.)

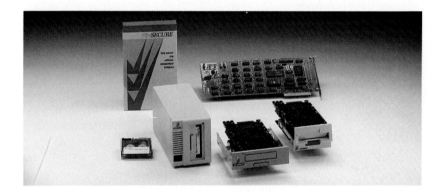

FIGURE 4.21

Cartridge tape unit. Such tape units are used with microcomputers to back up the contents of hard disk units, so that data is not lost if the hard disk units fail.

Most microcomputers have one of the following disk-drive configurations:

1. Two diskette drives
2. One diskette drive and one hard drive
3. Two diskette drives and one hard drive

When you are working with applications software and want to save the work you've done, you need to tell the software which disk drive to use to save the work. This is similar in concept to telling someone what drawer to put a folder in. To do this, you must follow certain disk-drive-naming conventions.

With DOS and IBM-type PCs, the first diskette drive is referred to as Drive A. The second diskette drive is referred to as Drive B. A hard disk is typically called Drive C. If an optical disk drive is also present, it may be called Drive D.

When you are using DOS or applications software, the drive letter is always followed by a colon (:) to represent the drive designation—that is, the colon is an essential part of the drive name.

Macintosh microcomputers do not use these disk-drive-naming conventions. Instead they use icons and labels (such as "hard disk") to represent disk drives. When you have hands-on practice in the lab or on your own computer, you will become familiar with disk-drive-naming—and file-naming—conventions.

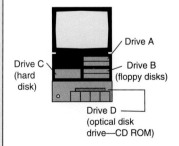

SUMMARY

- A *bit*, short for *binary digit*, is either 1 (on) or 0 (off). There are 256 possible combinations of bits used in binary *coding schemes*, the computer's language for representing data.

- Two commonly used coding schemes are the *American Standard Code for Information Interchange* (*ASCII*) and the *Extended Binary Coded Decimal Interchange Code* (*EBCDIC*).

- Both ASCII and EBCDIC use 8 bits to represent a character. Sometimes a *parity bit*, or *check bit*, is added for the purpose of error checking. Computers are designed to use either an *odd-parity scheme* or an *even-parity scheme*. In an odd-parity scheme, if an even number of 1s turns up in a character, an error message is displayed on the screen. The reverse is true of an even-parity scheme.

- Data is stored according to a *data storage hierarchy*:
  1. *Files*—at the top of the hierarchy. A file is made up of a group of related records (example—an inventory file about sporting goods).
  2. *Records*—second in the hierarchy. A record is made up of a collection of related fields (example—the items in inventory, such as baseballs, bats, gloves, rackets, etc.).
  3. *Fields*—third in the hierarchy. A field is a collection of related characters, or bytes, of data (example—inventory item identifiers, such as product number, product description, unit price, and quantity on hand).
  4. *Bytes*—fourth in the hierarchy. A byte is made up of 8 bits (example—a character in a field, such as the first number of the product number).
  5. *Bit*—lowest in the hierarchy; 0 or 1.

- Data is stored on a storage *medium* (plural = *media*), such as disk or tape.

- The process of storing data involves four steps:
  1. After input, the data to be recorded by a storage device temporarily resides in RAM.
  2. Software instructions determine where the data is to be recorded on the storage medium.
  3. The controller board for the storage device positions the recording device over the appropriate location on the storage medium.
  4. The recording mechanism is activated and converts electrical impulses to magnetic spots placed—according to a coding scheme, such as ASCII—on the surface of the medium.

- For disk storage, the recording mechanism is called the *read-write head*.

- Modern storage devices are usually *direct access storage and retrieval devices*—that is, any record can be accessed directly, without having to read through other records.

- The *diskette*, or *floppy diskette*, is a storage medium frequently used with microcomputers. Diskettes are made of a flexible plastic that is coated with a material that is easily magnetized. The disk is enclosed in a protective paper or hard plastic jacket.

- A diskette jacket has four openings:
  1. *Hub*—the round opening in the center, which fits over the center mount, or spindle, in the disk drive.
  2. *Data access area*—where the read/write head(s) of the disk drive is positioned. The read/write head(s) moves back and forth over the data access area as the disk(s) spins.

3. *Write-protect notch*—covered, it prevents the read/write head(s) from touching the surface of the disk(s), thereby preventing accidental erasure or overwriting of data.

4. *Index hole*—repeatedly passes a photoelectric sensing mechanism in the disk drive that activates a timing switch. The timing mechanism determines which portion of the diskette is over or under the read/write head(s).

- The *byte* is used to measure the capacity of a storage device:
  1. 1,024 bytes = 1 kilobyte (K)
  2. 1,024,000 bytes = 1 megabyte (MB)
  3. 1,024,000,000 bytes = 1 gigabyte (GB)
  4. 1,024,000,000,000 bytes = 1 terabyte (TB)

- Common diskette capacities range from 360 K to 1.44 MB.

- Diskettes are *single-sided* (data is recorded only on one side) or *double-sided* (data is recorded on both sides).

- The *recording density* measures the number of bits per inch (bpi) that can be written on the surface of the disk. The higher the density, the more data that can be recorded on the diskette. Diskettes are:
  1. *Single-density*
  2. *Double-density*
  3. *Quad-density*

- Data is recorded on disks in circular bands called *tracks*. Track *density* also affects how much data can be stored on a disk. Track density is measured in tracks per inch (tpi). Common tpi's today are 48, 96, and 135.

- After you insert a diskette into the disk drive, you must close the *disk drive gate,* or *door,* if your computer has one.

- Diskettes come in two standard sizes: 5¼ inches (with paper jackets) and 3½ inches (with hard plastic jackets).

- Diskettes are divided into eight or nine *sectors,* or equal wedge-shaped areas used for storage reference purposes. The intersection of a track and a sector indicates where to position the read/write head.

- *Hard-sectored* disks have the same number and size of sectors, fixed by the manufacturer. *Soft-sectored* disks are marked magnetically by the user with software commands. This process is called *formatting,* or *initializing.* Soft-sectored disks must be formatted before they can be used.

- The average speed (usually 150 to 300 milliseconds, or thousandths of a second) with which a computer locates instructions or data and loads a copy of it into RAM is called the *access time.* Access time is determined by four factors:
  1. *Seek time*—the time it takes to position the read/write head(s) over the proper track
  2. *Rotational delay,* or *latency*—the time it takes for the correct sector to rotate over the read/write head(s)
  3. The time it takes for the read/write head(s) to contact the disk(s)
  4. *Data transfer rate*—the time it takes to transfer the data or instructions from the disk(s) to RAM

- *Hard disks,* rigid platters usually 5¼ or 3½ inches in diameter, can store more data than diskettes—from 20 MB to more than a gigabyte of data. Hard disk drives can be *internal* (inside the computer) or *external* (outside the computer, connected to it by a cable).

- The interior of a hard disk drive is sealed in order to prevent any contamination, such as dust, from coming between the disk(s) surface and the read/write head(s), which floats about .5 to 1.25 millionths of an inch above the surface. Such an occurrence could cause a *disk crash* and subsequent loss of data.

- *Hardcards*, which are inserted into an expansion slot inside the system cabinet, are an alternative to hard disk drive units.

- *Hard disk cartridges* are removable cassette-like disk units with one or two platters.

- *Optical storage technologies* use a laser beam to pack information densely on a removable disk. Although optical disks can store more data than hard disks, or diskettes, their access time is slower.

- *Compact disk read-only memory* (CD-ROM) is an optical technology capable of storing 540–748 MB of data on a disk. The data is prerecorded on the disk by the manufacturer, so the user can only read it.

- *Write once, read many* (WORM), an optical storage technology, is like CD-ROM, except that the user can determine what the manufacturer records on the disk. Once recorded, however, the data can then only be read. A WORM disk can store 122–6,400 MB of data.

- *Erasable optical disks* allow the user both to record data on an optical disk and to erase it. Each stores about 281–3,200 MB. *Magneto-optical* (MO) disk drives combine erasable optical disk technology with traditional magnetic disk drive technology.

- Users should back up their work. If they don't, and their hard disk or diskette is damaged or destroyed, all the work is lost. *Cartridge-tape units*, or *streamers*, are often used for backup. (Hard disk cartridges are also used for backup.)

KEY TERMS

access time, p. 82
American Standard
   Code for Information
   Interchange (ASCII),
   p. 72
auxiliary storage, p. 70
binary code, p. 72
binary digit (bit), p. 71
byte, p. 79
cartridge-tape unit,
   p. 91
check bits, p. 72
compact disk read-only
   memory (CD-ROM),
   p. 89
data access area, p. 76
data storage hierarchy,
   p. 74
direct access storage
   and retrieval, p. 76
disk cartridge, p. 88
disk drive, p. 76
disk drive gate (door),
   p. 76

diskette, p. 76
double-density, p. 80
double-sided, p. 80
erasable optical disk,
   p. 90
Extended Binary Coded
   Decimal Interchange
   Code (EBCDIC),
   p. 72
field, p. 74
file, p. 74
floppy diskette, p. 76
formatting, p. 81
gigabyte (GB), p. 79
hard disk, p. 82
hardcard, p. 85
hub, p. 76
index hole, p. 77
initializing, p. 81
kilobyte (K), p. 79
latency, p. 82
medium (media), p. 75
megabyte (MB), p. 79
nonvolatile, p. 70

optical storage
   technologies, p. 88
parity bit, p. 72
primary storage, p. 70
quadruple-density, p. 80
read/write head, p. 76
record, p. 74
recording density, p. 80
rotational delay, p. 82
secondary storage, p. 70
sector, p. 81
seek time, p. 82
single-density, p. 80
single-sided, p. 80
terabyte (TB), p. 79
track, p. 80
track density, p. 80
volatile, p. 70
write once, read many
   (WORM), p. 89
write/protect notch, p. 76

EXERCISES

SELF-TEST

1. According to the data storage hierarchy, files are composed of:
   a. _____   b. _____   c. _____   d. _____

2. Two popular coding schemes for representing data are _____ and _____.

3. The term *bit* is short for _____.

4. All computers are designed to use either an even- or an odd-parity scheme. (true/false)

5. Diskettes have the following openings:
   a. _____   b. _____   c. _____   d. _____

6. 1,024 bytes is equal to 1 _____.

7. 1,024,000 bytes is equal to 1 _____.

8. The _____ measures the number of bits per inch (bpi) that can be written on the surface of a disk.

9. Diskettes are divided into eight or nine _____, or equal wedge-shaped areas.

10. All disks must be _____ before they can store data.

11. Diskettes come in two standard sizes: _____ and _____.

12. _____ _____ _____ are removable cassette-like disk units with one or two platters.

13. _____ _____ technologies use a laser beam to store large amounts of data on a removable disk.

14. Erasable optical disks are now available that enable users to both record data and erase it. (true/false)

15. Diskettes' recording densities can be categorized as one of the following:
    a. _____   b. _____   c. _____

16. The average speed with which a computer locates instructions or data on a disk and then loads a copy of it into RAM is called _____ _____.

17. For disk storage, the recording mechanism is called the _____ _____.

18. Diskettes are often referred to as _____ disks.

19. 1,000,000,000 bytes is approximately 1 _____.

20. Modern storage devices are usually direct access storage and retrieval devices. (true/false)

SOLUTIONS   (1) records, fields, bytes, bits; (2) ASCII, EBCDIC; (3) *binary digit*; (4) true; (5) hub, data access area, write/protect notch, index hole; (6) kilobyte; (7) megabyte; (8) recording density; (9) sectors; (10) formatted [or initialized]; (11) 3½ inches, 5¼ inches; (12) hard disk cartridges; (13) optical storage; (14) true; (15) single-density, double-density, quad-density; (16) access time; (17) read/write head; (18) floppy; (19) gigabyte; (20) true

SHORT ANSWER

1. How is data represented in primary and secondary storage devices?
2. Why is it important for a microcomputer to be configured with at least one diskette drive?
3. What is the significance of the terms *track* and *sector?*
4. What are the advantages of a hard disk over a diskette?
5. What does the term *disk crash*, or *head crash*, mean?
6. What is the purpose of a parity bit?
7. How can you damage a diskette?
8. Describe the four steps involved in storing data onto a disk.
9. What are some of the uses for CD-ROM technology?
10. What happens to data saved to secondary storage when the power is turned off?

PROJECTS

1. What type(s) of storage hardware is currently being used in the computer you use at school or at work? What is the storage capacity of this hardware? Would you recommend alternate storage hardware be used? Why? Why not?
2. Computer shopping. Using newspapers or magazines, find ads for the following types of storage devices: (a) 5¼-inch double-sided, quad-density diskette; (b) 3½-inch double-sided, double-density diskette; (c) 60 MB hard disk; and (d) 120 MB hard disk. For each device, list its price, name and address of the supplier, and explain why you think the device is a good purchase. Make some price comparisons.
3. Research the latest in erasable (rewritable) optical storage technology, such as MO drives. How is the technology being applied now? How do you think it will be applied in the future?
4. Computer shopping. You want to purchase a hard disk for use with your microcomputer. Because you don't care how much money the hard disk costs, you are going to buy one with the highest storage capacity you can find. Using newspapers or magazines, find a hard disk you would like to buy. What is its storage capacity? Its average access time? How much does it cost? Who is the supplier? Is it an external or an internal drive?
5. The Bureau of Electronic Publishing's product guide lists many products and publications available on CD-ROM, such as Compton's *Multimedia Encyclopedia*, Grolier's *Electronic Encyclopedia*, National Geographic's *Mammals*, CD Fun House, U.S. History, and Birds of America. Write for a copy of the catalog and identify some business and professional uses for some of the products. What hardware and software would you need to run the programs you are interested in?

    Bureau of Electronic Publishing
    141 New Road
    Parsippany, NJ 07054
    (800) 828-4766

CHAPTER 5

OUTPUT HARDWARE

What use is a computer system if you or others can't view the information you produce as a result of processing? Very little. In business, presentation is important—how you present yourself, your product, your information. Although computers may not be able to help you with your wardrobe or your public speaking skills, they *can* help you create clear and attractive informational presentations quickly. But because computers can produce beautiful, professional, seemingly error-free printouts or exciting colorful graphics on a screen, we are apt to think that the information is more believable than the same results scribbled on a yellow pad. In fact, the information that is output —the basis on which you and others will be making decisions—is no better than the quality of data that was input.

PREVIEW

When you have completed this chapter, you will be able to:

▪

Describe the basic forms of output and categories of output media and hardware

▪

Explain what hardcopy output devices are available, as well as the advantages and disadvantages of each

▪

Describe what softcopy output devices are available and the advantages and disadvantages of each

CHAPTER OUTLINE

<table>
<tr><td>

WHY IS THIS
CHAPTER
IMPORTANT?

</td></tr>
</table>

The success of a business today can depend to a large extent on how relevant and timely the information is that the computer can produce—that is, the output. Having the right information, in the right hands, in the best form, at the right time—these are the keys to effective decision making (Figure 5.1).

To be effective, information must be produced in a usable form. To achieve this goal, you may need to use more than one output device and output medium, such as a display on a video screen as well as paper and a printer. Each type of output device has advantages and disadvantages. Is the hardware going to make a lot of noise? What is the quality of the output produced? Is the hardware slow? Is the hardware expensive? Is it compatible with the equipment you already have? Can it handle large volumes of output? Can it handle color? Not all software programs work with all types of output devices. How do you know which output hardware device to use? Many questions must be answered before output hardware can be chosen or purchased. Most important, if you are the one choosing output hardware, you must determine what *form* of output is needed to meet your needs and the needs of everyone else using your microcomputer system.

FIGURE 5.1

What form of output is best? As a computer user in the business environment, your output needs will be determined by the kind of decisions you need to make to perform your regular job duties, the type of information that will facilitate those decisions, and the frequency with which you must make decisions.

HOW DO WE CATEGORIZE OUTPUT?

There are two basic categories of computer-produced output: (1) *output for immediate use by people* and (2) *output that is stored in computer-usable form for later use by the computer* (and eventually, of course, by people). Output can be in either hardcopy or softcopy form. **Hardcopy,** as defined earlier, refers to information that has been recorded on a tangible medium (generally meaning that you can touch it), such as paper or microfilm. **Softcopy** generally refers to the output displayed on the computer screen (Figure 5.2).

Output hardware is categorized according to whether it produces hardcopy or softcopy. Output for immediate use can be in either hardcopy form—such as paper—or softcopy form—such as on a display screen. Output in computer-usable form for later use by the computer is in hardcopy form—such as on disk or tape. This chart shows forms of output commonly used with microcomputers.

FIGURE 5.2

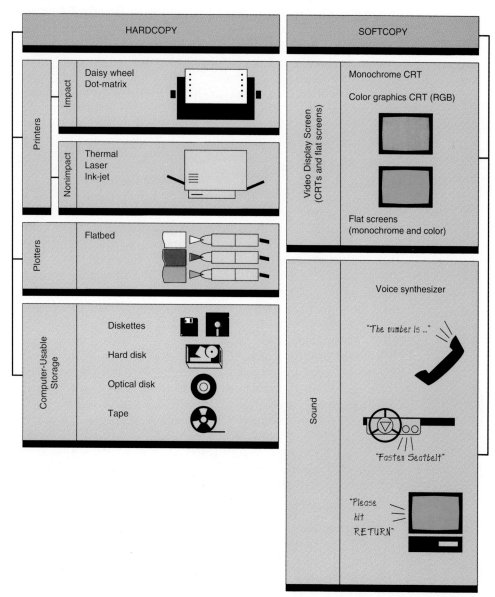

The advantages and disadvantages of each output medium must be considered to ensure that outputs are produced in the most usable form.

- When computer display devices are not readily available and information has some value over time, it is best produced as hardcopy.
- When computer display devices are readily available and information must be quickly accessible by a single user, it is best produced as softcopy.

Hardcopy output tends to have greater value over time, whereas softcopy output is best for displaying information that must be immediately accessible. The principal hardcopy output devices are printers and plotters—the different types and characteristics of these devices are described in detail in the next section. The principal softcopy output devices are cathode-ray tube video screens (CRTs), flat screens, and voice output systems.

HARDCOPY OUTPUT DEVICES

Among the wide variety of hardcopy output devices used with microcomputers, printers and plotters are used the most. A **printer** is capable of printing characters, symbols, and sometimes graphics on paper. Printers are categorized according to whether or not the image produced is formed by physical contact of the print mechanism with the paper. *Impact printers* do have contact; *nonimpact printers* do not. A **plotter** is used most often for outputting graphics because it can produce specialized and free-form drawings on paper. To suit the needs of many different users, different types of printers and plotters are available that have slightly different characteristics and capabilities—cost, quality, and speed.

IMPACT (CHARACTER) PRINTERS

An **impact printer**—also called a *character printer*—makes contact with the paper. It usually forms the print image by pressing an inked ribbon against the paper with a hammer-like mechanism. In one type of impact printer, called a *daisy wheel printer*, the hammer presses images of fully formed characters against the ribbon, just like a typewriter. The print mechanism in another type of impact printer, called a *dot-matrix* printer, is made of separate pin-like hammers that strike the ribbon against the paper in computer-determined patterns of dots.

DAISY WHEEL PRINTERS
Daisy wheel printers—often referred to as *letter-quality printers*—produce a very high-quality print image (one that is very clear and precise) because the entire character is formed with a single impact using a print "wheel" with a set of print characters on the outside tips of flat spokes (Figure 5.3). Daisy wheel printers can print around 60 characters per second (cps). This speed translates into approximately one page per minute.

The principal advantage of using daisy wheel printers is that they produce high-quality images. However, they do have some disadvantages, and their sales have declined dramatically as other types of printers have been perfected.

- They are too slow for many large-volume output situations.
- They are very noisy.
- To change the typeface style, the operator must halt the machine and change the print wheel.
- They cannot produce graphics.

DOT-MATRIX PRINTERS

Dot-matrix printers were developed with two objectives in mind: greater speed and more flexibility. Images are formed by a print head that is composed of a series of little print hammers that look like the heads of pins. These print hammers strike the ribbon individually as the print mechanism moves across the entire print line in both directions—that is, from left to right, then right to left, and so on. They can produce a variety of type styles and graphics without the operator having to stop the printer or change a print wheel. And, because they are impact printers, dot-matrix printers can be used with multipart forms.

Dot-matrix printers can print in either *draft quality* or *near-letter quality* (*nlq*) mode. The user determines which mode to operate in by pressing the appropriate button on the front of the printer. It takes longer to print in nlq mode because

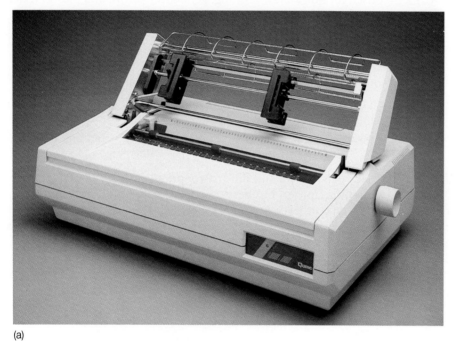

(a)

FIGURE 5.3

(a) Daisy wheel printer and (b) drawing of how a daisy wheel mechanism works. The daisy wheel spins and brings the desired letter into position. A hammer hits the wedge, which strikes the appropriate spoke against the ribbon, which hits the paper.

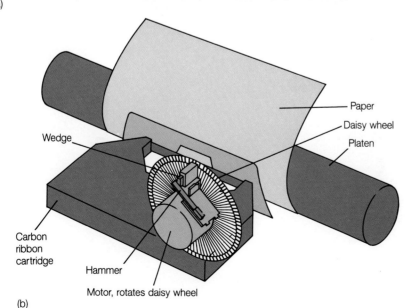

(b)

the print head makes more than one pass for each print line, creating a darker, thicker character (Figure 5.4). When the dot-matrix printer uses only one pass for each line, it's called *draft quality*. Nlq mode on the dot-matrix printer is used for professional correspondence and other high-quality print needs.

Figure 5.5 shows how a dot-matrix print head is constructed. The print head of a dot-matrix printer has either 9 pins or 24 pins (although other print head configurations are available, they aren't common).

Following are some of the characteristics that differentiate the two most common types of dot-matrix printers:

Nine-pin printers:

- Are less expensive
- Can print between 40 and 130 cps—between 1 and 2 pages per minute—depending on whether they're operating in draft or nlq mode
- Are best used for quick draft printing, generating forms, and jobs that don't require a high-quality image

Twenty-four-pin printers:

- Are more expensive
- Can print between 80 and 260 cps—between 1 and 4 pages per minute
- Produce a much more precise image than nine-pin printers—about 360 dpi, or dots per (square) inch
- Are best used in a heavy-volume environment where speed and quality are priorities

Table 5.1 compares daisy wheel and dot-matrix printers.

If you'd like to liven up your business reports with a little bit of color but can't afford an expensive type of color printer, a less expensive color dot-matrix printer may be the printer for you. **A color dot-matrix printer** uses the same technology as a monochrome dot-matrix printer, but it uses a color ribbon instead of a black ribbon. Color ribbons usually contain equal bands of black, yellow, red, and blue. Under software control, the colors can be blended to produce up to seven colors. Color ribbons cost up to three times as much as black ribbons.

FIGURE 5.4

To produce a near-letter-quality image with a dot-matrix printer, the character is printed twice; the second time the print head is positioned slightly to the right of the original image (a). (b) Shows a "real" (daisy wheel) letter-quality character for comparison. (c) Samples of dot-matrix output.

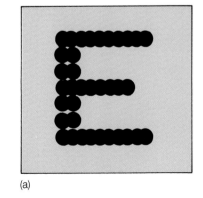

(a)

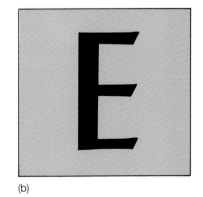

(b)

This is a sample of draft quality.
(c) This is a sample of near-letter quality.

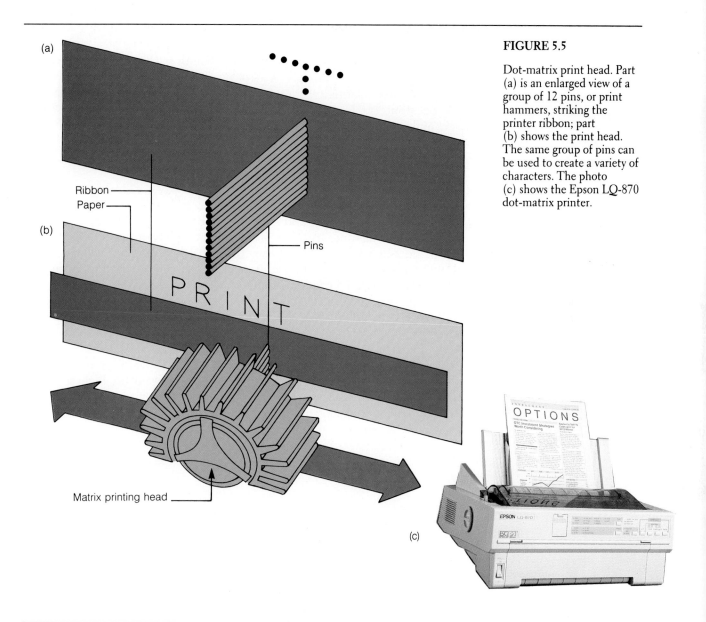

FIGURE 5.5

Dot-matrix print head. Part (a) is an enlarged view of a group of 12 pins, or print hammers, striking the printer ribbon; part (b) shows the print head. The same group of pins can be used to create a variety of characters. The photo (c) shows the Epson LQ-870 dot-matrix printer.

TABLE 5.1

Comparison of Daisy Wheel and Dot-Matrix (Impact) Printers

	Daisy Wheel	Dot-Matrix
Draft-quality speed	—	80–260 cps
Letter-quality speed	60–100 cps	40–80 cps (near-letter quality)
Image quality	Excellent	Good to very good
Cost	$500	$150–$2,000
Print mechanism	Daisy wheel	9-, 18-, or 24-pin print head
Advantages	Crisp, clear characters	Fast, can do graphics
Disadvantages	Slow, noisy, can't do graphics	Noisy, characters usually less clear
	Cannot print shades of gray	Cannot print shades of gray

NONIMPACT PRINTERS

Printers that do not strike characters against ribbon or paper when they print are **nonimpact printers**. The main categories of nonimpact printers are ink-jet printers, thermal printers, and laser printers. These printers generate much less noise than impact printers. However, if you're using a nonimpact printer, don't try to print on multiple-part carbon forms: Because no impact is being made on the paper, you'll end up with no copies!

Table 5.2 compares the various types of nonimpact printers.

INK-JET PRINTERS

Ink-jet printers (Figure 5.6) work in much the same fashion as dot-matrix printers in that they form images (text and graphics) with little dots. However, the dots are formed, not by hammer-like pins, but by tiny droplets of ink. The text these printers produce is letter quality (rather than near-letter-quality, which is produced by dot-matrix printers). These printers can match the speed of dot-matrix printers—between 1 and 4 pages per minute (ppm)—and they produce less noise. Ink-jet printers are often used to produce color proofs of posters, magazine layouts, and book covers, as well as color output for business presentations.

THERMAL PRINTERS

Thermal printers use colored waxes, heat, and special paper to produce images (Figure 5.7). No ribbon or ink is involved. For users who want the highest-quality desktop color printing available, thermal printers are the answer. However, they are also expensive, and they require special, expensive paper, so they are not generally used for high-volume output.

TABLE 5.2   Comparison of Nonimpact Printers

Type	Technology	Advantages	Disadvantages	Typical Speed	Approximate Cost
Ink-Jet	Electrostatically charged drops hit paper	Quiet; prints color, text, and graphics; less expensive; fast	Relatively slow; clogged jets; lower dpi	1–4 pages per minute	$800–$8,000
Thermal	Temperature-sensitive; paper changes color when treated; characters are formed by selectively heating print head	Quiet; high-quality color output of text and graphics; can also produce transparencies	Special paper required; expensive; slow	.5–4 pages per minute	$5,000–$22,000
Laser	Laser beam directed onto a drum, "etching" spots that attract toner, which is then transferred to paper	Quiet; excellent quality; output of text and graphics; very high speed	High cost, especially for color	4–25 pages per minute	$800–$20,000

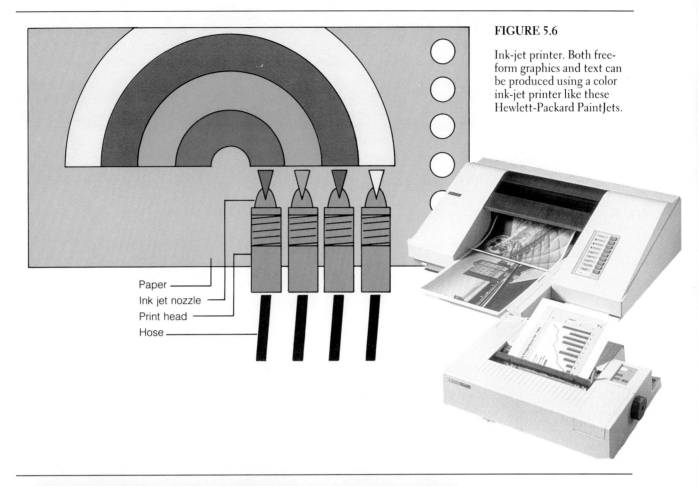

FIGURE 5.6

Ink-jet printer. Both free-form graphics and text can be produced using a color ink-jet printer like these Hewlett-Packard PaintJets.

Paper
Ink jet nozzle
Print head
Hose

FIGURE 5.7

Thermal printers produce images by using colored waxes, and heat to burn dots onto special paper. (Colored wax sheets are not required for black-and-white output because the thermal print head will register black dots on special paper.)

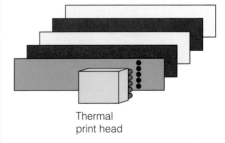

Thermal print head

LASER PRINTERS

Laser printer technology is much less mechanical than impact printing (that is, no print heads move, no print hammers hit), resulting in much higher printing speeds and quieter operation. The process resembles the operation of a photocopy machine (Figure 5.8). A laser beam is directed across the surface of a light-sensitive drum and fired as needed to record an image in the form of a pattern of tiny dots. The image is then transferred to the paper—a page at a time—in the same fashion as a copy machine transfers images, using a special toner.

The major advantages of laser printers are:

- Very high speed
- Low noise level
- Low maintenance requirements
- Very high image quality
- Excellent graphics capabilities

Laser printers can also generate text in a variety of type sizes and styles (called **fonts**), providing a business with the capability of outputting professional-looking near-typeset-quality reports and publications. Figure 5.9 shows examples of just a few of the types of fonts that can be generated using a laser printer. Most laser printers are capable of outputting a specific set of fonts. However, laser printers that include a built-in **page description language,** such as Adobe PostScript, provide greater flexibility by enabling users to generate fonts in almost any size and to produce special graphics effects. (Users can increase their font choices by purchasing "soft fonts" on diskettes and storing them on the hard disk to download—or load into RAM or the printer—whenever they want. However, their laser printer must be compatible with this technology.)

A variety of laser printers, each different in terms of cost, speed, and capabilities, are available for use with microcomputers today. In general, laser printers can be viewed as falling into three categories: (1) low end, (2) high end, and (3) color.

The laser printers that fall into the low-end category are the least expensive and can print between 4 ppm and 8 ppm. With printers in this range, 300-dpi images are common.

More expensive high-end laser printers can be purchased that are three to five times faster than low-end printers and generate clearer images (400–600 dpi). Printing between 15 and 25 ppm, these printers are appropriate in a networked environment where many users are sharing one printer.

Color laser printers are now available for less than $10,000—a recent break-through—and are frequently used in desktop publishing, especially in the magazine and newspaper businesses.

PORTABLE PRINTERS

Portable printers (Figure 5.10) are becoming more and more popular as portable computing using laptop computers has gained in popularity in the business environment. Many portable computer users, for example, need to print out sales reports or service estimates while on the road. So that a business traveler can carry both a 10-pound computer and a printer, **portable printers** are compact in size and typically weigh under 5 pounds. Nine-pin and 24-pin dot-matrix portable printers are available, as well as ink-jet and thermal printers.

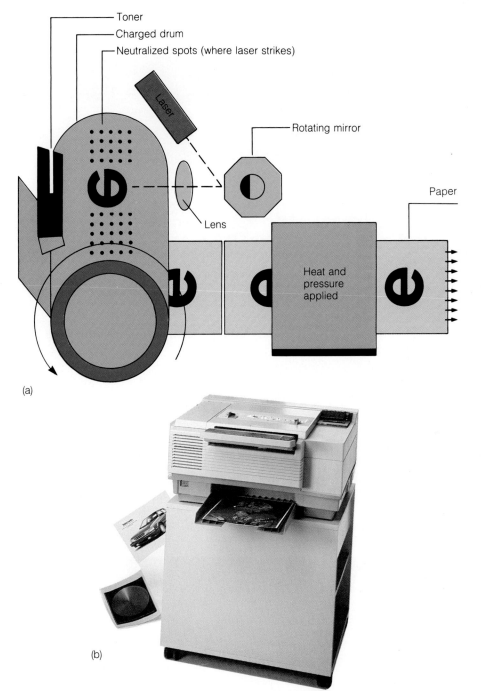

Toner
Charged drum
Neutralized spots (where laser strikes)

Laser

Rotating mirror

Paper

Lens

Heat and pressure applied

(a)

(b)

FIGURE 5.8

Laser printing. (a) A microprocessor controls a small laser beam that is bounced off a mirror millions of times per second onto a positively charged drum. The spots where the laser beam hits become neutralized, enabling a special toner (containing powdered ink and powdered rosin, an adhesive) to stick to them and then print out on paper, through the use of heat and pressure. The drum is then recharged for its next cycle. Part (b) shows the Tektronix Phaser III color laser printer (on top of a supply cabinet); part (c) is actual hardcopy laser output.

"I think there is a world market for about five computers."
--- Thomas J. Watson, founder of IBM (1943)

"I think there is a world market for about five computers."
--- Thomas J. Watson, founder of IBM (1943)

(c)

FIGURE 5.9   A set of characters and symbols in a particular size and style is called a *font*. This is a partial list of fonts as generated by the Hewlett-Packard LaserJet Series II.

FONT ID	NAME	POINT SIZE *	PRINT SAMPLE
S01	Dutch	10	ABCDEfghij#$@[\] ^ '{|}~123 ÀÂ°ÇÑ¿¡£§êéàèëöÅØåæÄÜßÁÐÒ
S02	Dutch BOLD	14	**ABCDEfghij#$@[\] ^ '{|}~123** **ÀÂ°ÇÑ¿¡£§êéàèëöÅØåæÄÜßÁÐÒ**
S03	Dutch BOLD	18	**ABCDEfghij#$@[\] ^ '{|}~** **ÀÂ°ÇÑ¿¡£§êéàèëöÅØåæÄÜß**
S04	Dutch BOLD	24	**ABCDEfghij#$@[\]** **ÀÂ°ÇÑ¿¡£§êéàèëöÅØ**
I00	COURIER	12	ABCDEfghij#$@[\]^'{|}~123 ÀÂ°ÇÑ¡¿£§êéàèëöÅØåæÄÜßÁÐÒ
I01	COURIER	12	ABCDEfghij#$@[\]^`{|}~123 íó┤╢╖╕╣║╗╝┐└┴┬├─┼╞╟╚╔╩╦╠═╬╧╨╤╥╙╘╒╓╫╪┘┌█▄▌▐▀απΦ

*12 points = 1 pica, and 6 picas = 1 inch.

FIGURE 5.10

Portable printer. This illustration shows a Kodak Diconix 150 Plus.

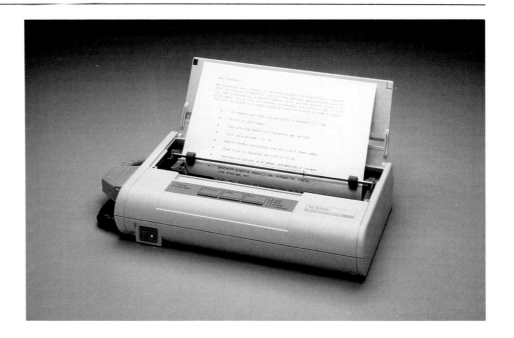

Plotters

A **plotter** (Figure 5.11) is a specialized output device designed to produce high-quality graphics—especially in the areas of drafting and design—in a variety of colors using inked pens. The type of plotter used with microcomputer systems is the **flatbed plotter,** which is designed so that the paper is placed flat and one or more pens move horizontally and vertically across the paper. These plotters use from two to eight pens to generate images.

Softcopy Output Devices

Softcopy output generally refers to the display on a monitor, the output device that many people use the most. The two main types of monitors are the cathode-ray tube (CRT) and the flat panel.

Cathode-Ray Tube (CRT)

The **cathode-ray tube (CRT)** (Figure 5.12) is probably the most popular softcopy output device used with microcomputer systems. The CRT's screen display is made up of small picture elements, called **pixels** for short. A pixel (Figure 5.13) is the smallest unit on the screen that can be turned on or off or made different shades. The smaller the pixels and the closer together they are (the more points that can be illuminated on the screen), the better the image clarity, or **resolution**. A screen resolution of 320 × 320 means the screen has horizontal and vertical rows of 320 pixels each to form images. This is medium resolution. Most users prefer higher resolutions, such as 640 × 480 or even 1,024 × 768.

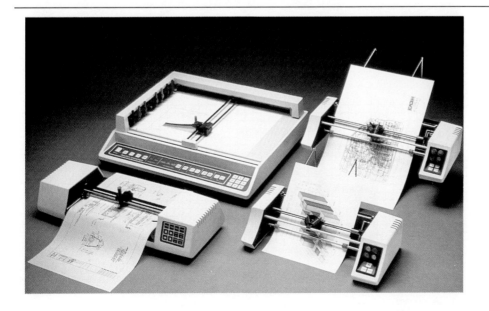

FIGURE 5.11

This illustration shows plotters from Houston instruments. The flatbed plotter is at the back, on the left.

FIGURE 5.12

The CRT's electron gun emits a beam of electrons that, under the control of the yoke's magnetic field, moves across the interior of the phosphor-coated screen. The phosphors hit by the electrons emit light, which makes up the image on the screen. The distance between the points of light is fixed by the shadow mask, a shield with holes in it that is used to prevent the dispersion of the electron beam.

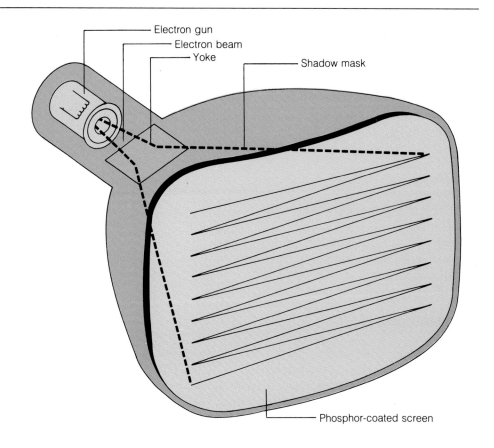

FIGURE 5.13

Each character on the screen is made up of pixels, or picture elements.

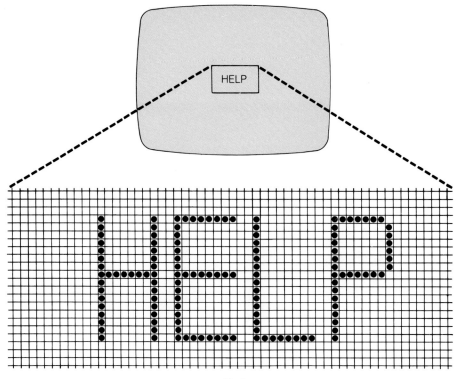

Pixels

U sing 70 Macintosh SE terminals located at nine campus polling places, Stanford University's student government, in April 1985, held the first totally computerized election in California history. Some 6,500 students cast ballots for the next year's Council of Presidents. Ironically, when none of the three slates won the top office, students returned to the polls a few weeks later and made their final choice using old-fashioned paper ballots.

Nevertheless, the first election was so revolutionary that it drew observers from local county registrars of voters and from the state capital. County election officials were concerned about possible fraud in electronic voting systems, but Stanford's terminals were not linked into a network, and buzzer alarms were written into the software to deter prospective hackers. To tally the results, election officials transferred the data voters recorded on the Macintosh hard disks onto floppy disks; the data was then tabulated at a single location. The biggest advantages of computerized balloting were the reduced costs of printing paper ballots (only a few were on hand for computerphobes) and the increased speed in tabulating returns.

Electronic voting may be the wave of the future, but computers are already being used extensively in politics and government. Political parties have long used computers for campaign purposes, primarily for fund-raising. Anyone who has ever contributed to a candidate or political party is sure to be in some database. Computers are also used to aim direct-mail pieces with very specific messages at selected audiences. Another use is to identify certain voter groups, such as those who tend to vote in Presidential elections but not in off-year congressional elections, in order to urge them to the polls.

Computers also came in for heavy use following the 1990 census, when state legislators used them to redraw boundaries of new election districts in ways that would most favor the party in power. For instance, in one system, a legislator could use computer graphics to call up his or her district on a screen, then shift the boundaries and get instant numbers of what the voting behavior, racial composition, and other population characteristics would be in the new district.

Census Bureau data is not available only to politicians, however. The bureau developed a computer map system called TIGER (for *Topologically Integrated Geographic Encoding and Referencing* system) that, when used with a database such as the 1990 census results or a company's own customer files, provides a detailed cartographic profile. TIGER can produce a map with 26 million street intersections and every city block, river, railroad line, or governmental entity in the country. The entire map comprises 16 billion lines. ▪

COMPUTERS AND CAREERS

POLITICS AND GOVERNMENT

CRTs have some disadvantages that recent technology has been trying to overcome, most notably:

1. Large size
2. High power consumption
3. Fragility

The CRT is rather large and bulky because of the need to separate the electron gun from the screen by a particular distance, so it is unsuitable as a display screen for portable computers. The CRT also tends to use a substantial amount of electric power, again making it unsuitable for use with portable computers, which occasionally need to run on batteries. Finally, as with a television, the CRT's glass tube and screen can be damaged if not handled carefully.

MONOCHROME AND COLOR MONITORS

A **monochrome monitor** (a monitor capable of displaying only a single-color image) and an **RGB color monitor** (RGB stands for *red, green, blue*) differ in two principal ways. First, they have different numbers of electron guns. A monochrome monitor has only one electron gun; however, as shown in Figure 5.14, an RGB color monitor has three electron guns. Second, the screen in an RGB color monitor is coated with three types—or colors—of phosphors: red, green, and blue. The screen of a monochrome monitor is coated with only one type of phosphor, which is often either green or amber in color.

The operational principles of both monitors are almost exactly the same. However, each pixel in an RGB monitor is made up of three dots of phosphors, one of each color. The three electron guns direct their beams together. Each gun is aimed precisely so that it can hit a specific color dot in each pixel. A wide variety of colors can be created by controlling—through software instructions—which guns fire and how long a burst they project at each dot. As you might expect, the control circuitry and software to direct the operation of an RGB monitor are somewhat more sophisticated and expensive than the corresponding components for a monochrome monitor.

CHARACTER-MAPPED DISPLAYS

Character-mapped display screens, such as the IBM monochrome monitor, can display only characters. (Note: As described in the next section, a character-mapped display screen may be able to display graphics if a video adapter card is plugged into the motherboard.) The patterns of pixels used to represent the standard characters displayed on a monitor (the alphabetic characters, numbers, and special symbols) in character-mapped displays are drawn from prerecorded templates (guides) stored in a video display ROM chip. When the user's software sends a request to display, for example, the letter A at a specific location, the template for that pixel pattern is looked up in the video display ROM chip. The electron gun then uses this pattern when it fires at the phosphors in the appropriate **character box**. The screen of a personal computer has 25 lines with 80 characters per line; this means that there are 2,000 positions on the screen where a predefined character can be placed.

BIT-MAPPED DISPLAYS

Because most software written today requires that the monitor be capable of displaying graphics, different types of video adapter cards were developed (Table 5.3). With appropriate software, sufficient RAM, and compatible monitors, these cards are plugged into the motherboard of a microcomputer to enable monitors to display **bit-mapped graphics**. To create the variety of images necessary to produce

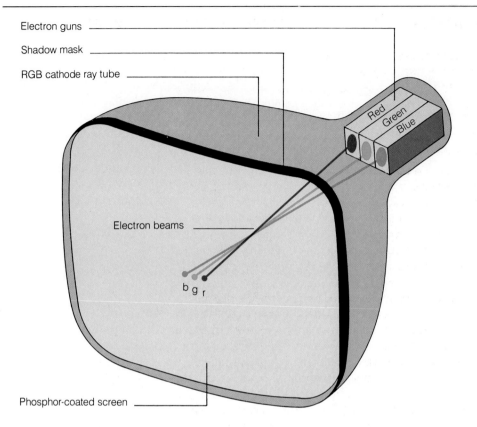

Electron guns

Shadow mask

RGB cathode ray tube

Red
Green
Blue

Electron beams

b g r

Phosphor-coated screen

FIGURE 5.14

RGB monitor. The workings of an RGB color monitor are similar to those of a monochrome CRT, except that the types of phosphors—red, green, and blue—are hit by three electron beams. Each pixel has three color dots that are activated to different degrees to produce a wide range of colors.

	Colors	Resolution (Pixels)	RAM Required
CGA (Color Graphics Adapter)	(1 bit/color) 4	320 × 200	
EGA (Enhanced Graphics Adapter)	(4 bits/color) 16	640 × 350	
VGA (Video Graphics Array)	(8 bits/color) 256 (4 bits/color) 16	320 × 200 640 × 480	 150 K
Super VGA	(8 bits/color) 256 (8 bits/color) 256	800 × 600 1,024 × 768	469 K 768 K
XGA (Extended Graphics Array)	(8 bits/color) 256 (16 bits/color) 65,536 (24 bits/color) 16,777,216	1,024 × 768 1,024 × 768 1,024 × 768	768 K 1,536 K 2,304 K

TABLE 5.3

PC Graphics Standards (Some RAM requirements for using particular color monitors at particular resolutions are also included.)

graphics, the computer needs to be able to direct each electron beam individually at each pixel on the screen, not just superimpose a template over a character box. This approach requires more sophisticated control circuitry, software, and RAM than is required by character-mapped displays.

Following are the common video graphics adapters (Figure 5.15):

- CGA (Color Graphics Adapter)—IBM PC video display circuit board that provides low-resolution text and graphics; CGA requires an RGB color display monitor and supports 4 colors at a resolution of 320 × 200. This standard has been superseded by EGA, VGA, Super VGA, and XGA.
- EGA (Enhanced Graphics Adapter)—IBM PC video display circuit board that provides medium-resolution (640 × 380) text and graphics and requires an RGB enhanced color display monitor to support 16 colors. This standard has been superseded by VGA, Super VGA, and XGA.
- VGA (Video Graphics Array)—IBM PC video display circuit board that is built into high-end models of IBM's PS/2 series that provides medium- to high-resolution (320 × 200 or 640 × 480) text and graphics; has 16 colors in its highest-resolution mode (640 × 480).
- Super VGA (Super Video Graphics Array)—VGA in a resolution mode of 800 × 600 or 1,024 × 768, and with 256 colors.
- XGA (Extended Graphics Array)—Video display circuit board that supports resolutions up to 1,024 × 768, with up to 16,777,216 colors.

In general, it's the circuitry that supports how many colors you can use and the monitor that determines the resolution. Macintosh computers and high-end IBM PS/2 models offer similar choices in monitor resolution modes and numbers of colors supported as do the adapter arrangements. However, these computers have the required circuitry built in on the motherboard, so they don't require extra boards (cards).

Users who work with sophisticated graphics or in desktop publishing often work in shades of gray on **gray-scale monitors**. Color monitors of high resolution that support a given number of colors can also be used at similar resolutions using the same number of gray shades. For example, a 256-color monitor will support 256 shades of gray.

FIGURE 5.15   Comparison of color adapter displays. (a) Monochrome VGA; (b) color Super VGA.

(a)

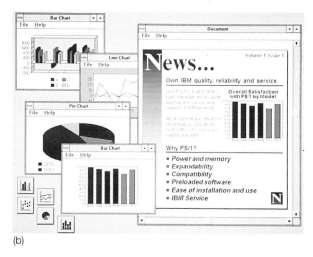

(b)

CRT SCREEN SIZE

A 1,024 × 768 resolution monitor allows you to pack 2½ times more images onto the screen than a 640 × 480 monitor does. But screen sizes are limited; if you have only a 14-inch monitor with 1,024 × 768 resolution, the images will be sharper, but they'll also be a lot smaller than on a 640 × 480 screen. Thus users who move to high-resolution monitors may also have to purchase larger ones. A 14-inch screen is fine for VGA, but 1,024 × 768 Super VGA would require a 16-inch or a 17-inch monitor for easy viewing.

Users working in graphics or desktop publishing often prefer an even larger screen: 19 inches or 20 inches, for example.

FLAT SCREEN TECHNOLOGIES

The disadvantages of the CRT—large size, high power consumption, and fragility, plus occasional flickering images—led to the development of **flat screen** technologies.

Flat screen technology is particularly useful for laptop and notebook computers, which can be used in the office and then taken home or on trips (Figure 5.16). Producing a truly lap-size, or laptop, computer—that is, one that is fully functional and weighs 15 pounds or less—has not been easy, and designing the video display has been the most difficult problem.

Interest in laptop computers encouraged researchers to explore different approaches to developing high-resolution, low-power-consumption flat screens with the same graphics capabilities as the traditional CRT. The most effective results to date have been achieved in three areas: liquid crystal display, electroluminescent display, and gas plasma display.

LIQUID CRYSTAL DISPLAY

The **liquid crystal display (LCD)** uses a clear liquid chemical trapped in tiny pockets between two pieces of glass. Each pocket of liquid is covered both front and back by very thin wires. In monochrome LCDs, when a small amount of current is applied to both wires, a chemical reaction turns the chemical a dark color—thereby blocking light. The point of blocked light is the pixel. In color LCDs, varying amounts of light pass through red, green, and blue filters.

FIGURE 5.16

CRT versus flat screen. As this photo shows, flat screen technologies have enabled manufacturers to produce personal computers small enough to be used on one's lap—the laptop computer.

LCD technology has progressed to the point that it rivals CRT technology in terms of resolution and the number of colors that can be displayed (Figure 5.17). In fact, since the screen is flat, text and graphics appear crisper than on the curved surface of the CRT, especially on the edges. In addition, images can be viewed from extreme angles with very little distortion. (Until recently, LCDs were susceptible to glare which forced the optimum viewing angle to be very narrow.)

ELECTROLUMINESCENT DISPLAY

Electroluminescent (EL) display (Figure 5.18) uses a thin film of solid, specially treated material that glows in response to electric current. To form a pixel on the screen, current is sent to the intersection of the appropriate row and column; the combined voltages from the row and the column cause the screen to glow at that point.

FIGURE 5.17

Three popular laptop computers that use a monochrome liquid crystal display: (a) NEC Prospeed 80386; (b) IBM PS/2 CL57 9X color LCD display; (c) Compaq SLT 386s/20; (d) Zenith Turbosport 386.

(a)

(b)

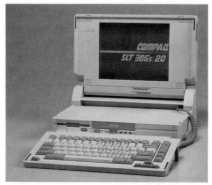

(c)

(d)

EL displays provide very high image resolution and excellent graphics capability. Several manufacturers are currently working on the development of electroluminescent displays with full-color capability. Most experts have predicted that this technology will soon match or even surpass all of the capabilities of the traditional CRT. Like LCD technology, the major limitation of this technology has been cost.

GAS PLASMA DISPLAY

The oldest flat screen technology is the **gas plasma display** (Figure 5.19). This technology uses predominantly neon gas and electrodes above and below the gas. When electric current passes between the electrodes, the gas glows. Depending on the mixture of gases, the color displayed ranges from orange to red.

The principal advantages of gas plasma display are:

- The images are much brighter than on a standard CRT.
- The resolution is excellent.
- Glare is not a significant problem.
- The screen does not flicker as it does on some CRTs.

The main disadvantages are:

- Only a single color is available (reddish orange).
- The technology is expensive.
- It uses a lot of power.
- It does not show sharp contrast.

FIGURE 5.18

Electroluminescent display. This Hewlett-Packard Integral computer uses an EL flat-panel display.

VOICE OUTPUT SYSTEMS

Voice output systems are relatively new and can be used in some situations in which traditional display screen softcopy output is inappropriate.

Voice output technology has had to overcome many hurdles. The most difficult has been that every individual perceives speech differently; that is, the voice patterns, pitches, and inflections we can hear and understand are different for all of us. It is not always easy to understand an unfamiliar voice pattern. At this point, two different approaches to voice output have evolved: (1) speech coding and (2) speech synthesis.

Speech coding relies on human speech as a reservoir of sounds to draw from in building the words and phrases to be output. Sounds are codified and stored on disk to be retrieved and translated back as sounds. Speech coding has been used in applications such as automobiles, toys, and games.

Speech synthesis relies on the use of a set of basic speech sounds that are created electronically without the use of a human voice.

Researchers are continuing to develop and improve voice output technologies for use with microcomputers. Many new products using voice output are expected to appear in the marketplace during the next decade. The largest application to date for the speech synthesis approach to voice output—converting text into "spoken" words—has many potential uses, including in reading machines for the blind (Figure 5.20). And, of course, sound output does not have to be in voice form; it can be music or special-effects sounds, such as the sound accompaniment for computer animation.

FIGURE 5.19

Gas plasma display. These popular laptop computers use gas plasma display: (a) GRiDCase 1500 Series; (b) Toshiba T5100; (c) IBM PS/2 P75 486.

(a)

(b)

(c)

SUMMARY

- Users must decide what *kinds* of output they require—based on the kind of information they need—before deciding which output hardware and media to use. They should also consider:
  1. How much noise the output equipment makes
  2. How fast it works
  3. How expensive it is
  4. Whether it is compatible with the equipment they already have
  5. How easily it can be upgraded

- The two basic categories of computer-produced output are:
  1. Output for immediate use by people
  2. Output stored in computer-usable form for later use by the computer (and people)

- Output is available in two forms:
  1. *Hardcopy*—refers to information that has been recorded on a tangible medium (you can touch it), such as paper or microfilm. When computer display devices are not readily available and information has some value over time, it is best produced as hardcopy.
  2. *Softcopy*—refers to the output displayed on the computer screen. When computer display devices are readily available and information must be quickly accessible, it is best produced as softcopy.

- Paper is the most widely used hardcopy output medium.

- The video display image on the computer screen is the most widely used form of softcopy output.

- Common hardcopy output devices used with microcomputers are:
  1. *Printers*—capable of printing characters, symbols, and occasionally graphics on paper. Printers are either:
     (a) *Impact printers*—the image is produced by physical contact of the print mechanism with the paper. Impact printers must be used to produce output on multipart forms with carbon layers.
     (b) *Nonimpact printers*—no contact with the paper by the print mechanism is required to form the image.

FIGURE 5.20

Xerox/Kurzweil Personal Reader, a breakthrough in technology for people who are blind, visually impaired, or dyslexic. The Personal Reader uses an optical scanner to convert typeset and typewritten material into speech. It can also be used to write and store information.

2. *Plotters*—used most often for outputting graphics because they can produce specialized free-form drawings on paper.

- Commonly used impact printers are:
  1. *Daisy wheel (letter-quality) printers*—produce a high-quality print image because the entire character is formed by a single impact by a print wheel with a set of characters on the outside tips of the wheel's spokes. Daisy wheel printers produce letter-quality output, but they are being phased out in favor of less expensive and more flexible printers.
  2. *Dot-matrix printers*—produce images with a print head composed of a series of little print hammers (usually 9 or 24) that look like the heads of pins.

- Although daisy wheel printers produce high-quality images, they also have several disadvantages:
  1. They are too slow for many large-volume output situations.
  2. They are noisy.
  3. To change the typeface style, the operator must halt the machine and change the print wheel.
  4. They cannot produce graphics or color output.

- Dot-matrix printers are more flexible, quieter, and faster than daisy wheel printers, and they can also produce graphics output. In addition, they can produce a variety of type styles without the operator having to stop the machine. However, their image quality is not as high as that produced by daisy wheel printers.

- Dot-matrix printers can print in *draft quality* (one pass of the print head for each line) or *near-letter-quality* (*nlq*) (two or more passes of the print head for each line).

- Twenty-four-pin dot-matrix printers are more expensive and faster than nine-pin printers, and they produce better-quality images. They are best used in a heavy-volume environment where speed and quality are priorities.

- *Color dot-matrix printers* use a multicolor ribbon instead of a black one.

- The main types of nonimpact printers are:
  1. *Ink-jet printers*—form images by spraying tiny droplets of ink (black or colors); text is letter quality and graphics can be output. These printers are about as fast as dot-matrix printers, and they are quiet.
  2. *Thermal printers*—use heat to produce images on special chemically treated paper. No ribbon or ink is involved. Although thermal printers are expensive, they produce excellent color output by using wax.
  3. *Laser printers*—use a laser beam to produce images in a process similar to that used by photocopiers. Laser printers are fast, quiet, have low maintenance requirements, and produce high-quality images, including graphics. They can also output text in a variety of fonts—type sizes and styles. Laser printers that have a built-in *page description language* (such as PostScript by Adobe Systems) provide greater flexibility to produce different fonts and special graphics.

- Laser printers are:
  1. *Low end*—less expensive, slower, produce lower-quality images
  2. *High end*—more expensive, faster, produce higher-quality images
  3. *Color*—expensive but effective

- *Portable printers* (9- and 24-pin dot-matrix, ink-jet, and thermal) have been developed for businesspeople to take on the road.

- *Plotters* are used for specialized output, such as blueprints of architectural designs.

- The *flatbed plotter* is the type of plotter most commonly used with microcomputers. It is designed so that the paper is placed flat and one or more pens move horizontally and vertically across the paper. Plotter output is available in color.

- The *cathode-ray tube* (*CRT*) is the most popular softcopy output device used with microcomputers. The CRT's screen is made up of *pixels* (*picture elements*); the smaller the pixels and the closer together they are, the better the image clarity, or *resolution*. The pixels are illuminated under software control by electron guns to form images.
- CRTs are:
  1. Large
  2. Power hungry
  3. Fragile
- CRTs can be *monochrome* or *RGB* (*red, green, blue*) *color*.
- Some CRTs, such as the IBM monochrome monitor, are *character-mapped displays*—they can display characters only and only according to template grid information stored in a video display ROM chip. Other CRTs are *bit-mapped displays*. They can display characters *and* free-form graphics because the electron beam can illuminate each individual pixel.
- *Color Graphics Adapters* (*CGA*), *Enhanced Graphics Adapters* (*EGA*), *Video Graphics Array* (*VGA*), *Super VGA*, and *Extended Graphics Adapter* (*XGA*) cards are available to upgrade a character-mapped monochrome monitor to display color bit-mapped graphics. (The card is inserted into an expansion slot in the system cabinet.) However, the resolution is determined by the monitor.
- *Flat screen technologies*, used with laptop computers, have been developed to overcome the disadvantages of the CRT: large size, high power consumption, and fragility.
- The three main types of flat screen technologies are:
  1. Liquid crystal display (LCD)
  2. Electroluminescent (EL) display
  3. Gas plasma display
- *Voice output systems*—including *speech coding* and *speech synthesis*—are a relatively new form of output used when traditional output is inappropriate.

KEY TERMS

Exercises

Self-Text

1. Output is available in two forms: _____ and _____.
2. _____ printers produce images with a print head composed of a series of little print hammers.
3. Printers are either _____ or _____.
4. _____ are used most often for outputting specialized graphics such as blueprints.
5. The most commonly used impact printers are _____ printers.
6. The video display image is the most widely used softcopy output. (true/false)
7. _____ _____ use heat to produce images on special chemically treated paper.
8. The _____ _____ is the most popular softcopy output device used with microcomputers.
9. Portable printers have been developed that can easily be taken on the road. (true/false)
10. Laser printers that have a built-in _____ _____ _____ provide even greater flexibility to produce different fonts and special graphics.
11. The image on a CRT is made up of _____, short for _____ _____.
12. CRTs can be _____ or _____.
13. CRTs are large, power hungry, and fragile. (true/false)
14. Three main types of flat screen technologies are:
    a. _____   b. _____   c. _____
15. Screen resolution is measured by vertical and horizontal lines of pixels. (true/false)
16. Voice output technology has advanced so far that most microcomputers are configured with voice output capabilities. (true/false)
17. The _____ plotter is the type of plotter most commonly used with microcomputers.
18. Some computer screens can display more than 16 million colors. (true/false)
19. Super VGA cards are used in Macintoshes. (true/false)
20. The more pixels that can be displayed on the screen, the better the _____ of the image.

Solutions   (1) hardcopy, softcopy; (2) dot-matrix; (3) impact, nonimpact; (4) plotters; (5) dot-matrix; (6) true; (7) thermal printers; (8) cathode-ray tube; (9) true; (10) page description language; (11) pixels, picture elements; (12) monochrome, color; (13) true; (14) liquid crystal display, electroluminescent display, gas plasma display; (15) true; (16) false; (17) flatbed; (18) true; (19) false; (20) resolution.

Short Answer

1. What advantages does the laser printer have over other printers?

2. In what ways do daisy wheel and dot-matrix printers differ? Which printer is used more?

3. What are the principal differences between how an image is formed on a monochrome monitor and on an RGB monitor?

4. What is the difference between a character-mapped display and a bit-mapped display?

5. Why has there been such interest in developing flat screen technologies?

6. What is the difference between hardcopy and softcopy? When might each be needed?

7. What must you consider before purchasing output hardware?

8. Compare ink-jet and thermal printers. How are they similar? Different?

9. What determines how many colors your monitor will display? What determines the monitor's resolution?

10. What is the main difference between a laser printer with a page description language and one without?

PROJECTS

1. Prepare an outline that indicates all the factors a user should consider when he or she is preparing to buy a printer.

2. Research the answer to the following questions: What is the state of the art in video display technology, and how is it currently being used? Is this technology being used only with microcomputers, or is it being used with all types of computers?

3. If you could buy any printer you want, what type (make, model, etc.) would you choose? Does the printer need to be small (to fit in a small space)? Does it need to print across the width of wide paper (11 × 14 inches)? In color? On multicarbon forms? Does it need to print graphics and typeset-quality text? Analyze what your needs might be and choose a printer (if necessary, make up what your needs might be). Review some of the current computer publications for articles or advertisements relating to printers. What is the approximate cost of the printer you would buy? Your needs should be able to justify the cost of the printer.

4. Visit a local computer store to compare the output quality of the different printers on display. Then obtain output samples and a brochure on each printer sold. After comparing output quality and price, what printer would you recommend to a friend who needs a printer that can output resumes, research reports, and professional-looking correspondence with a logo?

5. Explore the state of the art of computer-generated 3-D graphics. What challenges are involved in creating photo-realistic 3-D images? What hardware and software are needed to generate 3-D graphics? Who benefits from this technology?

6. At a computer store, compare the display quality of the following monitors: EGA, VGA, Super VGA, XGA, 16-bit Macintosh or Quadra, 24-bit Macintosh or Quadra. Which has the highest resolution? Displays the most colors? What size is the monitor you like best? How much does it cost and with what kind of microcomputer system is it compatible?

CHAPTER 6

APPLICATIONS SOFTWARE

Just as a hammer shouldn't be used to saw a board in half, a particular applications software package may not be suited for your particular processing task. Many different types of software tools are available for purchase today. To be an effective and efficient computer user, you must be able to evaluate your processing requirements and then choose the appropriate software tool to use to fulfill those requirements.

PREVIEW

When you have completed this chapter, you will be able to:

List and describe the different categories of applications software

Describe the uses for different types of general-purpose applications software

List some of the factors you should consider before purchasing applications software

Explain why applications software must be installed on your microcomputer system before it can be used

CHAPTER OUTLINE

Can you use a daisy wheel printer to print out a portrait of Abraham Lincoln? Can you use an RGB monitor to show the colors of the rainbow? With your knowledge of hardware, you know the answers to these questions. Different equipment has different uses. Likewise with software: A software program designed to handle text may not necessarily be used to draw charts and graphs or to manipulate rows and columns of numbers.

To help you begin to understand the differences among types of software, let us repeat the definitions we gave back in Chapter 1 for applications and systems software. **Applications software** is a collection of related programs designed to perform a specific task—to solve a particular problem for the user. The task or problem may require, for example, computations for payroll processing or for maintaining different types of data in different types of files. **Systems software** "underlies" applications software; it starts up the computer and functions as the principal coordinator of all hardware components and applications software programs. Without systems software loaded into the RAM of your computer, your hardware and applications software are useless. Both systems software and applications software must be purchased by the user (systems software is sometimes included in the price of a microcomputer).

This chapter focuses on applications software, and Chapter 7 covers systems software. You must understand the uses of—and the differences among—types of software so you will know what to use for a particular processing task.

CATEGORIES OF APPLICATIONS SOFTWARE

Custom software is written by programmers to meet the unique needs of an organization. However, most of the software you will be using is packaged software, also called **off-the-shelf software**, which is available at computer supply stores and by mail order. So many different types of applications software packages have come into the market that deciding which one to buy can require some investigation. Applications software is expensive. You can easily spend between $200 and $700 for a single package. In fact, individuals and companies typically spend much more on software than on hardware.

Just as the subject matter of a book determines what literary category it falls into (such as history, gardening, cooking, or fiction), the capabilities of an applications software program determine how it is categorized. Applications software falls into the following common categories:

- General business management
- Industry-specific
- Special disciplines
- Education
- Personal/home management
- General-purpose software for the user

General business management software, the largest group of applications software, includes products that cover the vast majority of business software needs, including accounting, inventory control, finance and planning, personnel, office administration, project management, and many others. However, some industries have very specialized applications software requirements; special *industry-specific software* is designed to meet these needs. Typical industries requiring specific products include specialized accounting services, advertising, agriculture and farm management, architecture, banking, construction, dentistry, engineering, legal services, leasing and rental companies, personnel agencies, property management, publishing, and others.

Special discipline software is a category set aside for such hobbies and special-interest areas as amateur radio, astrology, geography, mathematics, music, sports and leisure, visual arts, and others. *Education applications software* products focus on administration of educational institutions, computer-aided instruction (CAI), and special education. *Personal/home management software* includes products that relate to education, entertainment, finance, or home management.

This chapter highlights the types of **general-purpose applications software** you are likely to use in the business or professional environment. Specifically:

- Word processing
- Desktop publishing
- Electronic spreadsheets
- Database management systems
- Graphics
- Communications
- Integrated programs
- Computer-aided design, engineering, and manufacturing
- Applications software utilities

Don't worry if you don't know all these terms; you will by the end of the chapter. However, before we discuss the different types of general-purpose applications software, we need to go over some of the features common to most kinds of applications software packages.

COMMON FEATURES OF APPLICATIONS SOFTWARE

- **Cursor**—This is the blinking symbol that shows you where data—a character, a space, a command—will be entered next. It can be moved with the cursor-movement keys or with a mouse.

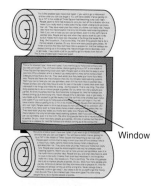

This is a cursor.

- **Scrolling**—This is the activity of moving images up or down on the display screen, so you can move to the beginning and the end of a document, for example. The portion of the file displayed on the screen is called a window. You can scroll by moving the cursor, using the PgUp and PgDn keys, by using the mouse to "click" on (select by pressing the mouse button) specified parts of the screen, or by using certain commands specified in the application package's documentation.

Window

- **Menu bar**—This is a row of command options displayed across the top or the bottom of the screen.

Menu bar

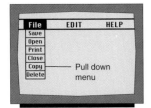

- **Pull-down menu**—This is a list of command options, or choices, that are displayed from the top of the screen downward when its title is selected from the menu bar. Pull-down menus can be opened by keystroke commands or by "clicking" (pressing) the mouse button while pointing to the title and then dragging the mouse pointer down.

- **Help screen**—This is on-screen instruction regarding the use of the software. The Help menu or options are accessed by clicking the mouse on the Help menu bar title or by using a specified function key (usually F1). The user then chooses the option he or she needs help with—such as printing a document.

WORD PROCESSING SOFTWARE

Word processing software offers capabilities that greatly enhance the user's ability to create and edit documents. It enables the user to easily insert, delete, and move words, sentences, and paragraphs—without ever using an eraser. Word processing programs also offer a number of features for "dressing up" documents with variable margins, type sizes, and styles. The user can do all these manipulations on screen, before printing out hardcopy.

Table 6.1 provides a list of some of the common features of word processing software packages. Figure 6.1 shows screens from the WordPerfect word processing program and Microsoft Word for the Macintosh. Besides WordPerfect and Microsoft Word, some popular word processing packages are WordStar, MultiMate Advantage, PC-Write, OfficeWriter, XyWrite III Plus, and Ami Professional.

Some word processing packages, including WordPerfect, Microsoft Word, and Ami Professional, provide desktop publishing features that enable users to integrate, or combine, graphics and text on a professional-looking page (Figure 6.2). Compared to dedicated desktop publishing packages (described shortly), word processing packages lack the ease with which different elements in a document can be placed and rearranged. However, the line that differentiates word processing packages and desktop publishing packages is blurring.

DESKTOP PUBLISHING SOFTWARE

Desktop publishing (DTP) is a combination of hardware—usually microcomputer, hard disk, laser printer, and scanner—and software that together provide near-typeset-quality output in a variety of sizes, styles, and type fonts (Figure 6.3). This technology can integrate graphics and text on a professional-looking page (Figure 6.4). Well-known desktop publishing software packages are Aldus PageMaker, Ready-Set-Go, Ventura, and Quark XPress. Desktop publishing software allows the user to combine into one file or output report, the elements from different files that have been generated using different software programs (Figure 6.5).

Desktop publishing software takes advantage of both the increased processing power and storage capacities of today's microcomputers and the flexibility in terms of output that a laser printer provides. For a laser printer to effectively combine text and graphics on a single page, a *page description language*, such as Adobe's PostScript, must be stored in the printer's memory and be usable by the software.

Desktop publishing software, often referred to as **page description software,** enables users to combine text and graphics in an organized format on a single page. Page description software falls into two categories—code-oriented and "what-you-see-is-what-you-get" (WYSIWYG). With a **code-oriented page description software** (Figure 6.6), formatting instructions are embedded (keyed) into a document in the form of codes. Code-oriented packages provide the user with more sophisticated desktop publishing options, compared to the WYSIWYG packages, and are based on traditional typesetting techniques, which also use formatting codes. There are two disadvantages to using this type of package. First, because of its high degree of sophistication, the user should have some typesetting experience before attempting to use the package. Second, the user can't see the final output until it's printed out. A user who is unfamiliar with how certain codes

TABLE 6.1	Some Common Word Processing Software Features
Correcting	Deleting and inserting. You simply place the cursor where you want to correct a mistake and press either the Delete key or the Backspace key to delete characters. You can then type in new characters. (Many packages offer shortcuts to deleting and inserting—for example, deleting many lines of text at one time by hitting a special sequence of keys.)
Block and move (or cut and paste)	Marking and changing the position of a large block of text; this can be done even between different documents, not just within the same document.
Check spelling	Many packages come with a spelling checker program that, when executed, will alert you to misspelled words and offer correct versions.
Thesaurus	Thesaurus programs allow the user to pick word substitutions. For example, if you are writing a letter and want to use a more exciting word than *impressive*, you can activate your thesaurus program and ask for alternatives to that word.
Mail merge	Most word processing programs allow the user to combine different parts of different documents (files) to make the production of form letters much easier, faster, and less tedious than doing the same thing using a typewriter. For example, you can combine address files with a letter file that contains special codes where the address information is supposed to be. The program will insert the different addresses in copies of the letter and print them out.
Scrolling	This feature allows the user to "roll" text up or down the screen; you can't see your long document all at once, but you can scroll the text to reach the point you are interested in. Most packages allow you to "jump" over many pages at a time—for example, from the beginning of a document straight to the end.
Search and replace	You can easily search through a document for a particular word—for example, a misspelled name—and replace it with another word.
Footnote placement	This feature allows the user to build a footnote file at the same time he or she is writing a document; the program then automatically places the footnotes at appropriate page bottoms when the document is printed.
Outlining	Some packages automatically outline the document for you; you can use the outline as a table of contents.
Split screen	This feature allows you to work on two documents at once—one at the top of the screen and one at the bottom. You can scroll each document independently.
Word wrap	Words automatically break to the next line; the user does not have to press Return or Enter.
Font choice	Many packages allow you to change the typeface and the size of the characters to improve the document's appearance.
Justify/unjustify	This feature allows you to print text aligned on both right and left margins (justified, like the main text in this book) or let the words break without aligning (unjustified, or ragged, like the text at the right side of this table).
Boldface/italic/underline	Word processing software makes it easy to emphasize text by using **bold**, *italic*, or <u>underlining</u>.

will affect the report may have to perform countless revisions. However, these programs usually require less RAM, less processing power, and fewer storage requirements than the WYSIWYG programs. Among the code-oriented packages being used today are SC-LaserPlus, from Graham Software Corporation, and Deskset, from G.O. Graphics.

FIGURE 6.1

Most word processing packages provide a number of different menus to use for editing your documents. Shown here is a PC Word-Perfect Edit menu and a Macintosh Microsoft Word screen showing the Fonts pull-down menu (different type sizes are listed at the top of the pull-down menu, and different type styles are listed at the bottom).

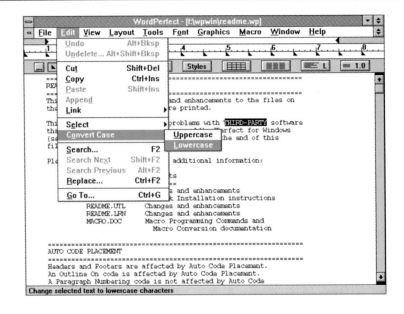

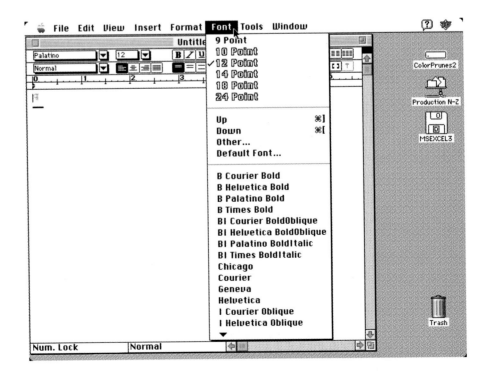

This figure illustrates the use of word processing software to integrate text and graphics on a professional-looking page.

FIGURE 6.2

LASER PRINTERS

Laser printer technology is much less mechanical than impact printing (that is, no print heads move, no print hammers hit), resulting in much higher speeds and quieter operation. The process resembles the operation of a photocopy machine: A laser beam is directed across the surface of a light-sensitive drum and fired as needed to record an image in the form of a pattern of tiny dots. The image is then transferred to the paper—a page at a time—in the same fashion as a copy machine, using a special toner.

Laser printers can also generate text in a variety of type sizes and styles (also called **fonts**) providing a business with the capability of outputting professional-looking typeset-quality reports. Most laser printers are capable of outputting a specific set of fonts and sizes. Laser printers that include a built-in **page description language** on a board inside the printer provide greater flexibility by enabling users to generate fonts in any size and to produce special graphics effects. The most popular page description language available is Adobe Systems' Postscript. Postscript printers are generally $1000–$2000 more than non-Postscript printers.

A variety of laser printers, each different in terms of cost, speed, and capabilities, is available for use with microcomputers today. In general, laser printers can be viewed as falling into three categories: (1) low-end, (2) high-end, and (3) color.

The laser printers that fall into the low-end category are priced between $1000 and $3000 and can print between 4 ppm and 8 ppm. With printers in this range, 300 dpi images are common. Laser printers that are priced around $1000 are providing businesses with a low-cost alternative to the high-end 24-pin dot matrix printers.

For $10,000–$20,000 a high-end laser printer can be purchased that is three to five times faster than a low-end printer and generates clearer images (400–

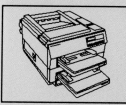

600 dpi). Printing between 15 and 25 ppm, these printers are appropriate in a networked environment where many users are sharing one printer.

FIGURE 6.3

Desktop publishing system. These newspaper professionals are using desktop publishing software to make up pages and insert art. Such systems usually comprise large color monitors, a laser printer, a scanner, and several hard disks, along with a microcomputer with mouse and DTP software.

FIGURE 6.4

Do it yourself! This ad was done in a short time using a microcomputer-based desktop publishing system.

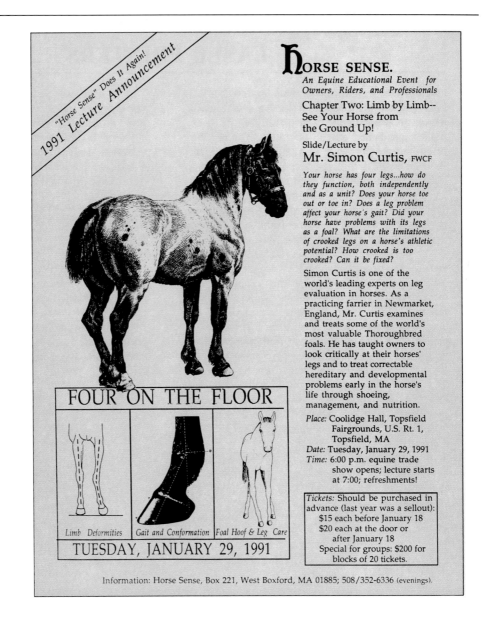

WYSIWYG programs (PageMaker from Aldus Corporation and Ventura Publisher from Xerox Corporation) allow the user to see the report on the screen as it will appear when it is printed out (Figure 6.7). For this reason, many people prefer the WYSIWYG programs over the code-oriented programs; users don't have to wait until they print to see what a document will look like. With a WYSIWYG program, the user chooses from lists of menu options to format the text. This type of desktop publishing software is more power-, memory-, and storage-hungry than code-oriented software.

Because it can lead to tremendous savings, desktop publishing can significantly affect any user who currently sends text or graphics out to a professional typesetter. Instead of hiring a typesetter to format documents and graphics into reports, which can be costly, with a desktop publishing system you can design the document yourself—once you have been trained to do it properly. Desktop publishing can offer the advantages listed on page 137.

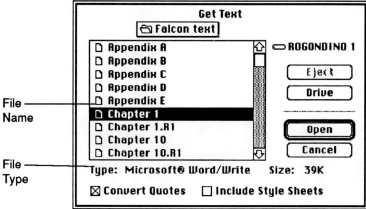

FIGURE 6.5

(a) Aldus PageMaker desktop publishing screens. The top screen shows that a text file is being imported into the desktop publishing program from a word-processing program (Microsoft Word). The bottom screen indicates that a graphics file is being brought in to be put on a page (TIFF = tagged image file format, a common bitmapped format for storing graphic images). (b) This diagram shows how DTP software uses files from other applications to produce documents with text and graphics.

File Name

File Type

(a)

Preview of Illustration

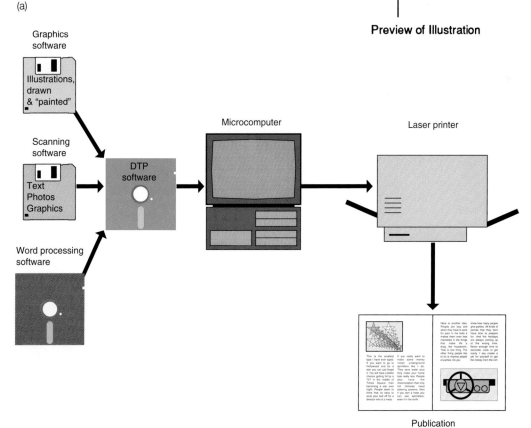

(b)

FIGURE 6.6   Code-oriented page description software. The top two lines (a bumper sticker) were printed
according to the codes shown below it, which is what the user would have seen on the
screen. The output was not displayed before it was printed.

DR. SCIENCE
He's not a real comedian

```
%!
/paperheight 11 72 mul def
/paperwidth 8.5 72 mul def
/width paperheight def
/height paperwidth 2 div def
/margin .375 72 mul def
/xcenter paperwidth 2 div def
/ycenter paperheight 2 div def

%xcenter ycenter translate
%.25 .25 scale
%xcenter neg ycenter neg translate

90 rotate
0 0 moveto paperheight 0 rlineto 0 paperwidth neg rlineto
paperheight neg 0 rlineto closepath 0 setlinewidth stroke

/bumpersticker
{
    /AvantGarde-Demi findfont setfont
    (ASS, DR. SCIENCE) dup stringwidth pop
    width margin sub margin sub exch div /points exch def
    /AvantGarde-Demi findfont
    [points 0 0 points 1.5 mul 0 0 ] makefont setfont
    margin margin 135 add moveto show

    /AvantGarde-DemiOblique findfont setfont
    (He's not a real comedian) dup stringwidth pop
    width margin sub margin sub exch div /points exch def
    /AvantGarde-DemiOblique findfont
    [points 0 0 points 1.5 mul 0 0 ] makefont setfont
    margin margin 20 add moveto show
} def

0 height neg translate
0 0 moveto width 0 rlineto stroke
bumpersticker
0 height neg translate
bumpersticker

showpage
```

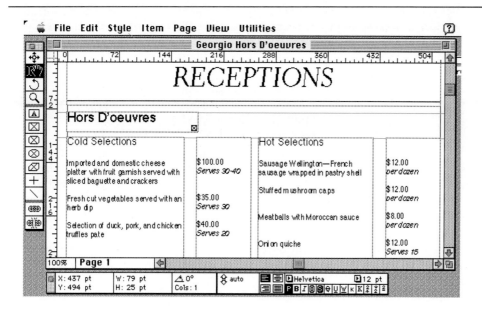

RECEPTIONS

Hors D'oeuvres

Cold Selections

Imported and domestic cheese
platter with fruit garnish served with
sliced baguette and crackers $100.00 *Serves 30-40*

Fresh cut vegetables served with an
herb dip $35.00 *Serves 30*

Selection of duck, pork, and chicken
truffles pate $40.00 *Serves 20*

Hot Selections

Sausage Wellington—French
sausage wrapped in pastry shell $12.00 *per dozen*

Stuffed mushroom caps $12.00 *per dozen*

Meatballs with Moroccan sauce $8.00 *per dozen*

Onion quiche $12.00 *Serves 15*

FIGURE 6.7

WYSIWYG document. The printed restaurant menu shown at the bottom was displayed on the computer screen (top) before it was printed out. The software documentation explains what the option symbols on the left and bottom sides of the screen mean.

- *You save money.* Sending a report, a newsletter, or a brochure out to a professional typesetter can easily cost a few hundred dollars.

- *You save time.* Using a desktop publishing system can cut the time spent on preparing documents by nearly 50%. Because you are preparing the report yourself electronically using a desktop publishing system, you can make any needed revisions immediately. The turnaround time necessary to make revisions when you are using a typesetter can easily add days onto a production schedule.

- *You maintain control.* You are in charge of the final output and production schedule.

A typical desktop publishing system, including a microcomputer with mouse, a laser printer, and page description software, costs around $10,000. This may sound like a lot of money, but when you consider that you might easily spend that much having just a few projects professionally designed and typeset, the cost doesn't look so bad. The cost of a desktop publishing system increases when certain other peripherals are included in the overall system; for example, an optical scanner for inserting drawings and photos into a report and a mouse and graphics tablet for drawing specialized images. Just remember—if you have the opportunity to choose a desktop publishing system, examine the features of the software programs you are most interested in first and then determine what microcomputers and peripheral devices the software is compatible with.

ELECTRONIC SPREADSHEET SOFTWARE

With **spreadsheet software,** based on the traditional accounting worksheet, the user can develop personalized reports involving the use of extensive mathematical, financial, statistical, and logical processing. Its automatic calculation abilities can save the user almost a lifetime of tedious arithmetic. The spreadsheet shown in Figure 6.8 was created by a beginner in less than an hour. This spreadsheet is designed to calculate expense totals and percentages.

Some of the terms you will encounter when using spreadsheets are listed in Table 6.2. Figure 6.9 shows a window (screen-size working area) of a Lotus 1-2-3 spreadsheet.

One of the most useful functions of spreadsheet software is the performance of "What if" analyses. The user can say: "What if we changed this number? How would future income be affected?"—and can get an immediate answer by having the spreadsheet software automatically recalculate *all* numbers based on the one change. Some spreadsheet packages, including versions 2.2 and 3.0 of Lotus 1-2-3, enable you to *link* spreadsheets together—this is called dynamic file linking. If a number, such as an expense amount, is changed in one spreadsheet, the change

FIGURE 6.8

Electronic spreadsheets (b) look much like spreadsheets created manually (a). However, when a number is changed in an electronic spreadsheet, all totals are automatically updated—certainly not the case when you work with a spreadsheet by hand!

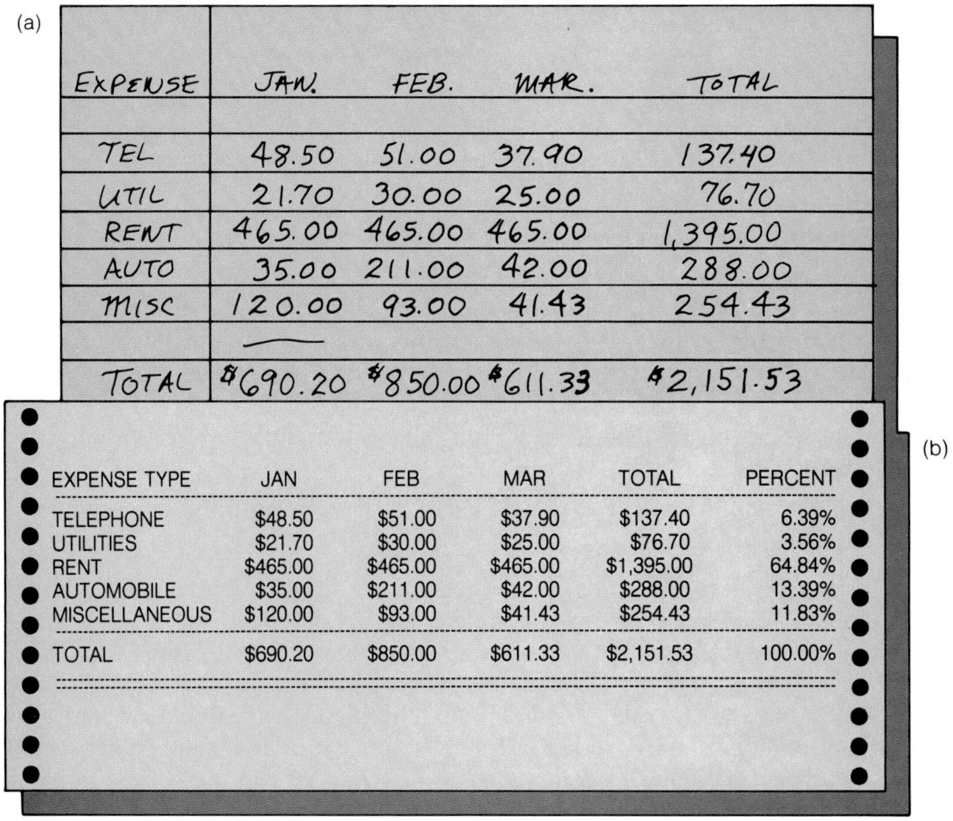

(a)

EXPENSE	JAN.	FEB.	MAR.	TOTAL
TEL	48.50	51.00	37.90	137.40
UTIL	21.70	30.00	25.00	76.70
RENT	465.00	465.00	465.00	1,395.00
AUTO	35.00	211.00	42.00	288.00
MISC	120.00	93.00	41.43	254.43
TOTAL	$690.20	$850.00	$611.33	$2,151.53

(b)

EXPENSE TYPE	JAN	FEB	MAR	TOTAL	PERCENT
TELEPHONE	$48.50	$51.00	$37.90	$137.40	6.39%
UTILITIES	$21.70	$30.00	$25.00	$76.70	3.56%
RENT	$465.00	$465.00	$465.00	$1,395.00	64.84%
AUTOMOBILE	$35.00	$211.00	$42.00	$288.00	13.39%
MISCELLANEOUS	$120.00	$93.00	$41.43	$254.43	11.83%
TOTAL	$690.20	$850.00	$611.33	$2,151.53	100.00%

TABLE 6.2

Common Spreadsheet
Terminology

Column labels	The column headings across the top of the worksheet area.
Row labels	The row headings that go down the left side of the worksheet area.
Cell	The intersection of a column and a row; a cell holds a single unit of information.
Value	The number within a cell.
Cell address	The location of a cell. For example, B3 is the address of the cell at the intersection of column B and row 3.
Cell pointer (cursor)	Indicates the position where data is to be entered or changed; the user moves the cursor around the spreadsheet, using the particular software package's commands.
Window	The screen-size area of the spreadsheet that the user can view at one time (about 8 columns and 20 rows). Most spreadsheets can have up to 8,192 columns and 256 rows; some have as many as 10,000 columns and more than 300 rows (AppleWorks).
Formula	Instructions for calculations; these calculations are executed by the software based on commands issued by the user.
Recalculation	Automatic reworking of all the formulas and data according to changes the user makes in the spreadsheet.
Scrolling	"Rolling" the spreadsheet area up and down, and right and left, on the screen to see different parts of the spreadsheet.
Graphics	Most spreadsheets allow users to display data in graphic form, such as bar, line, and pie charts.

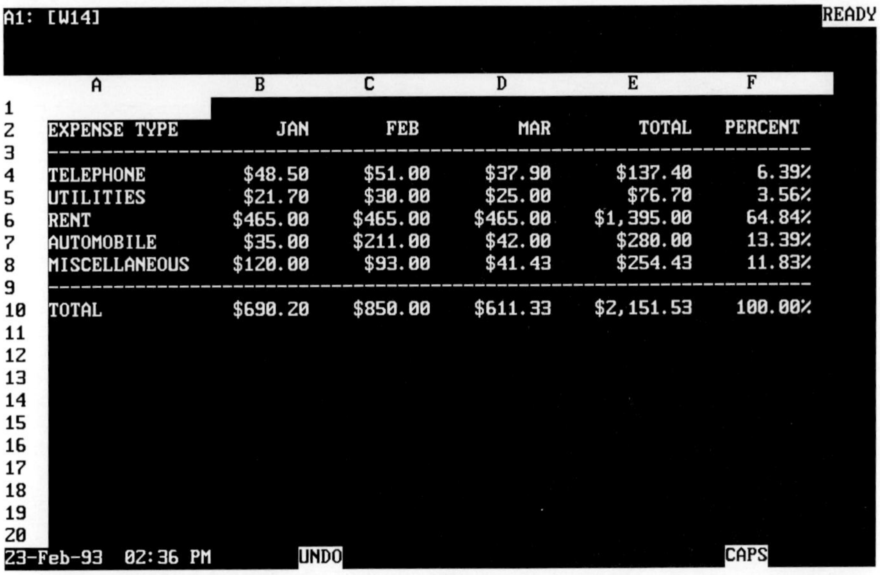

FIGURE 6.9

Window of a Lotus 1-2-3
spreadsheet

```
A1: [W14]                                                    READY

         A              B         C         D          E         F
 1
 2   EXPENSE TYPE       JAN       FEB       MAR       TOTAL    PERCENT
 3   -------------------------------------------------------------------
 4   TELEPHONE        $48.50    $51.00    $37.90    $137.40     6.39%
 5   UTILITIES        $21.70    $30.00    $25.00     $76.70     3.56%
 6   RENT            $465.00   $465.00   $465.00  $1,395.00    64.84%
 7   AUTOMOBILE       $35.00   $211.00    $42.00    $280.00    13.39%
 8   MISCELLANEOUS   $120.00    $93.00    $41.43    $254.43    11.83%
 9   -------------------------------------------------------------------
10   TOTAL           $690.20   $850.00   $611.33  $2,151.53   100.00%
11
12
13
14
15
16
17
18
19
20
23-Feb-93  02:36 PM         UNDO                           CAPS
```

is automatically reflected in other spreadsheet files that might be affected by the change.

Along with Lotus 1-2-3, popular spreadsheet packages are Microsoft Excel, Quattro, and Quattro Pro.

DATABASE MANAGEMENT SYSTEM SOFTWARE

Database management system (DBMS) software allows the user to store large amounts of data that can be easily retrieved and manipulated with great flexibility to produce meaningful management reports. With database management system software, also called a *database manager*, you can compile huge lists of data and manipulate, store, and retrieve it without having to touch a single filing cabinet or folder. Table 6.3 lists some common functions of database management software.

Two main categories of DBMS software exist:

- Flat-file systems
- Relational systems

Flat-file database management systems (also called **file management systems**) can deal with information in only one file at a time. They can't establish relationships among data stored in different files. **Relational DBMSs** can establish links by referring to fields (database hierarchy terms were described in Chapter 4, Figure 4.5) that store the same type of data in different databases. These links enable users to update several files at once or generate a report using data from different database files. Although flat-file DBMSs are perfectly suited for generating mailing labels, most business applications require the use of a DBMS with relational capabilities.

Popular DBMS packages include dBASE III Plus, dBASE IV, Paradox, Q&A, and Filepro.

TABLE 6.3

Common Functions of Database Management System Software

Create records	Group related data concerning one unit of interest—for example, one employee. A company's database would have one record for each employee.
Create fields	Group units of data within a record. A field might contain one employee's name, for example.
Retrieve and display	When the user issues database commands (determined by the particular DBMS program) and specifies the record and field needed, the DBMS program retrieves the record and displays the appropriate section of it on the screen. The user can then change data as necessary.
Sort	Data is entered into the database in a random fashion; however, the user can use the sort function of the DBMS program to output records in a file in several different ways—for example, alphabetically by employee last name, chronologically according to date hired, or by ZIP code. The field according to which the records are ordered is the *key field*.
Calculate	Some DBMS programs include formulas that allow the user to calculate, for example, averages or highest and lowest values.
Interact	Many DBMS programs can be integrated with other types of applications software—for example, with a spreadsheet program. In other words, the data in the DBMS program can be displayed and manipulated within the spreadsheet program.

GRAPHICS SOFTWARE

One picture is often worth a thousand words. Thus reports and presentations that include graphics can be much more effective than those that don't. **Graphics software** enables users to produce many types of graphic creations.

In general, **analytical graphics** are basic graphical forms used to make numerical data easier to understand. The most common analytical graphic forms are bar graphs, line charts, and pie charts—or a combination of these forms (Figure 6.10). The user can view such graphics on the screen (color or monochrome) or print them out. Most analytical graphics programs come as part of spreadsheet packages.

Presentation graphics are fancier and more dramatic than analytical graphics, and so the software that produces them is more sophisticated (Figure 6.11). Presentation graphics allow the user to function as an artist and combine free-form shapes and text to produce exciting output on the screen, on paper, and on transparencies and film (for slides and photos). Of course, the user can also produce output using bar graphs, line charts, and pie charts. Popular presentation graphics programs are Harvard Graphics, PC Paintbrush, Adobe Illustrator, CorelDRAW, Hollywood, and Persuasion.

Analytical graphics. Bar, line, and pie charts are commonly used to display spreadsheet data in graphical form.   **FIGURE 6.10**

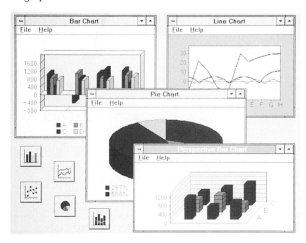
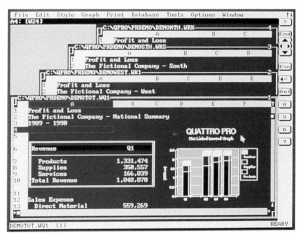

Presentation graphics software and software drawing tools provide the user with the means of producing sophisticated graphics.   **FIGURE 6.11**

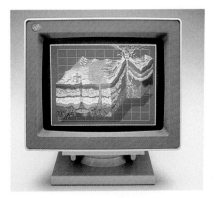
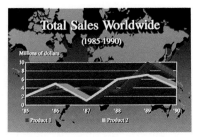

COMPUTERS AND CAREERS

SCIENCE AND SCHOLARSHIP

You like the outdoors and you're looking forward to a career in environmental science or wildlife management. It's a good thing, then, that we live in an age of computer technology.

Scientists in Idaho, looking for ways to preserve the nation's diversity of plants and animals, have combined satellite images of topography and vegetation with electronic data on land ownership. The result is a mapping system that identifies habitats rich in wild species that have been poorly managed by state and federal governments. The computerized maps help natural resource administrators save money by determining which tracts of land are highest in biological richness and should be acquired before they become targets of development.

At the University of Rhode Island and Brown University, researchers have used computers to recreate the flying patterns of birds. The work has caught the interest of Federal Aviation Administration officials, who are looking into whether the research might help produce a more efficient air traffic control system.

Using computers and aerial photographs taken over five-year intervals since the 1960s, scientists are attempting to track the past movement of coastal erosion and predict yearly movements of shorelines. With this data, suggests a panel of the National Academy of Sciences, government officials could delineate beach areas with imminent, intermediate, and long-term erosion risk and limit building in those areas.

Long used to help with research in the sciences, computers have also become tools of scholarship in other fields. A few years ago, a computer researcher at New Jersey's Bell Laboratories made a discovery that may be one of the most important in the history of art. Lillian Schwartz juxtaposed a self-portrait painted by Leonardo da Vinci with his world-famous painting of the Mona Lisa and found that the eyes, hairline, cheeks, and nose were identical. From this some scholars concluded that the Mona Lisa was in fact a self-portrait by da Vinci.

An exhibition at the IBM Gallery of Science and Art in New York showed that computer technology could be used to reveal new archeological insights from old ruins and artifacts. The ancient Roman port of Pompeii was buried in A.D. 79 in the volcanic eruption of Mount Vesuvius, preserving many details of everyday life. Recently, computer enhancement techniques were used to resurrect texts from charred papyrus documents found in Pompeii. Computers were also used to restore colors and background images to partially destroyed paintings. From a huge database, experts constructed a large computer-generated map of Pompeii that includes positions and shapes of buildings, baths, and other features.

Finally, computer research has been used to bring the maddeningly complex Chinese writing system into the modern world. With more than 50,000 characters, each composed of at least 1 of 214 root parts plus additional strokes, Chinese ideograms have not been adaptable to typewriters and other office technology. In the last decade, however, researchers have succeeded in designing systems that allow word processors to accommodate characters at speeds averaging 60 per minute. ■

Integrated Software

Integrated software represents the industry's effort to combine all the software capabilities that the typical user may need into a single package with a common set of commands and rules for its use. The objective is to allow the user to perform a variety of tasks without having to switch software programs and learn different commands and procedures to run each one. Integrated software combines the capabilities of word processing, electronic spreadsheets, database management systems, graphics, and data communications (using telephone lines, satellites, and other communications technology to transmit data and information) into one program.

Microsoft Works is a well-known integrated software package in business today; others are Framework III and Framework IV (Figure 6.12), Enable, and PFS: 1st Choice. SmartSuite for Windows integrates Lotus 1-2-3 spreadsheet software with Ami Pro word processing software, Freelance Graphics software, and cc:Mail messaging software.

Computer-Aided Design, Engineering, and Manufacturing

Industry, especially manufacturing, has probably experienced the greatest economic impact of computer graphics. Mechanical drawings that used to take days or weeks to complete can now be done in less than a day. Among other things, the drawings can be three-dimensional, rotated, shown in detailed sections or as a whole, automatically rendered on a different scale, and easily corrected and revised. But the use of computer graphics has evolved beyond the rendering of drawings; it is now used to help design, engineer, and manufacture products of all kinds, from nuts and bolts to computer chips to boats and airplanes.

FIGURE 6.12

Using integrated software. Because integrated software combines capabilities of several types of software programs, users are able to create a graphic presentation in one section of the screen while referring to data in a spreadsheet or a database— and perhaps later send the information to someone in another part of the country or the world. This Framework III Help screen lists what you can do to get started.

Computer-aided design (CAD) shortens the design cycle by allowing manufacturers to shape new products on the screen without having to first build expensive models (Figure 6.13). The final design data and images can be sent to a **computer-aided engineering (CAE)** system, which subjects the design to extensive analysis and testing that might be too expensive to do in the real world (Figure 6.14). From there, the product design may be sent to a **computer-aided manufacturing (CAM)** system, which makes use of the stored computer images in automating the machines (unintelligent robots) that manufacture the finished products (Figure 6.15). Computer simulation in industry has increased productivity enormously and made previously expensive procedures affordable.

COMMUNICATIONS SOFTWARE

Communications software allows users to access software and data from a computer in a remote location and to transmit data to a computer in a remote location—in other words, to establish *connectivity*. For example, the traveling business professional in Seattle, Wash., who needs to access client information daily from the company's main computer in San Diego, Calif., needs some communications software and a modem to enable his or her laptop computer to communicate long-distance. Popular microcomputer communications programs are ProComm, Smartcom II, Smartcom III, and Crosstalk XVI.

Communications software and hardware have become important to the computer user. Through systems connectivity the microcomputer is now able to share resources and services previously available only to users of large computer systems. Chapter 8 goes into the topic of communications in more detail.

FIGURE 6.13

CAD. This designer is using CAD software to design a valve to control missiles.

FIGURE 6.14

CAE. This national test facility is using a computer system to simulate and test space technology.

FIGURE 6.15

CAM. This computerized manufacturing plant produces high-quality cerium used in auto-exhaust catalysts, to help keep the air clean.

Applications Software Utilities

Many different types of **applications software utilities**—inexpensive programs that perform some basic "office management" functions—are available for purchase. These programs can be categorized as follows:

- Desktop management utilities
- Add-on utilities
- Disk utilities
- Keyboard and screen utilities

Depending on their function, the instructions in utility programs reside either in RAM or on disk. A **RAM-resident utility** is designed to be available at any time to the user because it resides in RAM at all times while the computer is on, even when the utility is not being used. In other words, once such a program is loaded into your computer (for example, from a diskette), a copy stays in RAM, "underneath" any applications software programs you may be using, until you turn the power off. As long as the power is on, you do not have to put the software disk back in the drive to use the utility program—you simply access it from RAM with certain keystrokes.

A **desktop management utility,** which is usually RAM-resident, allows the user to computerize many routine activities, including using a calculator, organizing an appointment calendar (Figure 6.16), taking notes, looking up words in a dictionary to make sure they are spelled correctly, and many more. The bottom line is that desktop manager software can save the user time. Sidekick and Pop-Up Windows are two popular desktop management packages.

Add-on utilities are usually RAM-resident and are used in conjunction with popular applications software packages. For example, to print wide electronic spreadsheets lengthwise on continuous-form paper (instead of across the width of the paper), many users use a program called Sideways. Allways, from Funk Software, is an add-on utility that is now sold with versions 2.2 and 3.0 of Lotus 1-2-3. This utility greatly enhances the way a spreadsheet appears in printed form through the use of stylized fonts in different sizes.

Disk utilities are usually purchased on floppy disks and then stored on hard disk. They provide users with a number of special capabilities, including:

- Recovering files that have been accidentally erased
- Retrieving damaged files
- Making automatic backup copies of a hard disk
- Organizing a hard disk by means of a menu system
- Compressing existing files on hard disk in order to free up room for additional files
- "Parking" the internal hard disk drive's actuator arm with the read/write heads in preparation for moving the computer; this way, disk damage can be avoided (not all computers need to have their disks parked before they are moved)

Keyboard utilities, such as Cursorific, are usually RAM-resident and enable you to change the way the cursor appears on the screen—usually by making it larger—so it is easier to see.

Screen utilities are used to increase the life of your screen. If your microcomputer is turned on and you don't use it for a period of a few minutes, a screen utility will automatically make the screen go blank. This saves your screen from having an image permanently burned onto the screen. When you press a key, the screen will again display the image that was showing previously.

We have mentioned only a few of the many utilities available. If your applications software package can't do something you want it to, there may be a utility that can. You can find out by phoning a computer software store.

HYPERTEXT AND MULTIMEDIA

Two new kinds of sophisticated applications software that do not easily fit into any of the preceding categories are hypertext and multimedia. **Hypertext** software—such as HyperCard, used on the Macintosh microcomputer, and Linkway, used on IBM PCs and PS/2 microcomputers—links basic file units comprising text and/or graphics with one another in creative ways. In HyperCard (Figure 6.17), a screen of information forms a record called a *card*; related groups of cards are organized into files called *stacks*. The user can work with the cards and stacks provided by the software program (for example, all the information in an encyclopedia) or create cards and stacks of text and graphics at will and combine them in all sorts of ways by using a mouse to click on "buttons" on the screen that move the user from card to card, and stack to stack. The user can program the sequences used to connect and combine cards and stacks, thereby discovering, sorting through, using, and presenting information in convenient or unusual ways.

Stackware, software packages that are collections of information created and used with HyperCard, is available at computer stores. For example, users can purchase "Research Stacks" consisting of five 800 K disks on selected subject areas—such as "Scientific Stacks," which include card stacks on amino acids, vitamin structures, galaxies, the ear, DNA structures, and the moons of Jupiter.

Multimedia is even more sophisticated than hypertext because it combines not only text and graphics but animation, video, music, and voice as well. In creating and presenting a multimedia product, one might, for example, use a Macintosh and HyperCard to create software programs that could integrate input data. The data could be input in the form of text and graphics through a scanner, animation through a special video camera, and sound through the use of a sound digitizer. The integrated data could be stored on a CD-ROM disk and then presented later on a television monitor and speaker that can run an optical disk or stored on tape and then run on a VCR. Text could also be printed out or stored on diskette or tape.

Multimedia sounds are available on disk for users with a Macintosh microcomputer, 2 MB of RAM, HyperCard, and applications software for sound management (such as HyperComposer). For example, Desktop Sounds v.1 includes the following sound effects: aircraft, animals, automotive, combat, comedy, crowds, household—and more.

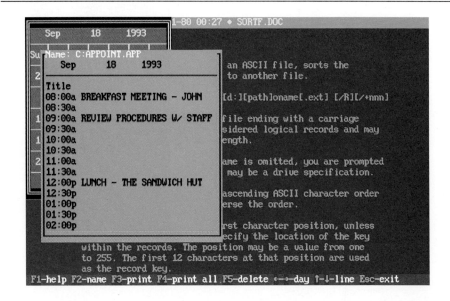

FIGURE 6.16

This desktop manager software utility allows the user to computerize many routine activities, such as keeping track of appointments.

FIGURE 6.17

HyperCard software provides a new kind of "information environment" for the Apple Macintosh computer. It stores information about any subject in the form of words, charts, sounds, pictures, and digitized photographs. Any "card" (piece of information) in any "stack" (related cards) can connect to any other card. (a) The Home card is the starting place for moving around in Hyper-Card. The various icons represent stacks for the user to click on, using a mouse. (b) An example of how HyperCard works.

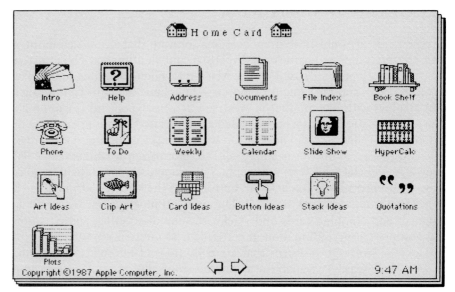

(a)

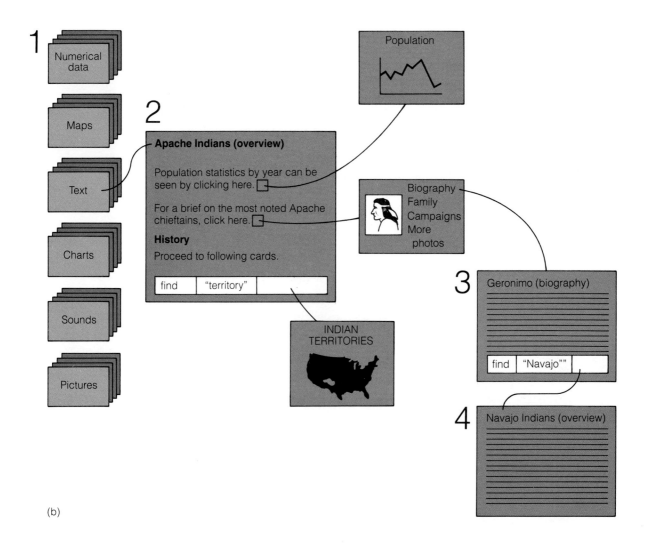

(b)

DECIDING WHAT TO PURCHASE

Computer software has become a multibillion-dollar industry. More than a thousand companies have entered the applications software industry, and they have developed a wide variety of products. As a result, the number of sources of applications software has grown. Applications software can be acquired directly from a software manufacturer or from the growing number of businesses that specialize in the sale and support of microcomputer hardware and software. Most independent and chain computer stores devote a substantial amount of shelf space to applications software programs; some businesses specialize in selling only software.

If you can't find off-the-shelf software—software that can be purchased off the shelf in a computer store—to meet your needs, you can develop your own. If you don't know how to do it yourself, you can have the computer professionals within your own organization develop custom software—software that is written to a particular organization's specifications—or you can hire outside consultants to do it. Unfortunately, hiring a professional to write software for you usually costs much more than off-the-shelf software.

Many software developers sell different versions of the same software application. Each version is usually designated by a different number—generally, the higher the number, the more current the version and the more features included with the package. For example, Lotus 1-2-3 is available in versions 2.2 and 3.0; WordPerfect for the PC in 4.2, 5.0, 5.1, and 6.0; Microsoft Windows in 3.0 and 3.1—and so on. In some cases, different versions are written to be used with particular microcomputer systems such as IBM compatibles or Macintosh microcomputers. If you buy a software package, make sure you have the version that goes with your microcomputer.

A user who buys a certain version of a software application may after a few months find that a later version of the same application is now available. This user has two choices: Either stay with the purchased version or upgrade (usually for a fee) to the later version. Because many users want the "latest," they will spend the extra amount for the most recent version of a software package, even if their current version satisfies all of their processing requirements.

Because there is so much to choose from, deciding what applications program—and then what version—to use requires very careful analysis. You should evaluate software applications by focusing on the following:

- *Quality of the documentation.* Using documentation that isn't written clearly and thoroughly can be very frustrating. Before purchasing an application, leaf through the documentation manual that accompanies the program to see if the instructions and reference information are clearly written and presented.

- *Ease of learning.* Just because the documentation for a particular application is good, it doesn't mean that the program is easy to learn. Because training can cost thousands of dollars, companies should evaluate how easy an application is to learn before purchasing it. A good way for a potential user to determine how easy a program is to learn is to ask friends or colleagues who are currently using it or to take a course at a community college or other training location.

- *Ease of use.* Some programs aren't easy to use on an ongoing basis. Before purchasing a package, ask people who are using the program if they enjoy using it. Are some procedures difficult to perform using this application?

- *Error handling.* It's human nature to make mistakes, and we don't want to go through tortuous procedures to correct them. When we make mistakes using applications software, we want the software to provide some helpful information on the screen that tells us what we did wrong. Ideally, the software should also tell us how to correct our mistakes. The documentation should tell you what "help" procedures are available.

- *Support.* Is there a phone number you can call if you have questions that relate to the software you are using? Most software development companies provide an 800 number that you can use.

If you want to try to keep track of all the software available, you can read software catalogs and directories. For example, magazines such as *Compute, PC World, Macworld, MacUser,* and *PC Computing* provide general users with reviews of many different kinds of software. *PC Magazine* and *InfoWorld* (Figure 6.18) also provide valuable guides to computer hardware, software, services, and related topics of interest.

FIGURE 6.18

(a) *PC Magazine.* This publication provides "Fact File," concise reviews of hardware and software in each issue.
(b) *InfoWorld* software review. *InfoWorld* magazine publishes reviews like this in every issue.

Criterion	(Weighting)	Score
Performance		
Basic editing	(60)	Very Good
Spelling checker/thesaurus	(60)	Good
Mail merge	(20)	Very Good
Layout	(60)	Excellent
Graphics	(50)	Excellent
Outlining	(20)	Satisfactory
TOC and indexing	(20)	Good
Style sheets	(20)	Very Good
Font support	(60)	Excellent
Footnoting	(25)	Excellent
Macros	(25)	Excellent
Printer support	(60)	Very Good
Compatibility	(60)	Very Good
Speed	(50)	Good
Documentation	(75)	Very Good
Ease of learning	(75)	Good
Ease of use	(130)	Good
Error handling	(40)	Good
Support		
Support policies	(20)	Excellent
Technical support	(20)	Good
Value	(50)	Good
Final score		**7.4**

PRODUCT SUMMARY

Company: WordPerfect Corp., 1555 N. Technology Way, Orem, UT 84057; (801) 225-5000.
List price: $495.
Requires: Macintosh Plus, SE, or II computer; 1 megabyte of RAM; hard disk; System 6.0.3 or later.
Pros: Includes a robust drawing utility and an improved user interface.
Cons: None significant, except the bug in the Styles function.
Summary: A feature-filled program capable of handling a wide range of sophisticated word processing duties.

INSTALLING APPLICATIONS SOFTWARE

Once you have bought your applications software package, you must install it to work with your microcomputer system. **Software installation** usually involves telling the software the characteristics of the hardware you will be using so that the software will run smoothly. When you purchase a software application, check to see that the documentation tells you how to install the software.

To install software, you first insert the applications software diskette as indicated by the package documentation. Then the installation program usually asks a number of different questions about your hardware. For example, the installation program will usually display on your monitor a list of the popular printers on the market. You will be instructed to choose the name of the printer that corresponds to the one you are using. If the printer you are using doesn't appear on the list, and you are given no generic choice, you must contact the support staff at the company who developed your software and tell them what printer you are using. (Use the 800 number given in the documentation.) They will respond in one of the following ways:

- Send you the printer driver for the printer you are using. A **printer driver** is a file stored on a disk containing instructions that enable your software program to communicate with or print with the printer you are using.

- Tell you to choose a different printer from the list. If the printer you are using operates similarly to one on the list, your printer can use the printer driver of the other printer. This is often referred to as *emulating* the characteristics of another printer. (To **emulate** means to imitate.)

You may also be asked other questions during the installation procedure:

- What is the make and model of the microcomputer you are using?
- Are you using a color monitor? If so, what kind?
- Are you using a monochrome monitor? If so, what kind?
- Are you using $5\frac{1}{4}$-inch or $3\frac{1}{2}$-inch diskettes?
- Are you using a hard disk?
- Where will you want the working copy of your applications software to be stored? On a diskette? On the hard disk?

Think about the answers to these questions *before* initiating the installation process. Once you have completed the installation procedure, your program will store most of your responses in a special file on the disk, which is referred to by your applications program when you load the software. In addition, if you will be using a hard disk, many installation programs automatically copy the program files to the hard disk for you. (*Note:* If you are using a hard disk, the installation process involves transferring *copies* of the programs that came on the diskettes in the applications package. Keep the original diskettes as backup in case your hard disk crashes. If you are using diskettes, make copies of the original package diskettes and use the copies as your working diskettes. The originals will serve as backups.)

Once the installation procedure is completed, you are ready to roll!

SUMMARY

- *Applications software* is a collection of related programs designed to perform a specific task, such as word processing or payroll management. Applications software is either purchased by the user *off the shelf* at a computer store or from a software outlet, or it is custom written for the user.

- *Systems software* "underlies" applications software; it starts up the computer and coordinates the hardware components and the applications software programs. Systems software usually comes with the microcomputer.
- Many categories of applications software exist. The most common are:
  1. *General business management*—covers the majority of business software needs—for example, accounting, inventory control, finance and planning, personnel, office administration, and project management.
  2. *Industry-specific*—meets needs of specialized businesses—for example, agriculture and farm management, architecture, banking, construction, dentistry.
  3. *Special disciplines*—covers hobbies and special-interest areas such as amateur radio, astrology, music, sports, and visual arts.
  4. *Education*—focuses on administration, computer-aided instruction (CAI), and special education.
  5. *Personal/home management*—covers uses at home relating to entertainment, instruction, finance, and home management.
  6. *General-purpose software* for the user—covers the basic types of software that general users are likely to encounter in business and professional life.
- The following are common general-purpose software types:
  1. *Word processing software*—which enables the user to easily create and edit documents, including inserting, deleting, and moving words, sentences, and paragraphs, and to easily alter the appearance of documents through the use of different type sizes and styles and through different text arrangements.
  2. *Spreadsheet software*—with which users can easily develop reports involving the use of extensive mathematical, financial, statistical, and logical processing. When a few numbers are changed, such reports can be automatically recalculated to provide "What if?" analyses.
  3. *Database management system (DBMS) software*—which allows the user to input, store, and manipulate large amounts of data to produce reports. The data can be manipulated in different ways, depending on the relationships of the data, which are determined by the software system. *Flat-file management systems (file management systems)* can't establish relationships among data stored in different files. They can deal with only one file at a time. *Relational database management systems* can establish relationships among data in different files by using *key fields* or common identifying characteristics.
  4. *Graphics software*—which gives the user the ability to make reports and other presentations more effective through the use of *analytical graphics*, common graph forms that make numerical information easier to understand, and presentation graphics, fancy free-form drawings.
  5. *Integrated software* enables the user to perform a wide variety of tasks that typically include creating documents, spreadsheets, databases, and graphs. Most integrated software packages also include communications capabilities.
  6. *Desktop publishing (DTP)* uses a combination of hardware and software to enable the user to combine text and graphics on the same page in a professional-looking, publishable format. The hardware used in a typical desktop publishing system typically includes a microcomputer, a hard disk, a laser printer, and a scanner. A *WYSIWYG* desktop publishing package lets you view on the screen what your document will look like when printed. To use a *code-oriented* desktop publishing package, the user must embed codes in the document. The effect of these codes can be viewed *after* the document is printed.
  7. *Computer-aided design (CAD) software* enables manufacturers to save much time and money because they can design products on the screen without having to construct expensive models. After the designs have been developed, they are sent to a *computer-aided engineering (CAE)* system, which subjects the design to extensive analysis and testing. From there, the product might be created using a *computer-aided manufacturing (CAM)* system, which uses unintelligent robots to manufacture the final product.

8. *Communications software* allows users to access software and data from and transmit data to a computer in a remote location.

9. *Applications software utilities* are inexpensive programs that perform some basic "office management" functions. These utilities are considered *RAM-resident utilities*, because they reside in RAM at all times while the computer is on, even when they aren't being used. These programs can be categorized as *desktop management, add-on, disk, screen,* and *keyboard utilities.*

■ When users buy applications software, they should evaluate the following:

1. *Quality of the documentation*—the instructions and presentations in the accompanying users' manual should be clear and easy to follow.

2. *Ease of learning*—the program should not be too difficult to learn how to use; ask others who have learned how to use the program.

3. *Error handling*—the program should offer on-screen help that tells the user when errors have occurred, and, ideally, how to correct them.

4. *Support*—the documentation should include an 800 number and other information about how to get professional assistance to solve software problems.

■ Applications software must be *installed* by the user before he or she can use it. Installation involves telling the software—through use of one of the software disks that came with the applications package—the characteristics of the hardware that the software will be running. The documentation includes instructions about how to install the software.

■ While installing software, you will see a list of printers on the screen from which you must indicate the one you will be using. If your printer is not on the list, call the 800 number. The software company may send you a *printer driver* on a disk, which will enable you to use your printer with the applications software, or it may tell you which printer on the list to choose.

■ Other on-screen questions often posed during installation are:

1. Make of microcomputer
2. Color or monochrome monitor
3. Brand of monitor
4. Size of diskettes being used (3½-inch or 5¼-inch)
5. Use of hard disk
6. Where copy of the applications software is to be stored

KEY TERMS

EXERCISES

SELF-TEST

1. _____ _____ is a collection of related programs designed to perform a specific task for the user.

2. List four categories of applications software utilities:
   a. _____   b. _____   c. _____   d. _____

3. _____ _____ _____ offers capabilities that enable the user to easily create and edit documents.

4. Applications software starts up the computer and functions as the principal coordinator of all hardware components. (true/false)

5. _____ _____ enables a computer in one location to share data with another computer in a remote location.

6. Programs that reside in RAM at all times are referred to as RAM-resident utilities. (true/false)

7. When evaluating an applications software package, you should focus on the following five characteristics:
   a. _____   b. _____   c. _____   d. _____   e. _____

8. The type of software that enables users to input, store, and manipulate large amounts of data so that reports can be produced is _____ _____ _____ _____.

9. If you need to develop a report that involves the use of extensive mathematical, financial, or statistical problems, what type of software application should you use? _____ _____ _____

10. Relational database management systems can't establish links among data stored in different files. (true/false)

11. List five questions that you may be asked during the process of installing software.
    a. _____   b. _____   c. _____   d. _____   e. _____

12. New applications software must be _____ by the user before it can be used.

13. List four tasks typically performed by disk utilities:
    a. _____   b. _____   c. _____   d. _____

14. _____ _____ software enables you to combine near-typeset-quality text and graphics on the same page in a professional-looking document.

15. Applications software utilities usually reside in RAM at all times. (true/false)

16. Users often spend more on software than they do on hardware. (true/false)

17. A _____ _____ is a file stored on a disk containing instructions that enable your software program to communicate with or print with the printer you are using.

18. Software installation usually involves telling the software what the characteristics are of the hardware you will be using, so that the software will run smoothly. (true/false)

19. Keyboard utilities enable you to change the way the cursor appears on the screen. (true/false)

20. _____ _____ gets its name from the fact that it can be purchased off the shelf in a computer store.

Solutions   (1) applications software; (2) desktop management utilities, add-on utilities, disk utilities, keyboard and screen utilities; (3) word processing software; (4) false; (5) communications software; (6) true; (7) quality of the documentation, ease of learning, ease of use, error handling, support; (8) database management system software; (9) electronic spreadsheet software; (10) false; (11) What is the make and model of the computer? Are you using a color or monochrome monitor? A hard disk? Where will you store your work?; (12) installed; (13) recovering files, making backup copies of a hard disk, organizing a hard disk, compressing files on disk to create more room; (14) desktop publishing; (15) true; (16) true; (17) printer driver; (18) true; (19) true; (20) off-the-shelf software

Short Answer

1. What should you consider before purchasing a particular applications software package?

2. What does spreadsheet software do?

3. What is the purpose of communications software?

4. What are applications software utilities?

5. What would a good use be for database management system software?

6. What do users need to install software?

7. Why do some people prefer using integrated software over other types of applications software?

8. What do the abbreviations CAD, CAE, and CAM mean?

9. What advantages can desktop publishing software provide?

10. What is the difference between applications software and systems software?

11. What is the list of options displayed across the top or bottom of the screen called? What is it used for?

12. What is an icon? What is it used for?

13. What is a Help screen, and how can the user display it?

14. What is scrolling?

Projects

1. Locate an individual or a company who is using some custom-written software. What does this software do? Who uses it? Why couldn't it have been purchased off the shelf? How much did it cost? Do you think there is an off-the-shelf program that can be used instead? Why/why not?

2. Attend a meeting of a computer users' group in your area. What is the overall purpose of the group? Software support? Hardware support? In what ways? Does it cost money to be a member? How many members are there? How does the group get new members? If you were looking to join a user group, would you be interested in joining this group? Why/why not?

3. Make a list of all the ways a student could use word processing software to make life easier. Look at Table 6.1 to get some ideas, read some reviews of word processing software in computer magazines, and read the copy on word processing packages in a computer store.

GLOSSARY

accessory programs Microsoft Windows software tools for organizing the user's desktop, including clock, notepad, calendar, calculator, and cardfile.

access time Average time to locate instructions or data from **secondary** (auxiliary) **storage** device and to transfer this to computer's **main memory** (RAM).

add-ins *See* **add-on utility.**

add-on memory board Circuit board with memory chips plugged into expansion slot on **motherboard** to increase capacity of microcomputer's **main memory.**

add-on (add-in) utility **RAM-resident** software purchased to enhance the features of other applications software products (to provide additional capabilities)—for example, to print output lengthwise instead of across the width of the paper or to improve appearance of the output. Add-on software is loaded *after* the applications software has been loaded.

addressing scheme Computer design feature that determines amount of **main memory** the CPU can control at any one time.

algorithm A set of standard operations that guarantees a solution to a problem in a finite number of steps.

Alt key Modifier key on the computer **keyboard;** when a modifier key is pressed along with another key, the function of that other key is modified. The applications software program determines how modifier keys are used.

American National Standards Institute (ANSI) Organization that develops standards for all **high-level programming languages** and related subjects.

American Standard Code for Information Interchange (ASCII) Pronounced *"as*-key." Standard bit code used in data communications, microcomputers, and many minicomputers.

amplitude Size of voltage or magnitude of wave form in data or voice transmission.

analog signal Signal that is continuously varying and that represents a range of frequencies; the telephone system is based on analog signals. *See* **digital signal.**

analytical graphics Graphic forms used to make numeric data easier to understand; the most common analytical graphics forms are bar chart, line chart, pie chart, and XY chart. Analytical graphics are usually *spreadsheet-based;* that is, they are created using a **spreadsheet** software package. *Compare* **presentation graphics.**

ANSI *See* **American National Standards Institute.**

antivirus software Software that identifies the existence of **viruses** in a computer system and may also eliminate viruses the software recognizes.

applications software Program or programs designed to carry out a specific task to satisfy a user's specific needs—for example, to calculate payroll and print out checks. *Compare* **systems software.**

applications software utility Inexpensive program—**RAM-resident** or retrieved from disk—that performs basic "office management" functions for the user. *See* **add-on utility; disk utility; keyboard utility; screen utility.**

arithmetic/logic unit (ALU) Part of the computer's **central processing unit (CPU)** that performs all arithmetic and logical (comparison) functions.

arithmetic operations The operations of addition, subtraction, multiplication, division, and exponentiation.

artificial intelligence The study of intelligence as a collection of information-processing tasks; it is concerned with using computer hardware and software to simulate human thought processes such as imagination and intuition.

ASCII *See* **American Standard Code for Information Interchange.**

asynchronous transmission In data communications, sending one character, or **byte** (8 bits), at a time, each byte preceded by a "start" bit and followed by one or two "stop" bits and an error check bit (or parity bit). An inexpensive and widely used but relatively slow form of data communication. Also called *start-stop transmission.*

auxiliary storage *See* **secondary storage.**

Backspace key Used to move the **cursor** to the left and to simultaneously delete the character to the left.

batch commands Commands used to create batch command files, which automate frequently used command sequences and make procedures easier for users unfamiliar with the computer's operating system. Batch command files are considered **external command files** because their instructions are not loaded into main memory (RAM) at the time the computer is booted.

batch file File created by the user that is a collection of **DOS** commands automatically executed when the user types the name of the batch file after the **system prompt.** This type of file is useful for executing a frequently used series of commands.

binary code Scheme for encoding data using **binary digits.**

binary digit (bit) In binary notation, either 1 or 0. The digit 1 represents an "on" electrical (or magnetic) state; the digit 0 represents an "off" state. A group of adjacent bits (usually 8 bits) constitutes a **byte,** or single character.

bit *See* **binary digit.**

bit-mapped display **Cathode-ray tube** screen display system in which each possible dot is controlled by a single character in memory. Also known as *dot-addressable* or *all-points addressable* display.

block operations By using block operations, a feature of **word processing,** it is possible to move, delete, and copy entire sentences, paragraphs, and pages by issuing commands to the software.

boot To start up the computer and load the necessary software instructions into **RAM.**

bus An "electronic highway" or communications path linking several devices and parts of the **central processing unit (CPU).**

bus network Electronic communications **network** with a number of computers connected by a single length of wire, cable, or optical fiber.

byte Group of contiguous bits, usually 8 bits, that form a character.

cache memory Special high-speed memory area that the CPU can quickly access; it comprises a small area of RAM created in addition to the computer's main RAM; a copy of the most frequently used data and instructions is kept in the cache so the CPU can look in the cache first—which makes the computer run faster. Cache memory is usually located right on the 386 or 486 microprocessor chip.

Caps Lock key Keyboard key used to place all the alphabetic keys into uppercase position—that is, capital letters only.

cartridge-tape unit Device that reads **magnetic tape** in cassette form; often used as alternative type of **secondary storage** to **hard disk** and as backup storage for hard disks.

cathode-ray tube (CRT) Electronic screen used with computer terminals to display data entered into a computer and information available from it (**softcopy** output); also called *video display screen.*

CD-ROM *See* **compact disk/read-only memory.**

cell In a spreadsheet program, this marks the intersection of a column and a row.

central processing unit (CPU) The "brain" of the computer; the part of the computer composed of electrical circuitry directing most of the computer system's activities. The CPU consists of the **control unit** and the **arithmetic/logic unit (ALU)**, connected by a **bus.**

CGA *See* **color graphics adapter.**

character *See* **byte.**

character box Fixed location on a video display screen where a standard character can be placed. Most screens can display 80 characters of data horizontally and 25 lines vertically, or 2,000 character boxes (called character-mapped display)—the number the electron gun can target. The more **pixels** that fit into a character box, the higher the **resolution** of the resulting image. Each character box is "drawn" according to a prerecorded template stored in read-only memory (ROM).

character-mapped display *See* **character box.**

character printer *See* **impact printer.**

characters per second (cps) Measure of speed of printers and other output devices.

check bit *See* **parity bit.**

child record In **hierarchical database**, record subordinate to **parent record.**

chip Collection of related (integrated) circuits—usually on a wafer made of **semiconductor** material (usually silicon)—designed to work together on a set of tasks; can be as little as ¼-inch square.

CISC *See* **Complex Instruction Set Computing.**

clock Device in **CPU** that synchronizes all operations in a **machine cycle.**

clock speed The speed at which the **CPU** completes its internal processing tasks; measured in **megahertz (MHz).**

clone A copy of a brand-name hardware component. This term typically refers to an IBM-compatible computer.

closed architecture Attribute of computers that cannot be upgraded by the use of expansion cards; the user cannot open the **system unit.** *Compare* **open architecture.**

coaxial cable Type of thickly insulated copper wire for carrying large volumes of data—about 1,800–3,600 voice calls at once. Often used in local networks connecting computers in a limited geographic area.

code-oriented Refers to **desktop publishing; page descrip-**

tion software that displays all the formatting codes on the screen, thus preventing the user from seeing what the page will actually look like until it is printed out. *Compare* **WYSIWYG.**

color dot-matrix printer Printer that uses the same technology as a monochrome **dot-matrix printer;** however, it uses a color ribbon instead of a black ribbon. Color ribbons usually contain equal bands of black, yellow, red, and blue.

color graphics adapter (CGA) Expansion card plugged into **expansion slot** in **system cabinet** that allows compatible **monitor** to display **bit-mapped graphics;** must be used with appropriate software; monitor displays four colors as well as monochrome images; used in IBM-type PCs.

color monitor *See* **RGB monitor.**

command syntax *See* **syntax.**

communications software Programs that allow users to access software and data from a computer in a remote location and to transmit data to a computer in a remote location.

compact disk/read-only memory (CD-ROM) Optical storage disk whose data is imprinted by the disk manufacturer; the user cannot change it or write on the disk—the user can only "read" the data. *Compare* **erasable optical disk; write once, read many (WORM).**

compatibility Capability of operating together; can refer to different models of computers, different types of hardware peripherals, and various systems and applications software—not all software is compatible with all computers and other types of hardware, and not all types of hardware are compatible with one another. Incompatibility can often be overcome with the use of **modems** and/or special hardware and software.

compiler Computer program that translates a **high-level programming language** program (**source code**) into **machine-language** instructions (**object code**) all at once. *Compare* **interpreter.**

Complex Instruction Set Computing (CISC) A microprocessor chip design used in most of today's **microprocessor chips.** *Compare* **Reduced Instruction Set Computing (RISC).**

computer Data processing device made up of electronic and electromechanical components that can perform computations, including arithmetic and logical operations. Also known as **hardware.** By itself, a computer has no intelligence.

computer-aided design (CAD) The use of a computer and special graphics software to design products.

computer-aided engineering (CAE) The use of a computer and special software to simulate situations that test product designs.

computer-aided manufacturing (CAM) The use of computers and special software to control manufacturing equipment; includes **robots.**

computer-assisted software engineering (CASE) tools Software tools used in systems design, development, and documentation.

computer-based information system Computer system for collecting data, processing it into information, and storing the information for future reference and output. The system consists of five components: **hardware, software, data/information, procedures,** and **people. (Connectivity** is sometimes a sixth component.) It has four major phases of activity: **input, processing, output,** and **storage.**

computer crime   Crime committed when a person uses computer technology or knowledge of computers in an illegal activity.

Computer Fraud and Abuse Act of 1986   U.S. law that allows the prosecution of people who gain unauthorized access to computers and databases.

computer graphics   *See* **analytical graphics; presentation graphics.**

computer literacy (competency)   Basic understanding of what a computer is and how it can be used as a resource; includes some experience with commonly used software packages, such as **word processing, spreadsheet,** and/or **database** software.

Computer Matching and Privacy Protection Act of 1988   U.S. law that sets procedures for using computer data for verifying a person's eligibility for federal benefits or for recovering delinquent debts.

computer professional   Person with formal education in technical aspects of computers—for example, a programmer, a systems analyst, or a computer operator.

computer system   *See* **computer-based information system.**

concentrator   Communications device that multiplexes (combines) low-speed communications lines onto one high-speed line; it is more "intelligent" than a **multiplexer** because it can store communications for later transmission.

connectivity   When one computer system is set up to communicate with another computer system, connectivity becomes the sixth system element, after **hardware, software, data/information, procedures,** and **people;** it describes the manner in which the systems are connected.

controller   Communications hardware device that supports a group of devices (terminals and/or printers) connected to a computer.

control program   *See* **supervisor.**

control unit   Part of the **CPU** that reads, interprets, and sees to the execution of software instructions.

CPU   *See* **central processing unit.**

cracker   Person who gains unauthorized access to a computer system for malicious purposes.

CRT   *See* **cathode-ray tube.**

Ctrl key   Modifier key on the computer keyboard; when a modifier key is pressed along with another key, the function of that other key is modified. The specific use of modifier keys is determined by the software program.

current disk drive   *See* **default disk drive.**

cursor   Indicator on video display screen that shows where next data—character, space, command—will be input.

cursor-movement keys   Computer keyboard keys, usually marked with arrows, that are used to move the **cursor** around the video screen.

custom software   Software that is written by a programmer to a particular organization's specifications.

daisy wheel printer   **Impact printer** with plastic or metal disk with typeface impressions of characters on outside tips of spokes; the print character is forced against ribbon and paper.

data   Raw, unevaluated facts, concepts, or instructions; after processing, data becomes **information.**

data access area   Exposed part of a **disk,** through which the

read/write head inside the disk drive "reads" and "writes" data from and to a disk.

database   Large group of electronically stored, integrated (cross-referenced) data that can be retrieved and manipulated to produce information.

database administrator   Person who cordinates all related activities and needs for a company's database, including: (1) database implementation; (2) coordination with the user; (3) backup; (4) recovery; (5) performance monitoring; and (6) system security.

database management system (DBMS)   Comprehensive software tool that allows users to create, maintain, and manipulate an integrated base of business data to produce relevant management information. A DBMS represents the interface between the user and the computer's **operating system** and **database.**

database management system (DBMS) software   Program that allows storage of large amounts of data in different files; the data can be easily cross-indexed, retrieved, and manipulated to produce information for management reports.

database structure   The characteristics of every **field** stored in a database; the method according to which a **database management system** organizes records.

data bus   Electronic communication link that carries data between components of the computer system.

data dictionary   Reference file in a **database management system** that stores information about data that is essential to the management of that data as a resource; it contans the data element names and definitions for all the data to be mantained in data files, to be generated as output, and to be created as input.

data file   *See* **file.**

data flow diagram   Graphic representation of flow of data through a system; standard **ANSI** symbols are used to represent various activities such as input and processing.

data independence   Attribute of data that is stored independently of applications programs being used, so that it is easy to access and change.

data integrity   Attribute of data that describes its accuracy, reliability, and timeliness; that is, if data has integrity, then it is accurate, reliable, and timely.

data manipulation language   Program that is part of **database management system** software and that effects input to and output from the **database** files; the technical instructions that make up the input/output routines in the DBMS.

data (information) processing   Operations for refining, summarizing, categorizing, and otherwise manipulating data into a useful form for decision making.

data redundancy   A situation that occurs when the same element of data appears and is maintained in more than one file; a high degree of data redundancy makes updating files difficult.

data storage hierarchy   The levels of data stored in a computer file: (1) **files** (broadest level), (2) **records,** (3) **fields,** (4) **bytes,** and (5) **bits** (narrowest level).

DBMS   *See* **database management system.**

decision support system (DSS)   A sophisticated computer-based information system for assisting high-level managers in planning and decision making on an on-demand basis.

dedicated backup system   Hardware and software used only for backup purposes.

dedicated graphics package   A software application that functions solely to provide the user with the capability to produce graphics.

dedicated line   Communication line created or leased by a company for its own transmission purposes.

default disk drive   The disk drive that is automatically affected by commands unless the user specifies another drive.

default values   The values, or determinations, that the software assumes are true, unless the user instructs the software otherwise.

Del key   Used to delete the character the **cursor** is positioned on.

demodulation   Process of using communications hardware to convert **analog** signals sent over a telephone line into **digital** signals so that they can be processed by a receiving computer.

desktop computer   *See* **microcomputer**.

desktop management utility   Software designed to be available at any time to the user by residing in main memory at all times (**RAM-resident**); it provides many routine office support functions such as calendar organization, dictionary, and calculator.

desktop publishing software   Programs that enable user to use a microcomputer, graphics scanners, and a desktop-sized laser printer to combine files created by different software applications packages to produce high-quality publications.

detail report   Computer-generated report for **operating** (low-level) **management** that contains specific information about routine activities; such reports are highly structured, and their form is predetermined.

digital   Pertaining to the use of combinations of **bits** to represent all quantities that occur in a computation.

digital convergence   The merger of the computer, communications, and the consumer electronics and entertainment industries so that all manner of devices exchange data and information in the digital format understood by computers. *See also* **digital**; *compare* **analog**.

digital signal   Signal that is discontinuous and discrete; it consists of bursts that form a transmission pattern. Computers communicate with each other in streams of **bits** transmitted as digital signals—a series of on and off electrical pulses. *See* **analog signal**.

digitizer   Input device that can be moved over a drawing or a photograph thereby converting the picture to computerized data that can be stored, printed out, or shown on a video display screen. The device can also be moved over an electronic digitizing tablet in order to communicate data to the computer.

digitizing tablet   *See* **digitizer**.

direct access storage and retrieval   Situation in which records are stored and retrieved in any order. Also called *random access*.

direct entry   Nonkeyboard input.

directory commands   **Internal command instructions** used in microcomputers to create **directory structures** on a storage device.

directory structure   The way a disk is organized into **subdirectories**.

disk   Revolving platter (**secondary storage** medium) on which data and programs are recorded electronically or optically (laser) in the form of spots representing electrical "on" and "off" states.

disk cartridge   Form of **secondary storage** consisting of a 5¼- or 3½-inch cartridge containing one or two platters and enclosed in a hard plastic case; the cartridge is inserted into the disk drive much like a music cassette tape.

disk drive   Device into which a **diskette (floppy disk)**, **hard disk**, or **disk pack** is placed for storing and retrieving data.

disk drive gate   Door of disk drive, which must be closed for the read/write operation to be performed. (Not all computers have disk-drive gates.)

diskette   Thin plastic (Mylar) disk enclosed in paper or plastic that can be magnetically encoded with data; standard diskettes are 5¼ or 3½ inches; also known as *floppy disks*.

disk operating system (DOS)   **Internal command instructions** for microcomputers; **MS-DOS** and **PC-DOS** have become the industry standard for IBM PC microcomputers; **OS/2** is used on IBM's PS/2 Series microcomputers; **Apple-DOS** and the **Macintosh operating system** are used on the Apple Company's microcomputers; **TRS-DOS** is used on Tandy/Radio Shack microcomputers. These disk operating systems are not generally mutually compatible.

disk utility   **Applications software utility** stored on disk; used to recover files that were accidentally erased, to make backup copy of a hard disk, and to organize a hard disk by means of a **menu**-driven system.

documentation   Written description of a system's or a software package's parts and procedures; can come in the form of a user's manual that tells the user how to operate a piece of hardware or run a particular software program, or it can be a large collection of volumes and printouts to be used by programmers and computer operators.

DOS   *See* **disk operating system**.

dot-matrix printer   **Impact printer** using pin-like hammers to strike a ribbon against paper in computer-determined patterns of dots, making possible a variety of type styles and graphics.

double-density   *See* **recording density**.

double-sided disk   Disk(ette) that stores data on both sides; a computer needs a **double-sided disk drive** to be able to read double-sided disks.

double-sided disk drive   Disk drive with **read/write heads** for both top and bottom surfaces of a disk.

drive A (A:)   Designation for the first **disk(ette) drive** in a microcomputer; the program diskette is usually inserted in this drive, which is often the left-hand or the upper drive.

drive B (B:)   Designation for the second **disk(ette) drive** in a microcomputer; the data diskette is usually inserted in this drive, which is often the right-hand or the lower drive.

drive C (C:)   Designation for the **hard disk** drive in a microcomputer.

editing   Process of changing text—for example, inserting and deleting.

electrically erasable programmable read-only memory (EEPROM)   Type of **read-only (ROM)** memory (chip) much the same as **erasable programmable read-only mem-**

ory except that changes can be made to an integrated circuit electrically—new instructions can be recorded—byte-by-byte under software control.

electroluminescent (EL) display Type of **video display screen** with light-emitting layer of phosphor and two sets of electrodes surrounding the phosphor layer—one side forming vertical columns (usually 512), the other side forming horizontal rows (usually 256). To form a **pixel** on the screen, current is sent to row-column intersection, and the combined voltages cause the phospor to glow at that point.

electronic banking Service enabling customers to access banking activities from home or private office via a terminal or personal computer connected to their telephones.

electronic bulletin board (BBS) **Information service** that can be reached via computer connected to telephone lines that allows user to place messages or read messages from other users.

electronic communications Movement of voice and data over short and long distances, such as by telephone or microwave, through the use of computers and communications hardware and software.

electronic mail (E-mail) Transmission and storing of messages by computers and E-mail software.

electronic shopping Service through which users can order merchandise by using microcomputers and electronic communications to browse through products listed on remote databases.

electronic spreadsheet software *See* **spreadsheet software.**

electronic surveillance The monitoring of workers' performances—often without their knowledge—through the use of computers and other electronic equipment.

emulate To operate in a manner similar to something else; for example, when the user installs software, if the make and model of the user's printer aren't listed on the software's list of supported printers but it operates similarly to one on the installation list, the user's printer has the same characteristics of, or emulates the one on the list.

encryption The encoding of data transmitted over communications lines from standard code into proprietary (secret) code to prevent eavesdropping.

Enter key Computer **keyboard** key pressed to execute a command that was entered by tapping other keys first.

erasable optical disk **Optical storage** disk whose data can be changed and erased. *Compare* **compact disk/read-only memory (CD-ROM); write once, read many (WORM).**

erasable programmable read-only memory (EPROM) Type of **read-only memory** in which, with the help of a special device using ultraviolet light, the data or instructions on an integrated circuit (**chip**) can be erased and new data can be recorded in its place.

ergonomics The science of human comfort and health, especially as it relates to the use of computers.

Esc key Most **software applications** allow the user to press this key to back out of, or cancel, the current command procedure.

ethics A set of moral values or principles that govern the conduct of an individual or a group.

event-initiated report Computer-based report generated for **middle management** only when certain conditions exist, such as changes requiring immediate attention (for example, equipment breakdown).

exception report Report generated for **middle management** that shows out-of-the ordinary data.

execution cycle (E-cycle) Activity in **CPU** that includes execution of instruction and subsequent storing of result in a **register.** *See also* **instruction cycle; machine cycle.**

expanded memory In a microcomputer, **main memory (RAM)** that has been added to exceed the conventional 640 K maximum; it consists of an add-on memory board and special driver software; used only in compatible 8088, 8086, 80286, and 80386 microcomputers.

expansion card *See* **add-on memory board.**

expansion slot In a microcomputer that has **open architecture,** an area within the **system cabinet** where expansion cards—such as color graphics adapter cards and expanded memory cards—can be inserted and plugged into the computer's circuitry.

expert system A computer program based on various **artificial intelligence** techniques that performs a specialized task at the level of a human expert; the expert system consists of knowledge gathered from human experts plus rules for using the system. It usually comprises: (1) a **natural language** interface with the user; (2) a knowledge base; (3) an inference machine to solve problems and make logical inferences; and (4) an explanation module to explain the conclusions to the user.

export To convert a file created by one application into a file format that can be used by another application.

Extended Binary Coded Decimal Interchange Code (EBCDIC) Pronounced "*eb*-see-dick." The most popular code used for IBM and IBM-compatible mainframe computers.

extended memory In a microcomputer, **main memory (RAM)** that has been added to exceed the conventional 640 K maximum; it consists of an **add-on memory board** and special driver software; used only in compatible 80286, 80386, and 80486 microcomputers.

external command file **DOS** command instructions that aren't loaded into **RAM** when you **boot** your computer. *See* **external command instructions.**

external command instructions General-purpose instructions kept in **secondary storage** for "housekeeping" tasks on microcomputers such as the sorting of files and formatting of disks; part of a computer's **systems software.** *See also* **internal command instructions.**

external modem **Modem** that is outside the microcomputer and uses its own power supply; it is connected to the computer by a cable.

facsimile *See* **fax.**

Fair Credit Reporting Act of 1970 U.S. law intended to keep mistakes out of credit bureau files; credit agencies are barred from sharing credit information with anyone but authorized customers.

fax A faxed item. *See* **fax machine.**

fax card An internal fax **modem** that differs from conventional modems in that it can send and receive both text and graphics and can typically send and receive at a faster rate.

faxing The process of transmitting a **fax.**

fax machine   Short for *facsimile machine*, a type of **scanner** that "reads" text and graphics and transmits them over telephone lines to a computer with a fax card (board) or to another fax machine.

fiber optics   Form of computer communications in which signals are converted to light form and fired by laser in bursts through thin (2,000ths of an inch) insulated glass or plastic fibers. Nearly 1 billion bits per second can be communicated through a fiber optic cable.

field   Group of related characters (bytes) of data. *See* **data storage hierarchy.**

field name   In a **database structure,** the unique name given to each field of data that is stored. A field name can be no longer than 10 characters.

field type   In a **database structure,** the specification of the kind of data that will be stored in a given **field** (character, numeric, date, logical, float, or memo).

field width   In a database structure, the width of each **field** must be defined by the user.

file   Group of related **records.** A file may contain data (data file) or software instructions (program file). *See* **data storage hierarchy.**

file management system   *See* **flat-file database management system.**

filename extension   One to three characters added to a filename to aid in file identification. The filename and the extension are separated by a dot.

filename length   Convention specified by different **operating systems**—for example, **DOS** specifies one to eight characters in filenames.

file server   A computer, usually a microcomputer, with large-capacity storage, that stores data and programs shared by a network of terminals; often the central unit in a **star network.**

file updating   A factor in **data redundancy** and **data integrity;** when an element of data in a **database** needs to be updated in *all* files that contain it.

flatbed plotter   Special-purpose output device for reproducing computer-generated drawings. Paper is placed flat and pens move horizontally and vertically across it.

flatbed scanner   Type of **scanner** that enables the user to scan text and graphics by placing each page to be scanned on a piece of glass that the scanning mechanism passes over.

flat-file database management system   Database management system software that can deal with data in only one **file** at a time; cannot establish relationships among data elements stored in different files.

flat screen technology   Video display screens for laptop computers; the screens are much thinner than a **cathode-ray tube (CRT).** *See* **electroluminescent display; gas plasma display; liquid crystal display.**

floppy disk   *See* **diskette.**

font   All the characters of one size in one particular typeface; includes numbers, punctuation marks, and upper- and lowercase letters.

footer   Descriptive information (such as page number and date) that appears at the bottom of each page of a document.

formatting   (1) Directing the computer to put magnetic **track** and **sector** pattern on a disk to enable the disk to store data or information. Also known as *initializing.* (2) In **word processing,** the alteration of text appearance by addition of underlining or boldface, change of margins, centering of headings, and so on. (3) In electronic **spreadsheet** processing, the alteration of numbers by the addition of dollar signs, percent signs, decimal places, and so on.

formatting commands   *See* **formatting** (2).

formula   In **electronic spreadsheets,** a mathematical expression that defines the relationships among various cells in the spreadsheet.

Freedom of Information Act of 1970   U.S. law that gives citizens the right to look at data concerning themselves that is stored by the U.S. government.

freeware   Free software that is often limited in its distribution (usually through a bulletin board service).

frequency   Number of times a signal repeats the same cycle in a second.

front-end processor   Computer used in a computer center to handle data transmission and communications from outside terminals and devices to allow the main computer to concentrate solely on processing applications as quickly as possible.

full-duplex transmission mode   Communications transmitted in both directions simultaneously.

function keys   Specialized keys on a microcomputer **keyboard** for performing specific tasks with applications software; the keys are used differently with each applications package; they are labeled F1, F2, F3, and so on.

fuzzy logic   Type of programming logic used in the development of **natural languages** and **artificial intelligence** projects; works by allowing partial membership in a set—for example, not black or white but gray, not fat or thin but a "little" fat.

gas plasma display   Used as **video display screen** in some **laptop microcomputers.** Gas plasma display uses three pieces of glass sandwiched together. The inner layer has numerous small holes drilled in it. The outer two layers are placed on both sides of the middle one, and the holes are filled with a gas mixture, usually a mixture of argon and neon. Both outer layers of glass have a thin grid of vertical and horizontal wires. A **pixel** appears at a particular intersection when the appropriate horizontal and vertical wires are electrified.

GB   *See* **gigabyte.**

general-purpose applications software   Type of applications software used in general business and professional environments; includes word processing, desktop publishing, spreadsheet, database management, graphics, communications, integrated, CAD, CAE, CAM, and utility software.

gigabyte (GB)   One billion bytes.

graphics monitor (terminal)   Screen that can display both **alphanumeric data** and graphics; different types can display one-, two-, or three-dimensional graphics. *Compare* **alphanumeric monitor (terminal).**

graphics software   Programs that allow the user to present information in pictorial form, often with text. *See* **analytical graphics; presentation graphics.**

graphic user interface   Software feature that allows user to select **menu** options by choosing **icons,** or picture, that represent particular processing functions; makes software easier to use, and typically employs a **mouse.** Macintosh microcomputers and Windows software use graphic user interfaces.

gray-scale monitor Monitor that displays different shades, or scales, of gray; the more levels of gray scale, the more realistically an image can be displayed. High-resolution gray-scale graphics files require a large amount of storage.

hacker Person who gains unauthorized access to a computer system for fun.

half-duplex transmission mode Two-way data communications in which data travels in only one direction at a time.

hand-held scanner Small input device used to scan printed documents on a limited basis to input the documents' contents to a computer.

hardcard Type of **secondary storage** device consisting of a circuit board with a disk that is plugged into a microcomputer **expansion slot.** A hard card can store up to 80 MB of data.

hardcopy Output recorded on a tangible medium (generally meaning that you can touch it) such as paper or microfilm. *Compare* **softcopy.**

hard disk Secondary storage device consisting of a rigid metal platter connected to a central spindle; the entire unit, including the **read/write heads,** is enclosed in a permanently sealed container. Hard disks store much more data than do **diskettes**—40 MB and up.

hardware Four categories of electronic and electromechanical computer components: input, storage, processing, and output hardware. *See also* **computer.** *Compare* **software.**

header Descriptive information (such as page number and date) that appears at the top of each page of a document.

Help facility Most **applications software** packages include a command that enables the user to display helpful information on the screen about a particular command.

Help key In many software applications, this key is used to obtain help information about the current command, a particular function key, or a particular topic.

Help screen *See* **Help facility.**

hierarchical database model The type of **database** organization in which data is arranged into related groups resembling a family tree, with **child records** subordinate to **parent records.** A parent record may have many child records, but each child record can have only one parent record. The record at the highest level is called the *root record.*

hierarchical network **Star networks** configured into a single multilevel system, with a single large computer controlling all network activity. However, a computer connected into the main computer can have a star network of devices connected to it in turn. Also known as a *tree network.*

high-level programming language Third-generation programming language designed to run on different computers with few changes—for example, **COBOL, FORTRAN,** and **BASIC.** Most high-level languages are considered to be procedure-oriented because the program instructions comprise lists of steps, or procedures, that tell the computer not only what to do but how to do it. Also known as *procedural language.*

hub Round opening in the center of a diskette, which enables the disk to fit over a spindle in the disk drive.

hypertext software Software that links basic file units called *nodes* (text, sound, and graphics) with one another in creative ways. The user typically sees index-type "cards" and

"card stacks" on the screen as well as other pictorial representations of file units (nodes) and combination choices; card and stack contents can be determined by the user or supplied in an **off-the-shelf software** package (stackware).

icon Picture that represents the different application programs and processing procedures you can execute. Macintosh programs and **Microsoft Windows** use icons extensively.

impact printer Also called *character printer;* output device that makes direct contact with paper, forming the print image by pressing an inked ribbon against the paper with a hammer-like mechanism. Impact printers are of two types. *See* **letter-quality printer; dot-matrix printer.**

import To retrieve a file created by another application into the current application.

index hole Hole in protective jacket enclosing **diskette** that enables the disk to be positioned over a photoelectric sensing mechanism. Each time the disk revolves, a hole in the disk passes under the index hole in the jacket and activates a timing mechanism that determines which portion of the disk is over or under the **read/write heads.**

information Raw **data** processed into usable form by the computer. It is the basis for decision making.

information center Company department staffed by experts in hardware, software, and procedures used in the company; the experts help users in all matters relating to computer use.

information service *See* **public databank.**

initializing *See* **formatting.**

ink-jet printer Nonimpact printer that resembles **dot-matrix printer** in that it forms images or characters with dots. The dots are formed not by hammer-like pins but by droplets of ink fired through holes in a plate.

input hardware Hardware that is used to collect data and convert it into a form suitable for computer processing. The most common input device is a **keyboard.**

instruction cycle (I-cycle) In the **CPU,** the operation whereby an instruction is retrieved from **main memory (RAM)** and is decoded, alerting the circuits in the CPU to perform the specified operation.

integrated software package Software combining several applications into a single package with a common set of commands. **Word processing,** electronic **spreadsheets, database management systems, graphics,** and **data communications** have been combined in such packages.

internal command files Files that contain **DOS** command instructions that are stored in **RAM** at all times. The instructions in these files are loaded into RAM when your computer is turned on (booted).

internal command instructions Operating system software instructions loaded into **main memory (RAM)** (when the microcomputer is booted), where they direct and control applications software and hardware; they remain in main memory until the computer is turned off. *See also* **external command instructions.**

internal modem Modem that is inside a microcomputer; it is located on a circuit board plugged into the computer's expansion slot and draws power directly from the computer's power supply. No special cable is required. *Compare* **external modem.**

international network **Network** providing intercontinental voice and data communications, often using undersea cable or satellites.

interpreter **Language processor** that converts high-level program instructions into **machine language** one instruction statement at a time. *Compare* **compiler.**

K (KB) *See* **kilobyte.**

keyboard Device resembling typewriter keyboard for entering data and computer-related codes. Besides standard typewriter keys, it has special **function keys, cursor-movement keys, numeric keys,** and other special-purpose keys.

keyboard utility **Applications software utility,** usually **RAM-resident,** used to change the way the **cursor** appears on the screen.

kilobyte (KB) 1,024 bytes.

language processor Program that translates applications programs wirtten in **high-level programming languages** and **assembly languages** into **machine language** so that the computer can process them. Also known as a *translator.*

laptop microcomputer Microcomputer using **flat-screen technology** that is small enough to be held on a person's lap.

laser printer Output device in which a laser beam is directed across the surface of a light-sensitive drum to record an image as a pattern of tiny dots. As with a photocopying machine, the image is then transferred to the paper a page at a time.

latency period *See* **rotational delay.**

license What the user really buys when purchasing copyrighted software—that is, a license to use the software.

light pen Pen-shaped input device consisting of a light-sensitive photoelectric cell that, when touched to a video display screen, is used to signal the screen position to the computer.

line chart Shows trends over time; the angles of the line reflect variations in a trend, and the distance of the line from the horizontal axis represents quantity. *See also* **analytical graphics.**

line-of-sight System that enables users to use their eyes to point at the screen to specify screen coordinates. These systems are being used by the handicapped.

liquid crystal display (LCD) Used as a flat **video display screen** in some laptop microcomputers. LCD uses a clear liquid chemical trapped in tiny pockets between two pieces of glass. Each pocket of liquid is covered both front and back by thin wires. When current is applied to the wires, a chemical reaction turns the chemical a dark color, thereby blocking light. The point of blocked light is the **pixel.**

local area network (LAN) Communications **network** connected by wire, cable, or fiber optics link that serves parts of a company located close to one another, generally in the same building or within two miles of one another. LANs allow workers to share hardware, software, and data.

logical database design Detailed description of database structure from the user's perspective, rather than a technical perspective. It involves defining user information needs, analyzing data element requirements and logical groupings, finalizing the design, and creating the **data dictionary.** Every element of data necessary to produce required management information reports is identified, and the relationship among the records is specified. *Compare* **physical database design;** *see also* **schema, subschema.**

logical operations Operations consisting of three common comparisons: equal to, less than, and greater than. Three words used in basic logical operations are AND, OR, and NOT.

machine cycle In the **CPU** during processing, the **instruction cycle** and the **execution cycle** together, as they apply to one instruction.

machine language The language the **CPU** understands; data and instructions are represented as **binary digits.** Each type of computer responds to a unique version of machine language. Also known as **first-generation language.**

Macintosh Operating System The **operating system** designed by Apple Computers for the Apple Macintosh microcomputer.

macro Collection of procedures—a few high-level instructions that generate many machine-language instructions. Macros are created by the user and saved to disk, then used repeatedly to save time. A macro uses a few keystrokes to represent many.

magnetic tape Plastic ribbon coated with material that can be magnetized to record the **bit** patterns that represent data.

mainframe computer After the **supercomputer,** the most powerful type of computer; it is usually housed in a controlled environment and can support many powerful peripheral devices and the processing requirements of hundreds of users.

main memory The primary storage of a computer, where data and instructions are held for immediate access by the **CPU;** main memory is **volatile**—when the power is turned off, all data and instructions in memory are lost unless they have been saved to a **secondary storage** medium. Also known as *internal memory* and *RAM (random access memory).*

management Individuals responsible for providing leadership and direction in an organization's areas of planning, organizing, staffing, supervising, and controlling of business activities. Management may be low-level (operating or supervisory), middle-level (or tactical), or upper-level (strategic). *See also* **middle management, operating management, upper management.**

management information system (MIS) Computer-based processing and manual procedures within a company to provide useful and timely information to support useful and timely information to support decision making on all three levels of management.

MB *See* **megabyte.**

medium (*pl.* **media)** Type of material on which data is recorded—for example, paper, magnetic tape, magnetic disk, or optical disk.

megabyte (MB) 1,024 K—approximately 1 million characters.

megahertz (MHz) One million hertz; a measure of speed at which computers perform operations; **clock** speed.

memory *See* **main memory.**

menu List of options, or choices, offered to the user by the software; menus can be pulled down or popped up from the **menu bar** across the screen.

menu bar Row of on-screen **menu** options.

merging Bringing together information from two different files.

metropolitan area network (MAN) Computer-based **network** that links computer resources scattered among various office buildings in a city. *Compare* **local area network** and **wide area network**.

microcomputer Small, general-purpose computer system that uses a microprocessor chip as its **CPU**. It can usually be used by only one person at one time; can be used independently or as a **terminal**. Also known as *personal computer, desktop computer*.

microprocessor Integrated circuit (chip) containing the CPU circuitry for a microcomputer.

Microsoft Windows **Graphic user interface** software used with MS-DOS.

microwave system Communications technology using the atmosphere above the earth for transmitting signals point to point from tower to tower. Such systems are extensively used for high-volume as well as long-distance communication of both data and voice in the form of electromagnetic waves similar to radio waves but in a higher frequency range. Microwave signals are said to be "line-of-sight" because they cannot bend around the curvature of the earth.

middle management Level of management dealing with decisions that cover a broader range of time and are less structured than decisions made by **operating (low-level) management**. However, middle management deals with decisions that are more time-specific and more structured than decisions made by **upper-level (strategic) management**. Also called *tactical management*.

millions of instructions per second (mips) Unit of measure for speed at which a computer processes software instructions.

minicomputer Computer that is similar to but less powerful than a **mainframe computer;** it can support 2–50 users and computer professionals.

mips *See* **millions of instructions per second**.

modeling tools Program and systems design tools such as **computer-assisted software engineering (CASE), data flow diagrams, systems flowcharts,** and so on.

modem Device for translating **digital signals** from a computer into **analog signals** for transmission over wire telephone lines and then back into digital signals again for processing (a modem must be hooked up at each end of the transmission). Modem stands for MOdulate/DEModulate. (Modems are not needed for transmission over **coaxial cable** or **fiber optics cable**.)

monitor Device for viewing computer output. Also known as **cathode-ray tube (CRT); screen; video display screen**.

monochrome monitor Device for viewing text and in some cases graphics in a single color, commonly green or amber. It has only one electron gun. *Compare* **RGB monitor**.

motherboard Main circuit board in a microcomputer system. It normally includes the **microprocessor chip** (or **CPU**), **main memory (RAM)** chips, all related support circuitry, and the **expansion slots** for plugging in additional components. Also known as *system board*.

mouse Hand-held input device connected to a microcomputer by a cable; when the mouse is rolled across the desktop, the pointer moves across the screen. A button on the mouse allows users to make **menu** selections, issue commands, and position the **cursor**.

MS-DOS *See* **disk operating system**.

multimedia Sophisticated software that combines basic text and graphics along with animation, video, music, and voice.

multiplexer Device that allows several terminals to share a single communications line.

multiprocessing Activity in which an **operating system** manages simultaneous execution of programs with two or more **CPU**s. This can entail processing instructions from different programs or different instructions from the same program. *Compare* **multitasking**.

multiprogramming *See* **multitasking**.

multitasking Activity in which more than one task or program is executed at a time. A small amount of each program is processed, and then the **CPU** moves to the remaining programs, one at a time, processing small parts of each. Also known as *multiprogramming*.

natural language Programming language designed to resemble human speech. Similar to **query language**, it eliminates the need for user to learn specific vocabulary, grammar, or syntax. Also known as *fifth-generation language*.

network Collection of data communications hardware, computers, communications software, communications media, and applications software connected so that users can share information and equipment. *See also* **international network; private network; public network; ring network; star network; token ring network**.

network database model Type of **database** organization similar to **hierarchical database model** but allowing multiple one-to-many relationships; each **child record** can have more than one **parent record**. Access can be from a number of points, not just the top.

network fileserver Computer to which approximately 10 other microcomputers can be connected so that data and programs can be shared.

networking The connecting of computers and other hardware peripherals so they can share hardware, software, and data resources.

nonimpact printer Output device that does not make direct contact with paper when it prints. *See* **ink-jet printer; laser printer; thermal printer**. *Compare* **impact printer**.

nonvolatile storage Type of storage that is relatively permanent—such as data saved to disk or tape; that is, computer instructions and data are not lost when the power is turned off. *Compare* **volatile storage**.

numeric data Data that can be mathematically manipulated. *Compare* **alphanumeric data**.

numeric keys (keypad) The keys labeled 0–9 on the computer **keyboard;** used to enter numbers for mathematical manipulation.

Num Lock key When a computer **keyboard** combines the **numeric keys** with the **cursor-movement keys,** the Num Lock key must be pressed before numbers can be entered via the numeric keys. Then the Num Lock key is pressed again to restore the function of the cursor-movement keys.

object code Program consisting entirely of machine-language instructions. *Compare* **source code**.

object-oriented programming A means of creating software programs by using discrete units or modules (objects) of program instructions and refining and combining them, instead of writing each single instruction from scratch every time a new software program is created.

OCR   *See* **optical character recognition**.

off-the-shelf software   **Applications software** that can be purchased in a computer store, as opposed to software that is custom-written by a programmer.

on-demand report   Report requested by **middle management** on a case-by-case basis.

open architecture   Attribute of computers that can be upgraded by the use of expansion cards, such as **expanded memory** and **VGA**; the user can open the **system cabinet** and insert expansion cards in the computer's **expansion slots**. *Compare* **closed architecture**.

operating management   The lowest level of management, which deals with **structured decisions** and daily operations. Also called *supervisory management*. *Compare* **middle management** and **upper management**.

operating system (OS)   Set of **internal command instructions** or programs to allow a computer to direct its own resources and operations and run all other programs, including **applications software**; in microcomputers, called a *disk operating system*.

Operating System/2 (OS/2)   IBM **systems software** intended to take advantage of 80286 and 80386 microprocessors (such as in the IBM PS/2 Series of microcomputers) and support multitasking and software applications requiring up to 16 MB of main memory (RAM); more powerful than **MS-DOS**.

operational decision maker   Low-level manager who typically makes **structured decisions** regarding daily business operations.

optical character recognition (OCR) software   Software used to scan characters or text from a piece of paper into the computer's memory.

optical storage   **Secondary storage** technology using a high-power laser beam to burn microscopic spots in a disk's surface coating. Data is represented by the presence and the absence of holes in the storage locations (1s and 0s). A much lower-power laser beam is used to retrieve the data. Much more data can be stored in this way than with traditional storage media, and it is faster and cheaper.

output   Computer-produced text, graphics, or sound in **hardcopy** or **softcopy** form that can be used immediately by people, or computer-produced data stored in computer-usable form for later use by computers and people.

output hardware   The purpose of output hardware is to provide the user with the means to view information produced by the computer system. Information is output in either **hardcopy** or **softcopy** form.

page description language (PDL)   Part of **desktop publishing software**; this **high-level language** defines printer output and thus allows a **laser printer** to combine text and graphics from different files on a single page. If an **applications software** program generates output in a PDL, the output can be printed on any laser printer that supports it.

parent record   In **hierarchical database**, the record higher in the structure than a **child record**. Each child can have only one parent—that is, each record may have many records below it but only one record above it, which is a *one-to-many relationship*. Deletion of a parent record automatically deletes all child records.

parity bit   An extra (ninth) **bit** attached to the end of a **byte**; it is used as part of an error-checking scheme. Computers are designed to use either an odd-parity scheme or an even-parity scheme, in which the total number of 1s in each byte, including the parity bit, must add up to an odd number or an even number.

PC-DOS   *See* **disk operating system**.

pen-based computing   Uses special software to allow user to write directly on the display screen to input data.

periodic report   Report for middle management produced at predetermined times—for example, payroll report, inventory status report.

physical database design   Hardware view of a database that identifies on what tracks, sectors, etc. various segments of the database are stored; also called the *internal view*, or *physical view*.

pixel   Picture element; a glowing phosphor on a **cathode-ray tube (CRT)** screen. Small pixels provide greatest image clarity (**resolution**).

plotter   Output device used to create **hardcopy** drawings on paper in a variety of colors. *See also* **drum plotter; electrostatic plotter; flatbed plotter**.

portable printer   Printer that is compact and typically weighs less than 5 lbs.

power supply   **Hardware** component that provides power to other hardware components; housed in the microcomputer's **system unit**.

presentation graphics   Graphic forms that go beyond simple **analytical graphics** (bar charts, line charts, pie charts); sophisticated presentation graphics software allows the user to function as an artist and combine free-form shapes and text.

primary storage   *See* **main memory**.

printer   Output device that prints characters, symbols, and sometimes graphics on paper. *See also* **impact printer; nonimpact printer**.

printer driver   File stored on a disk containing instructions that enable a software program to communicate, or print, on the user's printer.

Privacy Act of 1974   U.S. law that restricts U.S. governmental agencies in the way they share information about American citizens; it prohibits federal information collected for one purpose from being used for a different purpose.

private network   **Network** supporting the voice and data communications needs of a particular organization.

procedure   In an information system, specific sequence of steps performed to complete one or more information processing activities.

processing   The computer-based manipulation of **data** into **information**.

processing hardware   Hardware that is used to retrieve, interpret, and direct the execution of software instructions provided to the computer.

processing registers   In the **CPU**, the registers holding data or instructions being acted on. Their size determines the amount of data that can be processed in a single cycle.

program   Group of related instructions that perform specific processing tasks.

program independence   Attribute of programs that can be used with data files arranged in different ways—for example, some with the date first and expense items second and others with expense items first and date second. Program dependence means that a separate program has to be written to use each differently arranged data file.

programmable read-only memory (PROM) Type of **read-only memory (ROM)** chip in which data or program instructions are not prerecorded when it is manufactured; thus, users can record their own data or instructions, but once the data has been recorded, it cannot always be changed.

protocol In electronic communications, formal rules for communicating, including those for timing of message exchanges, the type of electrical connections used by the communications devices, error detection techniques, methods required to gain access to communications channels, and so on.

protocol converter Specialized intelligent **multiplexer** that facilitates effective communications between microcomputers and the main computer system.

prototyping tools Software programs used to build small-scale working models of a new system or parts of a system.

public databank Information service providing users with access, for a fee, to large databases.

public domain software Uncopyrighted software available free to users.

public network **Network** providing subscribers with voice and data communications over a large geographical area. Also known as *common carrier, specialized common carrier*.

pull-down menu **Menu** that contains options displayed down the screen rather than across a row.

quad-density *See* **recording density**.

query language Fourth-generation programming language that allows users to ask questions about, or retrieve information from, database files by forming requests in normal human language statements. Learning the specific grammar, vocabulary, and **syntax** is usually a simple task. The definitions for query language and for **database management systems software** are so similar that they are often considered to be the same.

QWERTY Term that designates the common computer **keyboard** layout, whereby the first six letters of the first row of lettered keys spell "QWERTY."

RAM *See* **random access memory**.

RAM-resident software Software always available to the user because it resides in **main memory (RAM)** at all times.

random access memory (RAM) The name given to the integrated circuits (**chips**) that make up main memory, which provides **volatile** temporary storage of data and program instructions that the **CPU** is using; data and instructions can be retrieved at random, no matter where they are located in main memory. RAM is used for storing **operating system** software instructions and for temporary storage of **applications software** instructions, input data, and output data. *See also* **internal command instructions**.

read-only memory (ROM) Type of memory in which instructions to perform operations critical to a computer are stored on integrated circuits (chips) in permanent, **nonvolatile** form. The instructions are usually recorded on the chips by the manufacturer. *Compare* **electrically erasable programmable read-only memory; erasable programmable read-only memory; programmable read-only memory; random access memory (RAM)**.

read/write head Recording mechanism in magnetic storage devices that "reads" (accepts) the magnetic spots of data and converts them to electrical impulses and that "writes" (enters) the spots on the magnetic tape or disk. Most disk drives have two read/write heads to access the top and bottom surfaces of a disk simultaneously.

record Collection of related **fields**. *See also* **data storage hierarchy**.

recording density Number of **bits** per inch (bpi) that can be written onto the surface of a magnetic disk. Disks and drives have three kinds of recording densities: (1) single-density, (2) double-density, or (3) quad-density. The higher the density number, the more data a disk can hold.

Reduced Instruction Set Computing (RISC) **Chip** design that allows microcomputers to offer very high-speed performance by simplifying the internal chip design and reducing the number of instruction sets. The RISC design enables a computer to process data about twice as fast as one based on the **CISC** design. *See* **Complex Instruction Set Computer**.

register Temporary storage location within the **CPU** that quickly accepts, stores, and transfers data and instructions being used immediately. An instruction that needs to be executed must be retrieved from **main memory (RAM)** and placed in a register for access by the **ALU (arithmetic/ logic unit)**. The larger the register (the more **bits** it can carry at once), the greater the processing power.

relational database model Type of database organization in which many tables (called *relations*) store related data elements in rows (called *tuples*) and columns (called *attributes*). The structure allows complex logical relationships between records in different files to be expressed in a simple fashion. Relational databases can cross-reference data and retrieve data automatically, and data can be easily added, deleted, or modified. Data can be accessed by content, instead of address, which is the case with **hierarchical database** and **network database models**.

removable media Storage hardware media that can be removed from the computer, such as a **diskette** or a **disk cartridge**.

resolution Clarity of the image on the **video display screen**; determined by the number of **pixels** that make up the screen images.

RGB (red/green/blue) monitor Video display screen for viewing text and graphics in various colors. It has three **electron guns,** and the screen is coated with three types of phosphors: red, green, and blue. Each **pixel** is made up of three dots of phosphors, one of each color, and is capable of producing a wide range of colors. *Compare* **monochrome monitor**.

ring network Electronic communications **network** in which messages flow in one direction from a source on the loop to a destination on the loop. Computers in between act as relay stations, but if a computer fails, it can be bypassed.

Right to Financial Privacy Act of 1979 U.S. law that sets strict procedures that U.S. governmental agencies must follow when they want to examine customer records in a bank.

RISC *See* **Reduced Instruction Set Computing**.

robot A programmable device consisting of machinery for sensory activity and mechanical manipulation and connected to or including a computer. Typically, these machines automatically perform some task normally done by human beings.

ROM *See* **read-only memory.**

root directory In the hierarchy of the **MS-DOS directory structure** when a microcomputer program is **booted,** the first directory displayed is the root directory. This directory contains subdirectories, which can in turn contain sub-subdirectories. The root directory is similar in concept to the filing cabinet.

root record In a **hierarchical database model,** the record at the highest level, or "top" of the tree. Root records, which are the key to the structure, connect the various branches.

rotational delay In a disk drive, the time required for the disk to revolve until the correct **sector** is under or over the **read/write heads.**

satellite system In electronic communications, a system that uses solar-powered satellites in stationary orbit above the earth to receive, amplify, and retransmit signals. The satellite acts as a relay station from microwave stations on the ground (called *earth stations*).

saving Activity of permanently storing data from a microcomputer's **main memory (RAM)** (primary storage) on disk or tape (**secondary storage**).

scanhead Scanning mechanism inside a **scanner.**

scanner (scanning device) Hardware device that "reads" text and graphics and converts them to computer-usable form; scanners "read" copy on paper and transmit it to the user's computer screen for manipulation, output, and/or storage.

scanning system A microcomputer (PC), a scanner, and scanning software. These systems enable users to convert a hardcopy picture or a photograph into a computer-usable graphics file that can be understood by a desktop publishing or graphics package.

schema Describes organization of **relational database** in its entirety, including names of all data elements and ways records are linked. A **subschema** is part of the schema.

screen *See* **monitor.**

screen utility Applications software utility, **RAM-resident,** used to increase the life of the computer video screen.

scrolling Activity of moving text up or down on the **video display screen.**

script language Communications software feature that enables the user to automate communications procedures.

search and replace In **word processing,** the activity of automatically searching for and replacing text in a document.

secondary storage Any storage device designed to retain data and instructions in permanent form. Secondary storage is **nonvolatile:** data and instructions remain intact when the computer is turned off. Also called *auxiliary storage. Compare* **primary storage.**

sector One of several wedge-shaped areas on a hard disk or diskette used for storage reference purposes. The point at which a sector intersects a **track** is used to reference the data location. *See* **hard-sectored disk; soft-sectored disk.**

security Controls built into a computer system to ensure the protection of data, hardware, and software from intrusions, sabotage, and natural disasters.

seek time In a disk drive, the time required for the drive to position the **read/write heads** over the proper **track.**

semiconductor Material (often silicon) that conducts electricity with only a little ("semi") resistance; impurities are added to it to form electrical circuits. Today, the integrated circuits (**chips**) in the **main memory (RAM)** of almost all computers are based on this technology.

semistructured decision Decision typically made at the **middle management** level that, unlike **structured decisions,** must be made without a base of clearly defined informational procedures.

setting time In a disk drive, the time required to place the **read/write heads** in contact with the disks.

shareware Software distributed on request—often through an electronic bulletin board service—for which a small fee is charged if the user decides to keep the software.

sheet-feed scanner Type of **scanner** that uses mechanical rollers to move paper over the **scan head.**

Shift key Computer **keyboard** key that works in the same way that a typewriter Shift key works: when pressed in conjunction with an alphabetic key, the letter appears as uppercase.

simplex transmission mode Communications transmission in which data travels only in one direction at all times.

single-density disk *See* **recording density.**

softcopy Output produced in a seemingly intangible form such as on a video display screen or provided in voice form. *Compare* **hardcopy.**

software Electronic instructions given to the computer to tell it what to do and when and how to do it. Frequently made up of a group of related programs. The two main types of software are **applications software** and **systems software.**

software installation Process of telling an **applications software** package what the characteristics are of the hardware you will be using so that the software will run smoothly.

software package **Applications software** and **documentation** usually created by professional software writers to perform general business functions.

software piracy The illegal copying of copyrighted software onto blank disks for unauthorized use.

source code Program written in **high-level programming language.** Source code must be translated by a **language processor** into **object code** before the program instructions can be executed by the computer.

spelling checker In **word processing,** programs that check a document for spelling errors.

spreadsheet area **Spreadsheet cells** that are visible on the screen.

spreadsheet software Software program enabling user to create, manipulate, and analyze numerical data and develop personalized reports involving the use of extensive mathematical, financial, statistical, and logical processing. The user works with an electronic version of the accountant's traditional worksheet, with rows and columns, called a *spreadsheet.*

star network Electronic communications **network** with a central unit (computer or **file server**) linked to a number of smaller computers and/or terminals (called *nodes*). The central unit acts as traffic controller for all nodes and controls communications to locations outside the network.

storage hardware Devices that accept and hold computer instructions and data in a form that is relatively permanent, commonly on magnetic disk or tape or on optical disk.

string Designated sequence, or group, of text characters.

structured decision Predictable decision that can be made about daily business activities by following a well-defined set of routine procedures; typically made by **operating (low-level) management**.

subdirectory Second level in the **MS-DOS** directory hierarchy; equivalent to a file drawer in a file cabinet (**root directory**), it can contain sub-subdirectories.

subschema Part of the **schema** of a **relational database;** it refers to the way certain records are linked to be useful to the user.

summary report Report for **middle (tactical) management** that reviews, summarizes, and analyzes historical data to help plan and control operations and implement policy formulated by **upper (strategic) management**. Summary reports show totals and trends.

supercomputer The largest and most powerful computer; it is about 50,000 times more powerful than a **microcomputer** and may cost as much as $20 million. Supercomputers are housed in special rooms; the next most powerful computer is the **mainframe**.

super video graphics array (S-VGA) Expansion card plugged into **expansion slot** in **system cabinet** that allows compatible monitor to display **bit-mapped graphics** in color; must be used with appropriate software; displays up to 256 colors at a very high **resolution**.

supervisor The "captain" of the **operating system,** it remains in a microcomputer's **main memory** and calls in other parts of the operating system as needed from **secondary storage** and controls all other programs in the computer. In a **multitasking** environment, a supervisor coordinates the execution of each program. Also known as *control program*.

surge suppressor Devices into which the user plugs a microcomputer system and which, in turn, are connected to the power line. They help to protect the power supply and other sensitive circuitry in the computer system from voltage spikes.

synchronous transmission Form of transmitting groups of characters as blocks with no start and stop bits between characters. Characters are sent as blocks with header and trailer bytes (called **synch bits**) inserted as identifiers at the beginnings and ends of blocks. Synchronous transmission is used by large computers to transmit huge volumes of data at high speeds. *Compare* **asynchronous transmission**.

syntax Rules for using a command.

system board *See* **motherboard**.

system files Files that must be stored on the disk **DOS** is loaded from.

system prompt Characters that display on the screen to indicate what **disk drive** is current and what **subdirectory** is current (if the **Prompt command** has been used).

system requirements Refers to the hardware and software that is required to use a particular software application.

systems development life cycle (SDLC) Formal process by which organizations build **computer-based information systems**. Participants are users, information processing staff, management of all departments, and computer specialists. The SDLC is used as a guide in establishing a business system's requirements, developing the system, acquiring hardware and software, and controlling development costs. It is often divided into six phases: (1) analyze current system; (2) define new system requirements; (3) design new system: (4) develop new system; (5) implement new system; (6) evaluate performance of and maintain new system.

systems flowchart Systems development modeling tool used to diagram and document design of a new system and present an overview of the entire system, including data flow (points of input, output, and storage) and processing activities.

systems software Programs that are the principal interface between all hardware, the user, and applications software; comprise **internal command instructions, external command instructions,** and **language processor**. *Compare* **applications software**.

system unit Main computer system cabinet in a microcomputer, which usually houses the power supply, the **motherboard,** and some storage devices.

TB *See* **terabyte**.

teleconferencing Electronic linkage of several people who participate in a conversation and share displayed data at the same time.

terabyte (TB) One trillion bytes.

thermal printer Nonimpact printer that uses heat to produce an image. The print mechanism heats the surface of chemically treated paper, producing dots as characters. No ribbon or ink is used.

thesaurus Lists of words that have similar meaning to a given word; feature of word processing programs.

timesharing System that supports many user stations or terminals simultaneously. A **front-end processor** may be used to schedule and control all user requests entering the system from the **terminals,** enabling the main computer to concentrate solely on processing.

token ring network Electronic communications **network,** in which each computer obtains exclusive access to the communications channel by "grabbing" a "token" and altering it before attaching a message. This altered token acts as a message indicator for the receiving computer, which, in turn, generates a new token, freeing up the channel for another computer. Computers in between the sender and the receiver examine the token and regenerate the message if the token is not theirs. Thus, only one computer can transmit a message at one time.

touch screen Video display **screen** sensitized to receive input from the touch of a finger.

track (1) On **magnetic tape** a channel of magnetic spots and spaces (1s and 0s) running the length of the tape. (2) On **disks,** a track is one of the circular bands.

trackball Input hardware device that functions like a **mouse** but doesn't need to be rolled around on the desktop; the ball is held in a socket on the top of the stationary device.

track density Number of **tracks** on magnetic medium. Common track densities are 48 tracks per inch (tpi) and 96 tpi. Track density affects capacity.

transaction log Complete record of activity affecting contents of a **database** during transaction period. This log aids in rebuilding database files if they are damaged.

transaction processing system (TPS) Operating-level information system that processes a large volume of transactions in a routine and repetitive manner; supports day-to-day business operating activities, or transactions. *Compare* **decision support system (DSS)**.

translator   *See* **language processor**.

tree network   *See* **hierarchical network**.

uninterruptible power supply (UPS)   Device used to protect hardware from the damaging effects of a power surge; also keeps the system running for about 15–30 minutes, providing the user with enough time to save work and shut the system down.

UNIX   **Operating system** initially created for **minicomputers**; it provides a wide range of capabilities, including **virtual storage, multiprogramming, and timesharing**. Although machine independent, it is not yet widely used on microcomputers because no standards have yet been developed for it.

unstructured decision   Decision rarely based on predetermined routine procedures; involves the subjective judgment of the decision maker and is mainly the kind of decision made by upper management.

upper management   The level of management dealing with decisions that are broadest in scope and cover the longest time frame. A manager at this level is also known as a *strategic decision maker*. *Compare* **middle management; operating management**.

user   Person receiving the computer's services; generally someone without much technical knowledge who makes decisions based on reports and other results that computers produce; also called *end-user*. *Compare* **computer professional**.

video display screen   Device for viewing computer output. Two main types are **cathode-ray tube (CRT)** and **flat screen**.

video graphics array (VGA)   Expansion card plugged into **expansion slot** in **system cabinet** that allows compatible monitors to display **bit-mapped graphics** in color; must be used with appropriate software; displays 16 colors at a resolution higher than **EGA**.

Video Privacy Protection Act of 1988   U.S. law that prevents retailers in the United States from selling or disclosing video-rental records without the customer's consent or a court order.

virtual memory   **Operating system** element that enables the computer to process as if it contained an almost unlimited supply of **main memory**. It enables a program to be broken into modules, or small sections, that can be loaded into main memory when needed. Modules not currently in use are stored on high-speed disk and retrieved one at a time when the operating system determines that the current module has completed executing. Also known as *virtual storage*.

virtual reality   A computer-simulated reality that can interact with all the senses.

virus   Bugs (programming errors) created intentionally by some programmers, usually "hackers" or "crackers," that consist of pieces of computer code (either hidden or posing as legitimate code) that, when downloaded or run, attach themselves to other programs or files and cause them to malfunction.

voice input device   Input device that converts spoken words into electrical signals by comparing the electrical patterns produced by the speaker's voice to a set of prerecorded patterns. If a matching pattern is found, the computer accepts it as a part of its standard "vocabulary" and then activates and manipulates displays by spoken command. Also known as *voice recognition system*.

voice mail   Electronic voice-messaging system that answers callers with a recording of the user's voice and records messages. Messages can be forwarded to various locations; local telephone companies provide voice mail services; voice mail systems are also used within companies.

voice output system   Synthesized or taped sound; computer output used in situations where other **softcopy** output is inappropriate, as in automotive systems.

voice recognition system   *See* **voice input device**.

volatile storage   Form of memory storage in which data and instructions are lost when the computer is turned off. *Compare* **nonvolatile storage**. *See also* **random access memory (RAM)**.

warm boot   Loading **DOS** into **RAM** *after* the computer has been turned on.

warranty   An agreement between the user and a hardware manufacturer. If something fails in the computer system within a certain period of time, the manufacturer should repair it at no cost.

wide area network (WAN)   Computer-based **network** that links communications resources scattered around a country or the world. *Compare* **local area network** and **metropolitan area network**.

window   Most **video display screens** allow 24–25 lines of text to be viewed at one time; this portion is called a *window*. By moving (scrolling) text up and down the screen, other windows of text become available.

Windows   *See* **Microsoft Windows**.

word processing   Electronic preparation of text for creating, editing, or printing documents.

word processing software   Program enabling user to create and edit documents by inserting, deleting, and moving text. Some programs also offer formatting features such as variable margins and different type sizes and styles, as well as more advanced features that border on **desktop publishing**.

word wrap   In **word processing**, when the **cursor** reaches the right-hand margin of a line it automatically returns (wraps around) to the left-hand margin of the line below and continues the text; the user does not have to hit a key to make the cursor move down to the next line.

write once, read many (WORM)   **Optical disk** whose data and instructions are imprinted by the disk manufacturer but whose content is determined by the buyer; after the data is imprinted, it cannot be changed. *Compare* **compact disk/read-only memory (CD-ROM)**; **erasable optical disk**.

write-protect notch   On a **diskette**, a notch in the protective cover that can be covered to prevent the **read/write head** from touching the disk surface so that no data can be recorded or erased.

WYSIWYG (what you see is what you get)   Page description **software** that allows the user to see the final version of a **desktop publishing** document on the screen before it is printed out. *Compare* **code-oriented**.

INDEX